POLITICAL SCIENCE AND HISTORY

MOORISH REMAINS IN SPAIN

POLITICAL SCIENCE AND HISTORY

Additional books and e-books in this series can be found
on Nova's website under the Series tab.

POLITICAL SCIENCE AND HISTORY

MOORISH REMAINS IN SPAIN

ALBERT F. CALVERT

Copyright © 2019 by Nova Science Publishers, Inc.

All rights reserved. No part of this book may be reproduced, stored in a retrieval system or transmitted in any form or by any means: electronic, electrostatic, magnetic, tape, mechanical photocopying, recording or otherwise without the written permission of the Publisher.

We have partnered with Copyright Clearance Center to make it easy for you to obtain permissions to reuse content from this publication. Simply navigate to this publication's page on Nova's website and locate the "Get Permission" button below the title description. This button is linked directly to the title's permission page on copyright.com. Alternatively, you can visit copyright.com and search by title, ISBN, or ISSN.

For further questions about using the service on copyright.com, please contact:
Copyright Clearance Center
Phone: +1-(978) 750-8400   Fax: +1-(978) 750-4470   E-mail: info@copyright.com.

NOTICE TO THE READER

The Publisher has taken reasonable care in the preparation of this book, but makes no expressed or implied warranty of any kind and assumes no responsibility for any errors or omissions. No liability is assumed for incidental or consequential damages in connection with or arising out of information contained in this book. The Publisher shall not be liable for any special, consequential, or exemplary damages resulting, in whole or in part, from the readers' use of, or reliance upon, this material. Any parts of this book based on government reports are so indicated and copyright is claimed for those parts to the extent applicable to compilations of such works.

Independent verification should be sought for any data, advice or recommendations contained in this book. In addition, no responsibility is assumed by the Publisher for any injury and/or damage to persons or property arising from any methods, products, instructions, ideas or otherwise contained in this publication.

This publication is designed to provide accurate and authoritative information with regard to the subject matter covered herein. It is sold with the clear understanding that the Publisher is not engaged in rendering legal or any other professional services. If legal or any other expert assistance is required, the services of a competent person should be sought. FROM A DECLARATION OF PARTICIPANTS JOINTLY ADOPTED BY A COMMITTEE OF THE AMERICAN BAR ASSOCIATION AND A COMMITTEE OF PUBLISHERS.

Additional color graphics may be available in the e-book version of this book.

Library of Congress Cataloging-in-Publication Data

ISBN: 978-1-53616-510-4

Published by Nova Science Publishers, Inc. † New York

CONTENTS

Preface		vii
Introduction		xi
Chapter 1	Cordova	1
Chapter 2	Seville	91
Chapter 3	Toledo	163
Chapter 4	Moorish Ornament	187
Index		413
Related Nova Publications		417

PREFACE[*]

The inception of my work on The Alhambra, to which this book is designed to be the companion and complementary volume, was due to the disappointing discovery that no such thing as an even moderately adequate souvenir of the Red Palace of Granada, "that glorious sanctuary of Spain," was in existence. It was written at a time when I shared the very common delusion that the Alhambra was the only word in a vocabulary of relics which includes such Arabian superlatives as the Mosque at Cordova, the Gates and the Cristo de la Luz of Toledo, and the Alcazar at Seville. I had then to learn that while the Alhambra has rightly been accepted as the last word on Moorish Art in Spain, it must not be regarded as the solitary monument of the splendour and beauty with which the Arabs stamped their virile and artistic personality upon Andalus.

In the course of frequent and protracted visits to Spain I came to realise that the Moors were not a one-city nation; they did not exhaust themselves in a single, isolated effort to achieve the sublimely beautiful. Before the Alhambra was conceived in the mind of Mohammed the First of Granada, Toledo had been adorned and lost; Cordova, which for centuries had commanded the admiration of Europe, had paled and waned beside the increasing splendour of Seville; and the "gem of Andalusia" itself had been wrested from the Moor by the victorious Ferdinand III. But each in turn had been redeemed from Gothic tyranny by the art-adoring influence of the Moslem. Their dominion, their politics, and their influence is a tale of a day that is dead, but it survives in the monuments of their Art, which exist to the glory of Spain and the wonder of the world. The Arabian sense of the beautiful sealed itself upon Cordova, and made the city its own; it blended with the joyous spirit of Seville; it forced its impress upon the frowning forehead of Toledo. To see the Alhambra is not to understand the wonders of the Alcazar; the study of Moorish wizardry in Toledo does not reveal, does not even prepare one, for the bewildering cunning of the Mosque in Cordova.

---

[*] This is an edited, augmented and reformatted version of "Moorish Remains in Spain" by Albert F. Calvert, originally published by London: John Lane Company, dated 1906.

In Cordova—this gay, vivacious overgrown village, which gleams serene in a setting of vineyards and orange groves—the spirit of the Moors still breathes. Rome wrested the city from Carthage; the Goths humbled it to the dust. But, under the Moors, Cordova became the centre of European civilisation, the rival of Baghdad and Damascus as a seat of learning, the Athens of the West, and second only in sanctity to the Kaaba of Mecca. Its Cathedral first came into being as a temple of Janus; it has been both a basilica and a mosque. But the magic art of the Mohammedan, which effaced the imprint of the Roman spear, has survived the torch of the Holy Inquisition, and to-day Cordova is the most exquisitely beautiful Moorish monument in Spain.

In Seville, on the spot where Roman, Visigoth, and Moslem have each in turn practised their faith, the Cathedral bells now hang above the Arabian tower of the mosque, and the spire of the temple of the faithful has become the world-famous Giralda, which dominates the city. Moorish fountains and patios are found at Malaga, and Granada, and Toledo, but one comes to "La Tierra de Maria Santisima" to see them at their loveliest, while the Alcazar is perhaps the best preserved and most superbly-decorated specimen of the Moorish citadel-palace that Europe has to show.

Menacing, majestic, and magnificent in its strength and splendid isolation, Toledo, guarded by its Moorish masonry, a rock built upon a rock, has been described by Padilla as "the crown of Spain, the light of the world, free from the time of the mighty Goths." The light of the world has dwindled in the socket of modern progress, the Moor has left his scars upon the freedom of the Goth; but Toledo, which was old when Christianity was born, presents an epitome of the principal arts, religions, and races which have dominated the world for the last two thousand years.

In the three cities of Cordova, Seville, and Toledo, in which the hand of the Moor touched nothing that it did not beautify, I have found the supplement to the art wonders that I attempted to describe in my book upon the Alhambra; and, encouraged by the cordiality of the welcome extended to that volume in Spain and America, as well as in this country, I have followed the course which I therein adopted, of making the letterpress subservient to the illustrations. While immersed in authorities, and tempted often by the beauties of the scenes to indulge the desire to emotionalise in words, I have never permitted myself to forget that my purpose has been to present a picture rather than to chronicle the romance of Spanish-Morisco art.

For the historical data, and some of the descriptions contained in this book, I have levied tribute on a large number of authors. Don Pascual de Gayángos, the renowned translator of Al-Makkari; the *Handbook* and the *Gatherings* of Richard Ford; William Stirling-Maxwell's *Don John of Austria*; *The History of the Conquest of Spain*, by Henry Coppeé; Washington Irving's *Conquest of Granada*; Miss Charlotte Yonge's *Christians and Moors in Spain*; Stanley Lane-Poole's *The Moors in Spain*; the writings of Dr. R. Dozy, of Leipsic; Muhammed Hayat Khan's *Rise and Fall of the Muslim Empire in Spain*; Hannah Lynch's *Toledo*; Walter M. Gallichan's *Seville*; *The Latin-Byzantine*

Monuments of Cordova; *Monumentos Arquitectonicos de España*; Pedro de Madrazo's *Sevilla*—these, and many less important writers on Spain, have been consulted.

But with this wealth of literary material to hand, I have remembered that it is my collection of illustrations, rather than on the written word, that I must depend. From the nature of Arabian art, and the characteristic minuteness of the details of which Morisco decoration is composed, lengthy descriptions of architeture, unaccompanied by illustrations, become not only tedious but positively confusing to the reader, while, on the other hand, a sufficiency of illustrations renders exhaustive descriptions superfluous. I have striven to do justice to the subject in this direction, not without hope of achieving my purpose, but with a vast consciousness of the fact that, neither by camera, nor brush, nor by the pen, can one reflect, with any fidelity, the effects obtained by the Moorish masters of the Middle Ages. In their art we find a sense of the mysterious that appeals to one like the glint of moonlight on running water; an intangible spirit of joyousness that one catches from the dancing shadows of leaves upon a sun-swept lawn; and an elusive key to its beauty, which is lost in the bewildering maze of traceries and the inextricable network of designs. The form, but not the fantasy, of these fairy-like, fascinating decorations may be reproduced, and this I have endeavoured to do.

A. F. C.
"Royston," Hampstead, N. W.
1905.

INTRODUCTION

The conquest of Spain by the Moors, and the story comprised in the eight centuries during which they wielded sovereignty as a European power, forms a romance that is without parallel in the history of the world. Under Mohammedan rule Spain enjoyed the first and most protracted period of comparative peace and material prosperity she had ever known. She had been plundered by Carthage and Phœnicia, ground beneath the iron heel of Rome, devastated and enslaved by those Christianised but corrupt barbarians, the Visigoths. All the evils and demoralisation arising from successive waves of bloody conquest and decadent voluptuousness had been sown in the breast of Spain. The squandered might of Carthage had left the country a prey to the vigorous Roman; the degenerate Roman had been banished by the rugged, victorious Goth, who, after two centuries of security and sensual ease, was to be made subject to the warlike and enlightened Moor. Once more the land was to be overrun and the face of the country was to be scarred with fire and the sword; once more the people were to learn to serve new masters and conform to new laws. Of a truth the last state must have seemed worse than the first to the Romanised Spaniards. Carthage had brought chains, but it had also introduced artificers and a form of Government; the Roman eagles had been accompanied by Roman engineers and road-builders; the Goths erected upon the broken altars of mythology temples to the living God. But it now seemed that the whips of ancient foes were to be replaced by the scorpions of their new taskmasters; the Christianity which the East had sent them was to be uprooted by the Eastern infidels.

Such must have been the prospect before Spain, and even before the rest of Europe, when Tarik returned in 710 to Ceuta, from a marauding expedition upon the coast of Andalusia, and reported to Musa, the son of Noseyr, the Arab Governor of North Africa, that the country was ripe for conquest and well worth the hazard of the cast. Twenty years later the Moslems had overrun Spain, captured Bordeaux by assault and advanced to the conquest of Gaul. It is passing strange to reflect that these far-reaching, epoch-making events had not been undertaken as the result of a deep-laid scheme of national expansion or religious enterprise. According to tradition the foundation of the Moslem supremacy in Spain was instigated by the hatred of a single traitor, Count Julian, the Governor of Ceuta, and his treachery was inspired by the dishonour of one young girl—Julian's daughter, Florinda.

At the beginning of the eighth century, when the Moors had extended their possessions up to the walls of Ceuta, which was held for Roderick, King of Spain, by Count Julian, the Count, in accordance with the custom among the Gothic nobility, had sent his daughter to the Court of Roderick, at Toledo, to be educated among the Queen's gentlewomen in a manner befitting her rank and lineage. The rest is the old story of a beautiful, unprotected girl, a lascivious guardian, and a father thirsting for vengeance. So far Count Julian had defended Ceuta against the Moors with unbroken success, now he came to Toledo to relieve the king of the custody of his daughter, and repay the breach of trust which Roderick had committed by making a compact with the king's enemies. On the eve of his departure from the capital, the king requested the Count to send him some hawks of a special variety that he desired for hunting purposes, and the vengeful noble pledged himself to supply his master with hawks, the like of which he had never seen.

But Count Julian found the Saracenic hawks less keen for the hunting he had in view than he expected. That old bird of prey, Musa, listened to the alluring tales of the richness and beauty of Spain, but doubted the good faith of his long-time enemy, who proposed that the Moors should invade this promised land in Spanish ships, lent to them for the purpose. But the love of conquest and the lust of loot, which had inspired and sustained the Arab arms in all their territorial campaigns, overcame the natural hesitancy of the Moorish Governor, and in 710 Musa despatched Tarik with a small expedition to spy out the state of the Spanish coast. So successful was the mission, and so rich the plunder they brought back, that in the following year he adventured an army of 7,000 men under Tarik for the spoliation of Andalusia. Tarik, who landed at the rock of Gibraltar—Gebal Tarik, which still bears his name—captured Carteya, and encountered the army of Roderick, who had hurried from the North of his dominions to repel the invaders, on the banks of the Guadalete.

Washington Irving, in the *Conquest of Spain*, has related, in his brilliantly picturesque style, the old legend of the prophecy of Roderick's overthrow and the mystery surrounding his death. The king was proof against the solemn warnings of the old warders of the tower of Hercules,—the tower of "jasper and marble, inlaid in subtle devices, which shone in the rays of the sun,"—wherein lay the secret of Spain's future, sealed by a magic spell, and guarded by a massive iron gate, and secured by the locks affixed to it by every successive Spanish king since the days of Hercules. Roderick came not to set a new lock upon the gate, but to burst the bolts of the centuries and reveal the mystery that his predecessors had gone down into their graves without solving. All day long his courtiers urged him vainly against his own undoing, and the custodians laboured at the rusty locks, and at evening he entered the mighty, outer hall, rushed past the bronze

Introduction xiii

warder, penetrated the inner chamber, and read the inscription attached to the casket, which Hercules had deposited in the gem-encrusted tower. "In this coffer is the mystery of the Tower. The hand of none but a King can open it; but let him beware, for wonderful things will be disclosed to him, which must happen before his death." In a moment the lid is prized open, the parchment, folded between plates of copper, is brought into the light of day, and the king has read the motto inscribed upon the border: "Behold, rash man, those who shall hurl thee from thy throne and subdue thy Kingdom."

Beneath the motto is drawn a panorama of horsemen, fierce of countenance, armed with bows and scimitars. As the king gazes wonderingly upon the picture, the sound of warfare rushes on his ear, the chamber is filled with a cloud, and in the cloud the horsemen bend forward in their saddles and raise their arms to strike. Amazed and terrorised, Roderick and his courtiers drew back and "beheld before them a great field of battle, where Christians and Moors were engaged in deadly conflict. They heard the rush and tramp of steeds, the blast of trump and clarion, the clash of cymbal, and the stormy din of a thousand drums. There was the flash of swords and maces and battle axes, with the whistling of arrows and hurling of darts and lances. The Christian quailed before the foe. The infidels pressed upon them, and put them to utter rout; the standard of the Cross was cast down, the banner of Spain was trodden underfoot the air resounded with shouts of triumph, with yells of fury, and the groans of dying men. Amidst the flying squadrons, King Roderick beheld a crowned warrior, whose back was turned towards him, but whose armour and device were his own, and who was mounted on a white steed that resembled his own war horse, Orelia. In the confusion of the fight, the warrior was dismounted and was no longer to be seen, and Orelia galloped wildly through the field of battle without a rider."

The vision he had witnessed in the Tower of Hercules must have recurred to Roderick when he saw the Moorish army encamped against him by the waters of the Guadalete, but he must have noted its numbers with surprise, and contemplated his own host with complacency. For Tarik, even with his Berber reinforcements, only counted 12,000 men, and nearly four score thousand slept beneath the standard of Spain. If ever prophecy was calculated to be found at fault it must have seemed to be so that day, and Tarik published his estimate of the enormity of the odds that were against him when he cried to his army of fatalists, "Men, before you is the enemy, and the sea is at your backs. By Allah, there is no escape for you, save in valour and resolution." But valour and resolution belonged to the Spaniards as well as to the Moors; and, but for the action of the kinsmen of the dethroned King Witiza, who deserted to the side of the Saracens in the midst of the seven day battle, the Moorish conquest would have been delayed, if not even entirely abandoned. But Witiza's adherents turned the tide of battle against Roderick, the Spaniards broke and fled, and Orelia galloped riderless through the field. Tarik, in a single encounter, had won all Spain for the infidels.

Without hesitation, and in defiance of the commands of Musa, who coveted the glory that his lieutenant had so unexpectedly won, Tarik proceeded to make good his mastery of the entire Peninsula. He despatched a force of seven hundred horsemen to capture Cordova; Archidona and Malaga capitulated without striking a blow; and Elvira was taken by storm. City after city surrendered to the victorious invaders, and the principles of true chivalry, which the Moors invariably observed, reconciled the vanquished Spaniards to their new conquerors. The common people welcomed the promise of a new era, while the nobles fled before the advancing armies, and abandoned the country to the enemy. With the surrender of Toledo, Tarik had added a new dominion to the crown of Damascus. Musa left Ceuta in 712 with 18,000 men to join Tarik at Toledo, taking Seville, Carmona, and Merida *en route*. The meeting of the Governor and his General at the capital revealed the first flash of that fire of personal jealousy and internecine conflict which kept Spain in a blaze throughout the eight centuries of the Moorish occupation.

To the intrepid warriors, who were bred to war and trained to the business of conquest, the Pyrenees represented, not a bar to further progress, but a bulwark from which they were to advance to the subjugation of Europe. The total defeat of the Saracens under the walls of Toulouse by the Duke of Aquitana in 721 turned their course westwards; and after occupying Carcasonne and Narbonne, raiding Burgundy and carrying Bordeaux by assault, they suffered a decisive defeat at the hands of the Franks, under Charles Martel, at the Battle of Tours in 733. The tide of Arabian aggression was arrested and rolled back; and although the Moors repulsed the Frankish invasion of Spain under Charlemagne, a bound had been put upon their empire-building ambitions, and they set themselves resolutely to accomplish the pacification of the kingdom they had already won. It is the boast of the Northern Spaniards, the hardy mountaineers of Galicia and Leon, of Castile and the Biscayan provinces, that they were never subject to Moslem rule. There is good warrant for their claim, and in truth the independence of the North was maintained, but the fact remains that the Moors had no desire for those bleak and unfruitful districts; and so long as the savage Basques did not disturb the security of Arabian tenure in the fertile South, they were left in the enjoyment of their dreary, frozen fastnesses, and their wind-swept, arid wastes.

The Moors had made themselves secure in the smiling country that, roughly speaking, lies South of the Sierra de Guadarrama; and here, with a genius and success that was unprecedented, they organised the Kingdom of Cordova. "It must not be supposed," writes Mr. Stanley Lane-Poole, "that the Moors, like the barbarian hordes who preceded them, brought desolation and tyranny in their wake. On the contrary, never was Andalusia so mildly, justly, and wisely governed as by the Arab conquerors. Where they got their talent for administration it is hard to say, for they came almost direct from their Arabian deserts, and their rapid tide of victories had left them little leisure to acquire the art of managing foreign nations. Some of their Counsellors were Greeks and Spaniards, but this does not explain the problem; for these same Counsellors were unable

Introduction

to produce similar results elsewhere; all the administrative talent of Spain had not sufficed to make the Gothic domination tolerable to its subjects. Under the Moors, on the other hand, the people were on the whole contented—as contented as any people can be whose rulers are of a separate race and creed—and far better pleased than they had been when their sovereigns belonged to the same religion as that which they nominally professed. Religion was, indeed, the smallest difficulty which the Moors had to contend with at the outset, though it had become troublesome afterwards. The Spaniards were as much pagan as Christian; the new creed promulgated by Constantine had made little impression among the general mass of the population, who were still predominantly Roman. What they wanted was—not a creed, but the power to live their lives in peace and prosperity. This their Moorish masters gave them."

The people were allowed to retain their own religion and their own laws and judges; and with the exception of the poll tax, which was levied only upon Christians and Jews, their imposts were no heavier than those paid by the Moors. The slaves were treated with a mildness which they had never known under the Romans or the Goths, and, moreover, they had only to make a declaration of Mohammedanism—to repeat the formula of belief, "There is no God but God, and Mohammed is His Prophet"—to gain their freedom. By the same simple process, men of position and wealth secured equal rights with their conquerers. But while the Moors thus practised the science of pacification, they were unable to conquer their own racial instincts, which found their vent in jealous blood feuds and ceaseless internal conflicts. In the field the Arabs were a united people; under stress of warfare their rivalries were forgotten; but the racial spirit of the conquerors reasserted itself when the stress of conquest gave place to "dimpling peace," and government by murder created constant changes in the administration. The Arabs and the Berbers, though they may be regarded as one race in their domination of Spain, were two entirely distinct and fiercely hostile tribes. The Berbers of Tarik had accomplished the conquest of Spain, but the Arabs arrived in time to seize the lion's share of the spoils of victory; and when the Berber insurrection in North Africa triumphed, their Berber brethren, who had been relegated to the least congenial districts of Estremadura, roused themselves to measures of retaliation, and carried their standards to the gates of Toledo and Cordova. In alarm, the Arab Governor of Andalusia sent for his compatriots of Ceuta to aid him, and he expiated his folly with his life. The African contingent routed the Berbers, murdered the Arab Governor, and set up their own chief in his place, until Abd-er-Rahman arrived from Damascus to unite all factions, for a while, under the standard of the Sultan of Cordova.

Figure 1. Cordova. The Mosque—Principal Nave of the Mihrab.

Figure 2. Cordova. The Mosque—Entrance To the Mihrab.

Figure 3. Cordova. Gates of Pardon.

Figure 4. View of the City and Bridge South of the Guadalquivir.

Figure 5. General View of the Interior of the Mosque.

Figure 6. Cordova. Façade and Gate of the Almanzor.

Introduction xix

Figure 7. Cordova. View of Interior of the Mosque 961-967.

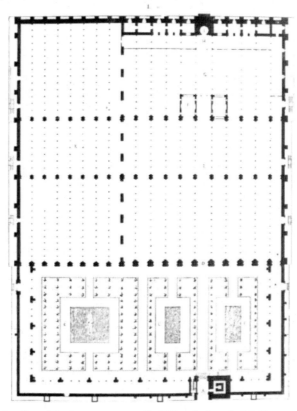

A—Gate of Pardon.
B—Bell Tower.
C—Orange Court.
D—Principal Entrance.
E—Mosque of the time 786-796.
F—Tribunal where the Mufti prays.
G—Portion of the time 961-967.
H—Hall where the Koran is kept.
I—Sanctuary.
K—Portion added in 988-1001.

Figure 8. Cordova. I. The Mosque. Plan in the Time of the Arabs 786-796, 961-967, 988-1001, 1523-1593.

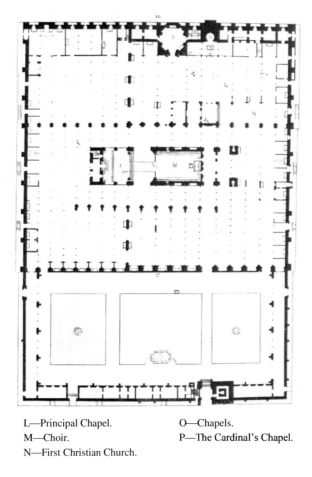

L—Principal Chapel.　　　　O—Chapels.
M—Choir.　　　　　　　　　P—The Cardinal's Chapel.
N—First Christian Church.

Figure 9. Cordova. II. The Mosque—Plan In Its Present State. 786-796, 961-967, 988-1001, 1523-1593.

Abd-er-Rahman, which signifies "Servant of the Merciful God," was a member of the deposed family of the Omeyyads, which had given fourteen khalifs to the throne of Damascus. The usurping khalif, Es-Deffah, "The Butcher," who founded the dynasty of the Abbasides, practically exterminated the Omeyyad family, but Abd-er-Rahman eluded his vigilance, and, after abandoning a project to make himself the Governor of North Africa, he determined to carry his princely pretensions to the newly-founded Spanish dominions. In Andalusia, the advent of the Omeyyads was hailed with enthusiasm. The army of the Governor deserted to the standard of the young pretender; Archidona and Seville were induced to throw open their gates to him by a piece of questionable strategy; he defeated the troops that opposed his march upon Cordova, and before the end of the year 756, or some fifteen months after setting foot in the country, all the Arab part of Spain had acknowledged the dynasty of the Omeyyads, which for three centuries was to endure in Cordova. Brave, unscrupulous, and instant in action, Abd-er-Rahman had recourse to every wile of diplomacy, of severity, and of valour to maintain his supremacy in Spain. He defeated and utterly annihilated an invading army sent against him by the Abbaside khalif, Mansur, and sent a sackful of the heads of his generals as a present to

Introduction xxi

their master; he won over the people of Toledo by false promises, and crucified their leaders; he had the Yemenite chief assassinated while receiving him as an honoured guest; he crushed a revolt of the Berbers in the North, and of the Yemenites in the South; he saw the forces of Charlemagne waste away in the bloody fastnesses of the Pyrenees. By treachery and the sword, by false oaths and murder, he triumphed over every rival and enemy until all insurrection had been crushed by his relentless might, and the Khalif Mansur was fain to exclaim: "Thank God, there is a sea between that man and me." In an eloquent tribute to his "daring, wisdom, and prudence," his old-time enemy thus extolled the genius of the conqueror: "To enter the paths of destruction, throw himself into a distant land, hard to approach and well defended, there to profit by the jealousies of the rival parties to make them turn their arms against one another instead of against himself, to win the homage and obedience of his subjects, and having overcome every difficulty, to rule supreme lord of all! Of a truth, no man before him has done this!"

But the tyrant of Spain was to pay a great and terrible price for his triumphs. He had established himself in a kingdom in which he was to stand alone. Long before his death he found himself forsaken by his kinsmen, deserted by his friends, abhorred by his enemies; on all sides detested and avoided, he immured himself in the fastnesses of his palace, or went abroad surrounded by a strong guard of hired mercenaries. His son and successor, Hisham, practised during the eight years of his reign an exemplary piety, and so encouraged and cherished the theological students and preceptors of Cordova, that they rebelled against the light-hearted, pleasure-loving Hakam, who succeeded him, and incited the people to open rebellion.

But while the insurrectionists besieged the palace, the Sultan's soldiers set fire to a suburb of the city; and when the people retired terror stricken to the rescue of their homes and families, they found themselves between the palace garrison and the loyal incendiaries. The revolt ended in a massacre, but the dynasty was saved, and the palace was preserved to become the nucleus of the gorgeous city which Hakam's son, Abd-er-Rahman II, was to fashion after the style of Harun-er-Rashid at Baghdad. Under this æsthetic monarch, Cordova became one of the most beautiful cities in the world. Its palaces and gardens, its mosques and bridges were the wonder of Europe; its courtiers made a profession of culture; its arbiter of fashion again asserted himself as the first man in the empire.

In such a city, and at such an epoch, it was natural, even inevitable, that Christianity should assert itself as a protest against the fashion of the age. But so tolerant was the Mohammedan rule in religious matters, that the too exalted spirit of the Cordovan Christians was hard put to it to find some excuse for its manifestation of discontent. While the sultan and his nobles found their pleasure in music, poetry, and other æsthetic if less commendable indulgences, the prejudices of the devout were always respected. Prosecution for religious convictions was unheard of, and the only way that the Christians could achieve martyrdom for their faith was by blaspheming the creed of their Moslem rulers. These early fanatics, whose religious rites and beliefs had been treated with respect by the Mohammedans, and who knew that by Moslem law he who blasphemes the Prophet Mohammed or his religion must die, voluntarily transgressed the law for the purpose of achieving their object. In spite of warnings, of protests, and of earnest counsel, these suicidal devotees cursed the name of the Prophet, and expiated their wilful fanaticism with death. With the exception of this period of religious mania, which was bewailed by the general body of Christians, and regarded with unfeigned sorrow by the Mohammedan judges, the tolerance of the Moors to the Christians was as unvarying as it was remarkable.

After the execution, in the year 859, of Eulogius, a fanatical priest, and the leader of these misguided martyrs, who was fruitlessly entreated by his judges to retract his maledictions against the Prophet and be restored to freedom, the mad movement flickered and died out. But the devotion displayed by the Cordovan Christians had made its effects felt in widespread rebellion in the provinces, and a series of incapable sovereigns had reduced the throne to the state of an island surrounded by a rivulet of foreign soldiers, in a country bristling with faction jealousies and discontent. Spain had fallen a prey to anarchy, and the end of Mohammedan rule appeared imminent. Petty kings and governors had thrown off their allegiance; Berbers, Arabs, Mohammedan Spaniards and Christians had each asserted their absolute independence; and the sultan at Cordova was "suffering all the ills of beleaguerment." The last vestige of the power of the Omeyyads was falling away when Abd-er-Rahman III came to the throne to reconquer Spain, and bring the rebel nobles to their knees. The new sultan was a lad of twenty-one, but he knew his countrymen, and he realised that after a century of lawlessness and wasting strife, the people were ripe for a strong and effectual government. The Cordovans were won by his handsome presence and gallant bearing. The boldness of his programme brought him adherents, and the weariness of internecine warfare, which had devastated the country, prepared the rebellious provinces for his coming. Seville opened her gates to receive him, the Prince of Algarve rendered tribute, the resistance of the Christians of Regio was overcome, and Murcia volunteered its allegiance. Toledo alone, that implacable revolutionist, rejected all Abd-er-Rahman's overtures, and confidently awaited the issue of the siege. But the haughty Toledans had not reckoned upon the metal of which the new despot was made. Abd-er-Rahman had no stomach for the suicidal tactics of scaling impregnable precipices, but he was possessed of infinite patience. He calmly set himself to build a town on the mountain over against Toledo, and to wait until famine should compel the inhabitants to capitulate. With the fall of Toledo, the whole of Mohammedan Spain was once more restored to the sultans of Cordova. The power, once regained, was never relaxed in the lifetime of Abd-er-Rahman. The Christians of Galicia might push southward as far as the great Sierra, Ordono II. of Leon might bring his marauding hosts to within a few leagues of Cordova, and cause Abd-er-Rahman to exert all his personal and military influence to beat back the obstinate Northerners, but the

Introduction   xxiii

stability of the throne was never again imperilled. During his fifty years of strenuous sovereignty, the great Abd-er-Rahman saved Spain from African invasion and Christian aggression; he established an absolute power in Cordova that brought ambassadors from every European monarch to his court; and he made the prosperity of Andalusia the envy of the civilised world. This wonderful transformation was effected by a man whom the Moorish historians describe as "the mildest and most enlightened sovereign that ever ruled a country. His meekness, his generosity, and his love of justice became proverbial. None of his ancestors ever surpassed him in courage in the field, and zeal for religion; he was fond of science, and the patron of the learned, with whom he loved to converse."

In 961, Abd-er-Rahman III, the last great Omeyyad Sultan of Cordova, died. His son Hakam II employed the peace which he inherited from his illustrious father in the study of books and the formation of a library, which consisted of no fewer than four hundred thousand works. But in his reign, the note of absolute despotism which had re-established the Empire of Cordova, was less evident; and when at his death, his twelve-year-old son, Hisham II., ascended the throne, the government was ripe for the delegation of kingly power to favourites and ministers. The Sultana Aurora, the Queen Mother, had already abrogated that power, and was wielding an influence that Abd-er-Rahman III would not have tolerated for an instant, and her favourite—an undistinguished student of Cordova, named Ibn-Aby-Amir—was waiting to turn her influence and favour to his own advantage. This youth, who is known to history as Almanzor, or "Victorious by the grace of God"—a title conceded to him by virtue of his many victories over the Christians— was possessed of pluck, genius, and ambition in almost equal proportions; and by the opportunity for their indulgence which the harem influence afforded, he made himself virtual master of Andalusia.

In his capacity of professional letter-writer to the court servants, Almanzor won the patronage of the Grand Chamberlain, and his appointment to a minor office brought him into personal contact with Aurora—who fell in love with the engaging young courtier— and with the princesses, whose good graces he assiduously cultivated. His charm of manner and unfailing courtesy gained for him the countenance of many persons of rank, and his kindness and lavish generosity secured him the allegiance of his inferiors. By degrees he acquired a plurality of important and lucrative posts; he earned the gratitude of the Queen Mother by arranging the assassination of a rival claimant who opposed the accession of her son Hisham to the throne; and he volunteered to lead the sultan's army against his insurrectionary subjects of Leon. Almanzor was without military training or experience, but he had no misgivings upon the score of his own ability, and his faith in himself was justified. His victories over the Leonese made him the idol of the army; and on the strength of his increased popularity he appointed himself Prefect of Cordova, and speedily rendered the city a model of orderliness and good government. By a politic impeachment of the Grand Chamberlain for financial irregularities, he presently succeeded his own patron in the first office in the State, and became supreme ruler of the kingdom.

Almanzor had allowed no scruple or fear to thwart him in his struggle for the proud position he had attained, and he now permitted nothing to menace the power he had so hardly won. He met intrigue with intrigue, and discouraged treachery by timely assassination. He placated hectoring, orthodox Moslems; he curtailed the influence of his formidable rival, Ghalib, the adored head of the army; he conciliated the Cordovans by making splendid additions to the mosque; he terrorised the now jealous Aurora and the palace party into quiescence; and he kept the khalif himself in subjection by the magnetism of his own masterful personality. His African campaigns extended the dominion of Spain along the Barbary coast, and his periodical invasions of Leon and Castile kept the Northern provinces in subjection, and his army contented and rich with the spoils of war. The Christians had terrible reason to hate this invincible upstart, and it is not surprising to read in the Monkish annals, the record of his death transcribed in the following terms: "In 1002 died Almanzor, and was buried in hell." But if his death meant hell to Almanzor, as the Christians doubtless believed, it meant the recurrence of the hell of anarchy for the Kingdom of Spain.

Within half a dozen years of the great Chamberlain's death, the country which had been held together by the might of one man, was torn to pieces by jealous and tyrannical chiefs and rebellious tribal warriors. Hisham II was dragged from his harem seclusion, and the reins of Government were thrust into his incompetent hands. He failed, and was compelled to abdicate, and another khalif was set up in his place. For the next twenty years khalifs were enthroned and replaced in monotonous succession. Assassination followed coronation, and coronation assassination, until the princes of every party looked askance at the blood-stained throne, where monarchs and murderers played their several intimate parts. Outside the capital, anarchy and devastation was ravaging the country. Berbers and Slavs were carrying desolation into the South and East of the country, and in the North the Christians were uniting to throw off their dependence. Alfonso VI was selling his aid to the rival chieftains in their battles amongst themselves, and storing up his subsidies against the day when he would undertake the re-conquest of Spain. The Cid had established his Castilian soldiers in Valencia, and the voluptuous, degenerate Mohammedan princes were panic-stricken by the growing disaffection and the instant danger which they were powerless to overcome.

In their extremity they sent for assistance to Africa, where Yusuf, the king of a powerful set of fanatics whom the Spaniards named Almoravides, had made himself master of the country from Algiers to Senegal. Yusuf came with his Berber hosts in 1086, defeated the Christians, under Alfonso, near Badajoz, and leaving three thousand of his men to stiffen the ranks of the Andalusians in maintaining the struggle, he returned to Africa. Four years later the Spanish Mohammedans again besought Yusuf to bring his legions against their Christian despoilers, offering him liberal terms for his assistance, and stipulating only that he should retire to his own dominions as soon as the work was completed. The Almoravide king subscribed the more readily to this condition, since his priestly counsellors absolved him from his oath, and had little difficulty in convincing him that his duty lay in the pacification of the unhappy Kingdom of Andalusia. Yusuf organised a force capable of contending with both the Christians of Castile and his Moorish allies. The capitulation of Granada provided him with the means of distributing vast treasure among his avaricious followers, and promises of even greater booty inspired them to further faithful service. Tarifa, Seville, and the rest of the important cities of Andalusia, fell before the treasure-hunting Berbers; and with the surrender of Valencia, on the death of the Cid, the re-conquest of Mohammedan Spain was practically completed. Order was temporarily restored, lives and property were once more respected, and a new era of peace and prosperity appeared to have begun.

Figure 10. Cordova. Ancient Arab Tower, Now the Church of St. Nicholas De La Villa.

But the degenerating influence of wealth and luxurious ease, which in the course of generations had sapped the manhood of Spain's successive conquerors, played swift havoc with the untutored Berbers. At the end of a score of years, the Castilians, led by Alfonso "the Battler," had resumed the offensive, sacking and burning the smaller towns, and carrying their swords and torches to the gates of Seville and Cordova. The Almoravides were powerless to resist their vigorous forays. The people of Andalus, recognising the powerlessness of their protectors, declared their independence, and rallied to the ranks of the score of petty chiefs who raised their standards in every city and castle in Andalusia, and who fought with, or bribed their Christian adversaries for the maintenance of their vaunted power.

Figure 11. Cordova. Orange Court In The Mosque, Moorish Style, Built 957, By Said Ben Ayout.

Figure 12. Cordova. Exterior of the Mosque.

Figure 13. Cordova. The Mosque—Section of the Mihrab.

At this crisis in the history of Spain, when the dominion of the enfeebled and dissolute Arab and Berber leaders was weakening before the resolute onslaughts of the rude, hard-living, and hard-fighting Christians of the North, a new force was created to turn the scale of Empire and prolong the rule of the Moslem in Europe. Before the Almoravides had been overthrown in Andalus, the Almoravides in Africa had been vanquished and dispersed by the mighty Almohades, who now regarded the annexation of Mohammedan Spain as the natural and necessary climax to the work of conquest. Andalusia had been a dependence of the Almoravide Empire; it was now to be a dependence of the Almoravides's successors. Between 1145 and 1150 the transfer was completed; but although the Almohades had wrested the kingdom from the Almoravides, they had not subdued the Christian provinces. The new rulers, under-estimating the potentiality of this danger, left the country to be governed by viceroys—an error in statecraft, which ultimately lost Spain to the Mohammedan cause. In 1195 they sent from Morocco a huge force to check the Christian aggressive movement, and the Northern host was routed at Alarcos, near Badajoz. That success was the last notable victory that was to arrest the slow, but certain, recovery of all Spain to Catholic rule. In 1212, the Almohade army suffered a disastrous defeat at the battle of Las Navas; in 1235 they were driven out of the Peninsula; three years later, on the death of Ibn-Hud, the Moslem dominion in Spain was restricted to the Kingdom of Granada; and, although this Moorish stronghold was destined to endure for another two and a-half centuries, it existed only as a tributary to the throne of the Christian kings of Spain.

For the purposes of this book, the history of Moorish Spain closes with the expulsion of the Mohammedans from Cordova, Toledo, and Seville. That more modern, and, in some ways more wonderful, Moorish monument—the Red Palace of Granada—I have dealt with in my book on "The Alhambra," to which this work is intended to be the companion and complement.

Chapter 1

CORDOVA

Of the four great cities of the Mohammedan domination in Spain, Cordova, as the seat of the Khalifate established by Abd-er-Rahman I., is rightly regarded as chief. The sun of the Moslem era shone with dazzling brilliance on Seville, and pierced the shadows of grim Toledo ere it set upon the decaying grandeur of Granada; but it had risen first on Cordova, and from "that abode of magnificence, superiority, and elegance" its glory had been reflected to the furthest corner of the civilised world. For Cordova, by reason of its climate, its situation, and its surroundings has, since the beginning of time, been one of the garden spots of Europe. The Carthaginians had aptly styled it "the Gem of the South," and the Romans had founded a city there in 152 B.C., which they called Corduba. But Corduba had sided with Pompey against Cæsar in the struggle for the mastership of the Roman Empire, and the mighty Julius visited this act of hostility with the destruction of more than half the city, and the massacre of 28,000 of its inhabitants. When the Goths made themselves rulers of Spain in the sixth century, they selected Toledo to be their capital, and Cordova sank into political insignificance. In 711, when Tarik had defeated Roderick near the banks of the Guadalete, he despatched Mughith with 700 horse to seize Cordova. Taking advantage of a fortuitous storm of hail, which deadened the clatter of the horses' hoofs, and assisted by the treachery of a Christian shepherd, the followers of the Prophet obtained an unopposed entry, and the city fell without a blow being struck. Forty-four years later Abd-er-Rahman I. established the dynasty of the Omeyyads of Cordova, and for three centuries the capital of Mohammedan Spain was to be, in the language of the old chronicler, Ash-Shakand, "the repository of science, the minaret of piety and devotion, unrivalled even by the splendours of Baghdad or Damascus."

Science has long since deserted Cordova; piety is not obtrusive there; its material magnificence has passed away. To-day the once famous city is a sleepy, smiling, overgrown village; a congregation of empty squares, and silent, winding, uneven streets, which have a more thoroughly African appearance than those of any other town in Spain.

Theophile Gautier has described its "interminable white-washed walls, their scanty windows guarded by heavy iron bars," and its pebbly, straw-littered pavement, and the sensitive spirit of De Amicis was caught by a vague melancholy in the midst of its whitewashed, rose-scented streets. Here, he writes, there is "a marvellous variety of design, tints, light, and perfume; here the odour of roses, there of oranges, further on of pinks; and with this perfume a whiff of fresh air, and with the air a subdued sound of women's voices, the rustling of leaves, and the singing of birds. It is a sweet and varied harmony that, without disturbing the silence of the streets, soothes the ear like the echo of distant music."

Plate 1. Cordova. Shell-like Ornaments in the Cupola of the Mihrab.

It has, as I have observed elsewhere, a charm that fills the heart with a sad pleasure; there is a mysterious spell in its air that one cannot resist. One may idle for hours in the sunshine that floods the deserted squares, and try to reconstitute in one's mind, that Cordova, which was described as "the military camp of Andalus, the common rendezvous of those splendid armies which, with the help of Allah, defeated at every encounter the worshippers of the Crucified." This indolent, lotus-fed, listless Cordova was once, says El-Makkari, "the meeting place of the learned from all countries, and, owing to the power and splendour of the dynasty that ruled over it, it contained more excellencies than any other city on the face of the earth." Another Mohammedan author, Al-hijari, Abu Mohammed, writing of the city in the twelfth century, said: "Cordova was, during the reign of the Beni-Merwan, the cupola of Islam, the convocation of scholars, the court of the sultans of the family of Omeyyah, and the residence of the most illustrious tribes of Yemen and Ma'd. Students from all parts of the world flocked thither at all times to learn the sciences of which Cordova was the most noble repository, and to derive knowledge from the mouths of the doctors and ulema who swarmed in it. Cordova is to Andalus what the head is to the body. Its river is one of the finest in the world, now gliding slowly through level lawns, or winding softly across emerald fields, sprinkled with flowers, and serving it for robes; now flowing through thickly-planted groves, where the song of birds resounds perpetually in the air, and now widening into a majestic stream to impart its waters to the numerous wheels constructed on its banks, communicating fresh vigour to the land."

Plate 2. Shell-like Ornaments in the Cupola of the Mihrab.

The extent of ancient Cordova has been differently stated, owing, no doubt, to the rapid increase of its population and the expansion of the buildings under the sultans of the dynasty of Merwan on the one hand, and, on the other, to the calamities and disasters by which it was afflicted under the last sovereigns of that house.

Plate 3. Cordova. Shell-like Ornaments in the Cupola of the Mihrab.

Plate 4. Cordova. Part of the ornamentation and keystone of one of the lower arches which gives light to the dome.

Cordova is, moreover, described by Mohammedan writers as a city which never ceased augmenting in size, and increasing in importance, from the time of its subjugation by the Moors until A.D. 1009-10, when, civil war breaking out within it, the capital fell from its ancient splendour, gradually decaying, and losing its former magnificence, until its final destruction in A.D. 1236, when it passed into the hands of the Christians.

From 711 until 755, when Abd-er-Rahman arrived in Spain to seize the new Moorish possession, which had fallen to the military skill and courage of Tarik's Berbers, the conquerors had been too fully employed in capturing cities to devote much leisure to beautifying their prizes; now, with the foundation of the Omeyyad power, Cordova was to reap the first fruits of comparative peace. But the repulsion of the Abbaside invasion, the subjugation of Toledo, and the suppression of the Berber revolt in the Northern provinces, long delayed the commencement of the great mosque which the sultan projected as "a splendid seal upon the works pleasing to the Almighty, which he had accomplished." By the building of the mosque, Abd-er-Rahman would secure a place for himself in Paradise, and would leave to his own honoured memory a Mecca of the West to which the followers of the Prophet could go in pilgrimage.

The treasury of Abd-er-Rahman was at this time in a flourishing condition, despite the large sums spent in adding splendour to the growing khalifate, and there appeared to be no difficulty in carrying out his project. But Umeya Ibn Yezid, the favourite secretary of the sultan, who, in his capacity of Katib, was instructed to make overtures for the purchase of the church on whose site the khalif intended to build the new mosque, soon found that the negotiations were beset by serious difficulties. The Christians held firm to the conditions of capitulation granted them by the Saracen conquerors of Cordova, and were not at all inclined to sell to Abd-er-Rahman the temple upon which he had set his heart. This building is described by Pedro de Madrazo as a spacious basilica, which they shared with the followers of the Prophet, since the Mohammedans, according to the practice established amongst them by the advice of the Khalif Omar, shared the churches of the conquered cities with the Christians, and, after taking Cordova, had divided one of the principal basilicas in two parts, one of which they conceded to the Cordovans, reserving the other, which they at once turned into a mosque, for themselves. The Christians had religiously paid the tribute exacted from them that they might keep their churches, bishops, and priests, but this had not protected them from unjust exactions and plunderings at the hands of the governors and representatives of the Eastern khalifs. Knowing this, Abd-er-Rahman was anxious to acquire the desired site without violence, and, with his natural sagacity, he perceived that the religious zeal of the native Christians was much less fervent than that of his own people. Captivity and affliction had damped the old ardour of the natives of Cordova, which, in his day, was no longer the heroic colony, so anxious for martyrdom, and so prodigal of its blood, as it was at the time when the flock of Christ was guided by the great Osius under the persecutions of Diocletian and Maximilian. Neither was it the Cordova which had endured wars, hunger, and plague sooner than be contaminated with Arianism, and the khalif knew, too, that in spite of the education given to the Christian youth in the schools and colleges of the monasteries, where many young priests and secular scholars promised to be a future danger to the Mohammedans, the Church at Cordova was suffering grievous wounds from the new doctrines of Migencio and Elipando. He was, therefore, the more surprised to receive a stubborn refusal to his offer, but the estimation in which he held the vanquished people and their leaders, led him to believe that he could overcome their obstinacy by quiet persistence, and by trusting to time to undermine their scruples. His policy was justified by its eventual success.

How did Abd-er-Rahman succeed in persuading the Christians to make so great a sacrifice? How came they to be induced to abandon their principal church to the infidels? Had not these walls been witnesses of the vows they had sworn at the most solemn epochs of their lives? Perhaps it was already a matter of indifference to them to see the ground, sanctified by the blood of their martyrs, defiled! "God Almighty alone knows" must be our only comment upon this unaccountable transaction, and we leave it thus in accordance with the practice adopted by the Arab historians, when they were at a loss for an explanation.

It is certain that under the reign of Abd-er-Rahman the Christians were no longer persecuted on account of their religion. They paid tribute, it is true, as a conquered people, but their faith was respected; they had their churches and monasteries, where they worshipped publicly; and it is not recorded that any of their priests were molested by the first Moorish king of the West. On the other hand, when they compared their present lot with that of the past, they must have considered themselves greatly fortunate, as they escaped the tyranny under which their fathers had suffered during the years from the cruel Alahor to the time of the covetous Toaba. It is certain that a new empire was rising in Cordova, which was very threatening to the law of Christ; but at first its menace was not revealed, and for this reason it was more to be feared. Its intentions were not published, but they were vaguely felt. Those who were wisest and most far-seeing could perceive, though still far off, the dark cloud of a bloody persecution drawing around the Church of Andalusia; but for the generality of the Christians there seemed to be no reason why the present toleration was not to continue, and it is certain that fear was not the motive that made them yield to the wishes of the khalif.

History is very reticent concerning this event; in fact, as Pedro de Madrazo admits, nothing definite has, up to the present, been discovered with regard to it. The probabilities are that the Bishop of Cordova, upon receiving the message of the Moorish king, called a council, and, after due discussion, resolved to part amicably with that which, despite the king's moderation, would without any doubt be taken from them by force, should they persist in their refusal. In parting with their church, and transferring their place of worship, they hoped, too, to be released from the odious proximity of the infidels, whose presence under the roof of their basilica must always have been looked upon as a desecration of the sacred building. And, finally, the advantages to be gained by removing their holy relics to a more suitable sanctuary may have decided them to accept the khalif's offer, under the condition that they should be allowed to re-build the basilica of the martyrs St. Faustus, St. Januaris, and St. Marcellus, which had been destroyed in recent years; and this being conceded to them by the khalif, the bishop authorised the transfer. The Arab ordered that the price agreed upon should be sent at once to the Christians, who were in turn to surrender their church forthwith, because Abd-er-Rahman, already advanced in years, was anxious that the edifice he was going to raise should be commenced without delay. No sooner had the Christians departed than Abd-er-Rahman left his villa in Razafa and took up his residence at the alcazar of the city, in order to superintend the projected work. The destruction of the old building was immediately proceeded with. Devoured with the desire to see the work completed, the indefatigable old man spent many hours each day on the scene, carefully examining the portions of the demolished buildings, which were to be utilised for the new mosque, and classifying them with rare skill. The whole city was filled with movement and commotion. There was not a trade amongst the people which did not receive fresh impetus from the new building. Whilst all were busy in the factories and workshop, in the woods, on the mountains, and on the roads from the hills to the city; whilst the furnaces and brick ovens were glowing; whilst the Syrian architect meditated on his plans and on those traced by the king's own hands, and the Katib wrote to Asia and Africa inviting the co-operation of famous artists; the people, lazy and curious, swarmed around the spacious foundations, and the whole city presented a scene of animation and excitement not easy to describe.

Abd-er-Rahman, who had a presentiment that he would not live to see the mosque finished, pushed on the work with all speed, that he might at least have the satisfaction of covering the arcades which formed its naves, and of inaugurating the cult of Islam with one of those eloquent harangues, which he was in the habit of addressing to his people on the days of "Juma," or Rest. Barely two years after the foundations were laid the square fortress of Islam rose above the groves by the river, surpassing in height the severe Alcazar of Rodrigo. A few more moons, and the interior walls, the superb colonnades of bold and unusual form,—the mosque of Cordova is probably the first edifice in which superposed arches were introduced—the graceful rows of double arches, the ample porticos, the handsome façade of eleven entrances, the rich side doors, flanked by fretted windows, and finally the incomparable roof of incorruptible wood, carved and painted, would be finished. Still a few more moons, and the "hotba," or harangue, for the health of Abd-er-Rahman was to be read to the people from the most beautiful "nimbar," or pulpit in the West, and repeated by two thousand believers as with one voice, drowning in the vibrating surge of an immense and thundering contempt the shamed hymns of the vanquished Nazarenes.

Not only was the mosque to be ready for the celebration of the public ceremonies on the first day of "Alchuma," but already the sanctuary loomed at the extremity of the principal nave towards the South, covered with rich and dazzling Byzantine ornamentation, the venerated copy of the holy house of Mecca. The great aljama was not yet complete, it is true, but the diligent architects would find a way to satisfy the impatience of the sultan by covering the walls with rich hangings from Persia and Syria. A profusion of Corinthian columns in the principal naves, and of bold marble pillars from the Roman monuments, sent from the provinces as presents to the monarch from his walies, would be in their place. The columns taken from the old basilica of the Visigoths, would be found in the secondary naves, with others, as yet unchiselled. The floor was to be covered with flowers and fragrant herbs, and the sacred precincts would be inundated with light and perfume, diffused by hundreds of candelabra and thuribles. The fortunate Abd-er-Rahman would be able at least once before he died to direct the rites of the religion, for the propagation of which he had made so many sacrifices, in his capacity of "Imam" of the law.

But it was not to be. That day the news spread through the city that the angel of death was seated by the bedside of the khalif; and soon after, the body of Abd-er-Rahman, the wise, the virtuous, and the victorious, lay in one of the chambers of his alcazar, wrapped in the white garments, distinctive of his great lineage. The sad event was announced to the people by Abd-er-Rahman Ibn Tarif, the superior of the Aljama of Cordova, from the very pulpit from which the dead monarch was to have addressed his subjects, and the crowds departed from the mosque exclaiming: "May the Amir rest in the sleep of peace, Allah will smile upon him on the day of reckoning."

The great glory of completing the mosque was reserved for Hisham, the favourite son of Abd-er-Rahman, to whom all the walies had sworn fealty as the rightful successor. This prince was at Merida when his father died, but he at once left that city for Cordova, where he made the mosque the object of his special solicitude.

Soon after his accession, Hisham consulted a famous astrologer as to his future. The learned man, who was called Abh-dhobi, at first refused to gratify the sultan's curiosity, but upon being pressed he said: "Thy reign, O Amir, will be glorious and happy, and marked by great victories; but, unless my calculations are wrong, it will only last some eight years." Hisham remained some time in silence upon hearing these words, but presently his face cleared, and he spoke thus to the astrologer: "Thy prediction, O Abh-dhobi, does not discourage me, for if the days given me still to live by the Almighty are passed in adoring Him, I shall say when my hour comes, 'Thy will be done.'"

Figure 14. Cordova. The Mosque. Portal on the North Side, Moorish Style, Built Under Hakam III, 988-1001.

This monarch's brief reign was rich in notable deeds. He repressed the rebellion of his two brothers Suleyman and Abdullah, carried the holy war as far as Sardinia, entered and sacked the town of Narbonne, and compelled the unhappy Christians to carry the clay of the demolished walls of their city upon their shoulders as far as Cordova, in order to build a mosque in his alcazar. Hisham made himself feared by the Franks, and he did much to establish the empire of Islam in Andalus, enlarging its capital, repairing its magnificent bridge, creating useful public institutions, and finally completing the grand mosque, which his father had commenced, founding and endowing in connection with it schools and colleges. Moreover, he did all this with the resources of the treasury, and with his lawful part of the spoils of conquest, without levying any extraordinary taxes.

Figure 15. Cordova. Exterior View of the Mosque.

Figure 16. Cordova. Exterior Angle of the Mosque.

Figure 17. Cordova. The Exterior of the Mosque.

Plate 5. Cordova. Curvelinear triangles resulting from the intersection of the arches sustaining the dome. Setting of the arches sustaining the dome.

Plate 6. Cordova. Ornament running below the Cupola. Setting of one of the lower arches which gives light to the dome.

Plate 7. Cordova. Curvelinear triangles resulting from the intersection of the arches sustaining the dome. Architrave of one of the Arches sustaining the Dome.

Plate 8. Cordova. Keystone of the arch of the Mihrab. Keystone of the arch of the right hand side gateway. Details de las Portados de la Maksurah.

Plate 9. Cordova. Arches of the Portal of the Mihrab.

Plate 10. Cordova. Detail of the Framing of the Side Gate. Detail of the Window placed over the Side Door. Detail of the Framing of the Arch of the Mihrab.

Plate 11. Cordova. Windows in an Alcove.

Plate 12. Cordova. Height of Vase Ft. 4 6 In. Diameter Ft. 2 11 In. Arab Vase of Metallic Lustre.

Plate 13. Cordova. Details of the Arches.

Plate 14. Centre Painting on a Ceiling.

Plate 15. Divan.

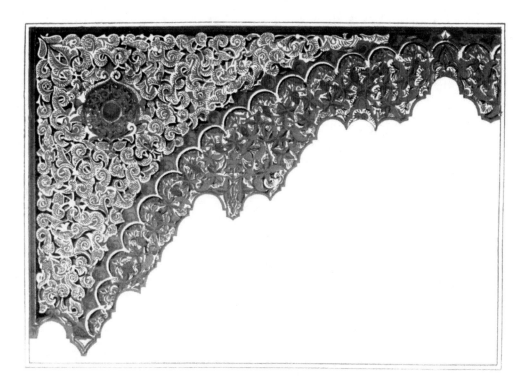

Plate 16. Detail of an Arch.

Tradition relates that there formerly was a bridge over the Guadelquivir, erected on the site of the present structure, about 200 years before the arrival of the Moors in Spain: but, this edifice being greatly decayed, it was rebuilt by the Arabs during the Viceroyship of Assamh, A.D. 720 or 721. This noble structure is four hundred paces, or one thousand feet, in length, and its breadth is twenty-two feet eight inches within the parapets. The passage over the bridge is a straight line from one end to the other; the arches are sixteen in number, and the buttresses of the piers are much stronger and better adapted for similar purposes than the modern tri-lateral cut-waters. Nearly eleven centuries have these buttresses withstood the rapid floods of the Guadelquivir, without sustaining any material injury. Although Hisham practically rebuilt the bridge, the labour did not contribute to his personal convenience. His great love of hunting caused the malcontents among his subjects to whisper that he had repaired the bridge to facilitate the outgoings and incomings of his hunting parties. The rumour reached the king, who vowed that he would never cross the bridge again—a vow he faithfully observed.

The great Aljama was completed in the year A.D. 793. The Emir Hisham took as great a personal interest in its progress as did his father, the walies of the provinces contributed to its decoration with the spoils from ancient monuments, the artificers with their genius, victors with their booty, the city with its workmen, the mountains of Cordova and Cabra by yielding the treasures of their quarries, Africa with the trunks of its imperishable larch-pines, and Asia by inoculating the growing Arabic-Spanish art with its genius of ornament, its aspirations and its poetry.

The superb mosque was finished, the workmen rested from their labours, and Hisham was confident that he had secured a place in the garden of everlasting joys. Let us look at this new house of prayer, majestically situated at the southern boundary of the great city, close to the green banks of the wide river of Andalus, occupying an area of 460 feet from north to south, and 280 from east to west, surrounded by high, thick battlemented walls, flanked by stout buttresses of watch towers, and surmounted by a lofty minaret. It is entered by the faithful by nine rich and spacious outer gates, and by eleven interior doors, four in the east and west sides, and a principal one to the north; the eleven in the inner façade communicating with an equal number of naves in the temple. The interior arrangement of this wonderful monument is most beautiful. There is a great courtyard, or atrium, with wide gates in the north, west, and east sides, having fountains for the ablutions and the purifications, and orange and palm groves. Then comes the immense body of the house of prayer, divided into eleven principal naves, running from north to south, and crossed at right angles by twenty-one smaller naves, which run from east to west. The elegant combination of the arcades, in which the pilasters are superposed on the columns, and the arches on other arches, leaving a passage for the light between the upper and lower columniation, is quite ideal. Finally, the mysterious hidden sanctuary, within which the Koran is kept, in whose precincts Oriental art has exhausted all the riches of its fascinating resources.

Figure 18. Cordova. The Bridge.

Figure 19. Cordova. View of the Mosque and the Bridge.

Figure 20. Cordova. Section of the Mosque of Cordova on the Line of the Plan L. M.

Figure 21. Cordova. Section of the Mosque of Cordova on the Line of the Plan N. O.

Figure 22. Cordova. The Gates of Pardon.

The eleven great doors leading from the courtyard to the mosque are superb double arches all in a row, sustained by beautiful marble columns, which, four by four, encircle the stout supporting pillars of stone in which they are consolidated. From the courtyard the interior of the mosque is seen through these eleven doors glittering with golden fires, and from the temple the courtyard, seen through these same doors, appears to be a glimpse of the longed-for Garden of Delights. The Mohammedan poet, Mohammed Ibn Mohammed Al-baluni, sings as follows of the holy House of Prayer, which surpasses in richness of colour, beauty of design, and boldness of ornamentation the most famous mosques of Arabia, Syria, and Africa:

"Abd-er-Rahman, for the love of God, and in honour of his religion, spent eighty thousand dinars of silver and gold."

"He laid them out in constructing a temple for the use of his pious nation, and for the better observance of the religion of Mahomet."

"Here the gold lavished on the panelled ceilings shines with the same brilliancy as the lightning, which pierces the clouds."

The design, as completed by the Sultan Hisham I. in the years 794-95, received considerable improvements at the hands of his successors. Indeed, it can be safely said that none of the sultans of the illustrious family of Omeyyad who reigned in Cordova failed to make some estimable addition, or contributed in some way to the decoration of the sumptuous building. Hakam's son, Abd-er-Rahman II, A.D. 822-852, ordered much "Gilt-work"—*Zak-hrafah*—to be made, but died before the work was completed. Mohammed, his son and successor—A.D. 852-886—continued the work undertaken by his father, and brought it to a close. Mohammed's son, Abdallah—A.D. 886-888—is also recorded as having made improvements in the building.

In the time of the Great Khalif, Abd-er-Rahman III, called An-nasir in order to distinguish him from the other monarchs of that name, the old minaret was pulled down by the advice of a wise architect, and a new one built on its site, whose vastness surpassed all other minarets in the world. Forty-three days were spent in sinking its foundations, which penetrated into the ground till water was struck, and three months sufficed for its construction. The superb tower is built of freestone and mortar in such a curious manner that, though it contains two staircases in its interior, each flight containing 107 steps, people can ascend to the top and go down again without seeing one another.

Figure 23. Cordova. A View in the Garden Belonging to the Mosque.

This elaborate tower measures fifty-four cubits from its foundations to the upper part of the open dome, to which the priest, who calls to prayers, turns his back, as he perambulates the projecting balcony, whose elegant balustrade surrounds the four walls like a graceful ring. From this balcony up to the top the tower rises eighty-three cubits more, being crowned with three beautiful apples, two of gold and one of silver, each three palms and a half in diameter, from which spring two lilies of six petals, supporting a pomegranate of purest gold. It has fourteen windows in its four faces. In two of these faces there are three intervals, and in the other two, two intervals, formed between columns of white and red jasper, and over the windows there is a crowning of solid arches sustained by small columns of the same jasper. These windows break up the mass of the walls in an admirable manner. The minaret is covered, both inside and out, with beautiful tracery in relief.

Abd-er-Rahman also rebuilt the wall which enclosed the mezquita to the north, looking towards the Orange Court, and he had the entire floor of the mosque levelled.

Figure 24. Cordova. The Mosque—Lateral Gate.

Figure 25. Cordova. Interior of the Mosque, or Cathedral.

In 961 A.D., Abd-er-Rahman III, the last great Omeyyad Sultan of Cordova died, and among his papers was discovered a diary, in his own handwriting, in which he had carefully noted down the days which he had spent in happiness and without any cause of sorrow. They numbered exactly fourteen. "O, man of understanding!" says the Arabian philosopher, "wonder and observe the small portion of real happiness the world affords even in the most enviable position! The Khalif An-nasir, whose prosperity in mundane affairs, and whose widely-spread empire became proverbial, had only fourteen days of undisturbed enjoyment during a reign of fifty years, seven months, and three days. Praise be given to Him, the Lord of eternal glory and everlasting empire."

The Sultan Hakam, as soon as he succeeded to the Khalifate, determined to enlarge the mosque, which was too small to accommodate the numbers of those who went there to perform the "azalas." He called together the architects and geometricians, who decided that the addition should extend from the "kiblah"—the point looking towards Mecca—of the mosque to the extreme end of the atrium, thus running the entire length of the eleven naves. The addition measured ninety-five cubits from north to south, and as much from east to west as the width of the whole mosque.

Figure 26. Cordova. Interior of the Mosque, Moorish Style, Built 961-967, Under Hakam II.

The passage to the alcazar, used by the khalif when he came to the "azalas," was intersected near the "nimbar," or pulpit, inside the "maksurrah." In the year 354 of the Hegirah the cupola, which crowned the "mihrab," or sanctuary, containing the Koran, in the addition to the mosque made by Hakam, was completed. In the same year the "sofeysafa," or enamelled mosaic work, was commenced in the mosque, and, by the order of Hakam, the four incomparable columns, which formerly had served as jambs for the doors of the old "mihrab," were set up again in the new one. It is related that while the addition was being made, a lively dispute arose as to the exact spot of the "kiblah," and it was finally decided to erect the sanctuary at the limit of the prolongation of the eleven naves, in the centre, looking directly to the south. Between the interior southern wall and the exterior, which was strengthened with round towers, a space of some fifteen feet remained. This was divided into eleven compartments, corresponding with the eleven naves of the mosque, that in the centre being destined for the sanctuary, and the others being reserved for the priests and other purposes. In this manner the "mihrab" was placed in the exact centre of the south side, with a wing on each side, of precise resemblance. In the west wing there was a secret passage leading from the mosque to the alcazar, which extended very near the west wall of the mezquita. The doors of this passage were arranged in a most intricate fashion, doubtless for the greater security of the palace, and they gave entrance to the interior of the "maksurrah," a sumptuous reserved space, communicating on the north, east, and west with the great naves, and on the south forming part of the interior wall of the mosque. This "maksurrah" was a privileged spot, enclosed by a sort of wooden grating, elegantly worked on both faces, and surmounted by turrets, the object of which was to cut off all communication with the sultan. This screen, measuring twenty-two cubits to its summit, gives its name to that part of the edifice which it occupies. Its ornamentation, as well as that of the new part of the central nave, extending from the old to the new "mihrab," is magnificent in the highest degree. The plan of the "maksurrah," properly speaking, was a large rectangle, divided into three parts, almost square, from which rose three Byzantine domes of rare beauty.

Figure 27. Cordova. The Mosque.

Figure 28. Cordova. The Mosque—Interior View.

Figure 29. Cordova. Interior View of the Mosque.

Figure 30. Cordova. The Mosque—General View of the Interior.

That in the centre served as a vestibule to the sanctuary, and was the most remarkable for its proportions, its outlines, and its decorations. This part of the mosque has been preserved in its principal features to the present day. The edifice has lasted nine centuries, and there is no indication that it will not endure for nine centuries more.

Over the festooned arches, which intersect each other, rise seven light and graceful horse-shoe arches, which disappear into the south wall, thus closing the picture and terminating the lower body of the sumptuous vestibule. Above these double arches runs an impost, beautifully worked and very graceful, embracing and crowning the four façades, and dividing the cupola into two zones—an upper and a lower. On this impost rest beautiful columns in pairs, oversetting great bold semi-circular arches, arranged with such art that they seem to imitate the curves of the interlaced garlands of a choir of beautiful odalisques, as the arches do not go from each column to the corresponding one of the next couple, but leave the intervening pair open. In this way, as there are two pairs of columns supporting the impost in each façade, eight principal arches are formed in the space in two great quadrilaterals placed opposite each other, their springing stones crossing and forming eight points of a star. There is an octagonal ring in the centre with eight graceful pendants, as an embellishment to the capitals of the eight pairs of columns. A horseshoe arch from point to point, to which a tablet of alabaster is fitted, leaves an uncertain prospect of the vault of heaven, which shines upon the cupola and the profusion of rich mosaic work with which it is adorned.

Between the elegant arches, which appear rather to hang from the cupola than to support it, the marvellous façade of the "mihrab" appears in the background, which glistens in the rays of the setting sun like a piece of brocade loaded with jewels, and which must have been dazzling as a fairy palace when, in the month of Ramadhan, the fourteen hundred and fifty-four lights of the great lamp shone under this enamelled "half-orange." This façade, in spite of its marvellous richness, does not show the smallest confusion in its ornamentation, each line is traced with the idea of giving greater beauty to the arch which forms the entrance to the sanctuary. It is composed of the arch with its spacious architrave and its smooth jambs with small columns, together with its "arraba" surrounded by Grecian frets, and a light series of arches without vacuums, upon which rest the imposts which divide the upper and lower bodies of the dome. But such is the profusion and splendour of the ornamentation of each of these parts that it is impossible to describe them. The keystones, the architrave, the circle drawn in squares, the panels, the trefoil arches and the tympana are incomparable, and the combination of Grecian frets with Persian and Byzantine ornaments and geometrical figures is as beautiful as it is bewildering. These last, moreover, do not preponderate as was the case later in the degenerate Mussulman ornamentation proper. Here the Grecian frets are the most important, being combined in a thousand different ways, the stems and leaves tracing the most graceful curves, and all uniting to form an elegant border, of the most capricious tracery. The whole of this ornamentation is of marble, delicately carved, now smooth and white, now covered with minute mosaic of various colours, and loaded with crystal and gold. The inscriptions seen here are also in gold, on a ground of crimson, or ultra-marine, alternating with the shining "sofeysafa."

"Sofeysafa" is an obscure word, which Don Pascual de Gayangos believes to be a transposition of the Arabic word Foseyfasa,[1] signifying enamel work of exceptional brilliancy, laid down by Greek workmen whom Abd-er-Rahman had brought to Cordova for the task.

Two columns are built into the jamb of the entrance arch to the sanctuary—one of black marble, the other of jasper, with lavishly carved capitals. If his blind enthusiasm did not deceive El-Makkari, the four columns were of green jasper and lapis-lazuli, two of each. An impost rests upon them as a cornice, and from this the arch springs; and on the impost an inscription in golden characters upon a crimson ground is written, which has the following meaning:

> "In the name of God, clement and merciful, let us give praise to Him, who directed us to this, for we could not have directed ourselves if we had not been directed by God, for which purpose the deputies of our Lord came with the truth. The priest Al-mostaner Billah Abdallah Al-Hakam, Prince of the Faithful—may God be faithful to him—ordered

---

[1] *Foseyfasa.* Gayangos tells us that the word is not in the Dictionaries, but that, according to an old Arabian writer, it is a substance of glass and small pebbles, crushed and baked together, uniting, with great variety of colour, great brilliancy, and beauty; it is sometimes mixed with silver and gold. One of the conditions of peace granted to the Emperor of Constantinople by the Khalif, Al-waléd, was that the Emperor should provide a certain quantity of *foseyfasa*, or enamelled work, for the great mosque at Damascus. Idrisi, in his description of the mosque of Cordova, says that the enamel which covered the walls of the "mihrab," came from Constantinople.

the president and prefect of his court, Giafar ben Abd-er-Rahman—may God be pleased with him—to add these two columns, since he laid the foundations in the holy fear of God, and with His good pleasure. This work was concluded in the month of Dhilhagia of the year 354 of the Hegirah."

Figure 31. Cordova. The Central Nave of the Mosque—961-967.

Figure 32. Cordova. The Mosque—Chief Entrance.

Figure 33. Cordova. Interior View of the Cathedral.

Figure 34. Cordova. Interior of the Mosque—Lateral Nave.

Figure 35. Interior of the Mosque—East Side.

Plate 17. Cordova.

Plate 18. Cordova. Detail of one of the niches of the Cupola. Mosaic keystones of the great arch of the Mihrab. Details of the Mihrab.

Plate 19. Cordova. Cufic inscription, over the arch of the Mihrab.

Plate 20. Cordova. Pieces of Wood used in the ancient covering of the Mosque. Details of the Interior of the Mosque.

From this inscription it would seem that two of the columns supporting the arch of "sofeysafa" were placed there by order of Hakam II., and that the others belonged to the old "mihrab," which had been demolished in order to lengthen the mosque; but no one is capable of saying to-day whether the black marble columns, or the jasper, were those added by the order of the magnificent khalif; and whether the inestimable gift which was deemed worthy of being commemorated in letters of gold was of lapis-lazuli or not. "God alone knows!"

The sanctuary is a small heptagonal space, with a pavement of white marble, a socle formed by seven great slabs of the same, and a dome, also of marble, shaped like a shell and made of a single piece, edged with an elegant moulding. The seven sides of the heptagon are decorated with exquisite trefoiled arches, supported by marble columns, with gilt capitals of delicate workmanship; the columns resting on a cornice, below whose modules runs a fascia, or fillet, of gilded characters carved in the marble of the slabs, which form the socle, or sub-basement.

Within this sanctuary was kept the famous "nimbar" of Hakam II, which was a sort of pulpit, according to the Arab historian, unequalled in the world, either for its materials or its workmanship. It was of ivory and precious woods—ebony, red and yellow sandal, Indian aloe, &c.—and the cost of it was 35,705 dineros and three adirmames. It had ten steps, and was said to consist of 37,000 pieces of wood joined by gold and silver nails, and incrusted with precious stones. It took nine years to build, eight artificers working at it each day. This pulpit, which must have been of mosaic of wood, jewels and metals of price, was reserved for the khalif, and in it was deposited also the chief object of veneration of all the Mohammedans of Andalusia, a copy of the Koran, supposed to have been written by Othman, and still stained with his blood. This copy was kept in a box of golden tissue studded with pearls and rubies, and covered with a case of richest crimson silk, and was placed on a desk or lectern, of aloe wood with golden nails. Its weight was so extraordinary, that two men could scarcely carry it.

Figure 36. Cordova. The Mosque—Detail of the Gate.

Figure 37. The Mosque—Façade of the Almanzor.

Figure 38. Cordova. View in the Mosque—961-967.

It was placed in the pulpit in order that the Imam might read in it during the "azala;" and when the ceremony was concluded, it was carried to another place, where it remained, carefully guarded, with the gold and silver vases destined for the great celebration of Ramadhan.

The chronicler, Ambrosio de Morales, says that the "nimbar" was a sort of chariot on four wheels, and that it had but seven steps. It was to be seen in the cathedral of Cordova as late as the middle of the sixteenth century, when it was dismembered, and its materials employed in the construction of a Christian altar.

The place, which from the slight indications of Edrisi appears to have served as treasure-room, was a sort of chapel, which is situated to-day not far from the site of the ancient "mihrab," to the north of the present "maksurrah." In this way it can easily be supposed that the noblest apartment of the mosque was completely closed to the people on the north and south sides; and, being occupied by the principal personages of the court, it would have been difficult for any irreverence to have been shown to the Imam or to the venerated "Mushaf"—Koran.

Figure 39. Cordova. The Mosque—A Gate on One of the Lateral Sides.

Figure 40. Cordova. The Mosque—Side of the Captive's Column.

The two "maksurrahs" remained, the one facing the other, both occupying exactly the same space; that is, at least, from east to west, supposing that they cut the three centre naves of the eleven which are in the mosque. Both these "maksurrahs," or screens, have disappeared; and at the present time we cannot form the slightest idea as to their design. Almost the only thing which has remained intact of that time is the sumptuous space of the three chapels occupied by the "maksurrah" of Hakam; and of the spaces occupied by the old "maksurrahs," only two disfigured chapels exist—that of the chief nave, and that of the next nave to the east. The latter is divided into two parts by a platform some feet above the floor of the mosque. In the upper portion the "Alicama" or preliminary for the prayer was made; and in the lower part, which still has the form of an underground chapel, the treasure was kept. The centre chapel, the present Chapel of Villaviciosa, was reserved for the khalif when he did not act as Imam; and in the west chapel, which exists no longer, was the seat of the Cadi of the Aljama. No trace of the original interior decoration of these chapels remains at the present day, and externally, only the arches facing the "mihrab," and which are similar to those of the façade of the vestibule, are left.

When everything had been completed internally to the satisfaction of Hakam, it occurred to him that the fountains in the Court of Ablutions did not harmonise with the grandeur of the mosque; he therefore commanded that they should be replaced by four splendid founts, or troughs, each cut out of a single piece of marble—two for the women in the eastern part, and two for the men in the west. It was his wish that these basins should be of magnificent proportions, and made from the same quarry. The work took much time, engaged many people, and necessitated the expenditure of a great deal of money; but it was happily executed, and the troughs were brought to their destination by a sloping way, specially constructed for the purpose, on great carts, each drawn by seventy stout oxen. The water, which was brought by the aqueducts of Abd-er-Rahman II, and was stored in a great reservoir covered with marble, flowed night and day; and after supplying the wants of the mosque, was carried off by three conduits to feed as many fountains for public use in the north, east, and west of the city.

Figure 41. Cordova. Mosque, North Side—Exterior of the Chapel of St. Pedro.

Figure 42. Cordova. General View of the Interior of the Chapel of the Masura and St. Ferdinand.

The great Vizier, Almanzor, considerably enlarged the mosque; many Christians, loaded with chains, being employed amongst the workmen. The eastern wall was thrown down, and the foundations of a new wall were laid one hundred and eighty feet from the old one, throughout the entire length from north to south. In the covered part of the building eight great naves were added, all of equal size, and having the same number of arches as those already existing; so that the thirty-three minor naves, which cut the principal naves at right angles, were lengthened one hundred and eighty feet, running from east to west. The new part formed thirty-five transverse naves, where there had formerly been only thirty-three, because the wing, with the residences which fell to the east of the "mihrab" which was not lengthened, occupied the space of the two extra naves. The prolongation of the minor naves was not carried out with the slavish and monotonous uniformity of modern days. The Arab architects did not understand symmetry as we do to-day, and they satisfied themselves with producing unity by means of variety, without seeking a forced correspondence of similar parts.

Figure 43. Cordova. Detail of the Chapel of Masura.

In the part added by Almanzor it was considered useless to give the same dimensions to the buttresses of the north wall as the primitive wall possessed, and consequently a space of six feet in length was gained from the principal naves at the north side. But as this extra width could not be given to the first of the lesser naves, as the height of the columns would not allow of it, the architect doubtless thought that instead of dividing up this small excess equally among the thirty-three arches in the length from north to south, it would be preferable and more effective to preserve the first three or four naves in line, adding a nave in the space gained by the diminution in the bulk of the buttresses, and by enlarging the succeeding naves wherever it seemed most convenient. As a result of this, the first transverse nave of the lengthened part, on account of the great narrowness of its intercolumniation, was not able to preserve the full span of its arches. It was necessary, therefore, to bring the latter nearer together and to break their curve, in order to keep the desired height, and thus probably for the first time, Pedro de Madrazo considers, was seen in the edifices of Arab Spain, the pointed arch which was destined to totally change the physiognomy of monumental art in the Middle Ages.

Figure 44. Cordova. The Mosque—Elevation of the Gate of the Sanctuary of the Koran.

    The arch, broken in this manner at the culminating point of its curve, presently adopted in this small nave all the varieties of decoration to which it was susceptible. Here in effect, in this small space of barely seven feet wide and one hundred and eighty-five long, architecture exhausted at one time, and at the first attempt, all the shapes of arches, which were to be employed in the four following centuries; a circumstance which was quite fortuitous. It was not the intention to dissimulate the enlargement of which we are speaking; on the contrary, it was decided to signalise it in an unmistakable manner, for which purpose a row of stout pillars was raised, where the old east wall stood, and where at present is the dividing line between the eleventh and twelfth greater naves, the pillars of which were suitably united to each other by great arches, springing from beautiful columns in pairs, built into the pillars. The old classical art would never have confided such wide spaces to supports so delicate as are these columns, which in couples send the bold festooned arches, which serve as an opening to the edifice of Almanzor, across to the opposite pair. But the architects of the time of Abd-er-Rahman I. and of Hakam II. had already successfully attempted a similar feat in the grand arcade of the inner façade, which looks on the Court, and in the strengthening arcade which divides the primitive mosque from its prolongation to the south, so there was no reason to fear its repetition. To-day we pass, with a certain respect, under these bold arches of eight metres elevation, and six, seven, and even eight metres in width, when we consider that they rest on columns of some three metres high, including their capitals; and only the stoutness of the pillars into which these graceful pairs are built assures us that they will not fall to the ground, wearied with such a supernatural effort.

Figure 45. Cordova. The Mosque—Gate of the Sanctuary of the Koran.

Figure 46. Cordova. The Mosque—Mosaic Decoration of the Sanctuary, 965-1001.

For the greater solidity of the wide edifice, added by Almanzor, a line of great pillars and arches, which marked the southern limit of the original mosque, was lengthened as far as the eastern wall, crossing at right angles the strengthening arcade already mentioned stretching from north to south; so that the actual Aljama was divided into four unequal parts, separated from each other, probably, by wooden screens and partitions. The part added by Hakam II., at whose extremities rose the old and the new "maksurrah," was called "The Noble Apartment," and was reserved for the nobility and the personages of the Court, the portion close to the "mihrab" being occupied by the ulema, alkatibes, almocries, and other ministers of the temple, and the Imam. The three remaining parts were for the people, and most likely the sexes were divided, for it is certain, from the assurances of an historian cited by Ahmed El-Makkari, that there were two doors inside the naves leading to the women's part.

Figure 47. Cordova. The Mosque—Right-Hand Side Gate within the Precincts of the "Maksurrah."

The art of the decorations of Almanzor's prolongation is not particularly attractive, the arches seem to be copied from those of the old door, and the only circumstance worthy of mention is that all the capitals of the columns are equal, and of the same form, in contrast with the great variety and richness of the capitals in the primitive mosque, and in the additions of Hakam II. The delicate and uniform construction of the mighty "hagib" may be mentioned as a purely archæological item, and also that the names of the artificers who made them are frequently to be seen in the foundations and shafts of the columns: e.g., Mondair, Mostauz, Motobarack, Fayr, Masud, Tasvir, Nassar, Kabir, Amin, Jalem-al-Amery, Hachchi, Tsamil, Bekr, Casim.

Figure 48. Cordova. The Mosque—Section of the Cupola of the Mihrab.

With the part added by Almanzor, the mosque is said to have formed a great rectangular quadrilateral 742 feet long from north to south, and 472 feet wide from east to west, enclosed by four great battlemented walls, fortified with square watch-towers, varying in height. The south wall, which reached a formidable height on account of the declivity of the ground, was adorned with nineteen towers, including those flanking it at both angles, which were more spacious and common to the two walls of east and west. The western wall had fourteen towers, and the north five, including the majestic minaret over the principal door; and, finally, the eastern wall was fortified by ten towers, all corresponding to the part which had to bear the pressure of the naves, and the wall of the Court at that side had no towers at all. The greater number of these towers remain, and the wide old walls also exist.

There were twelve outer gates to the mosque, ten leading into the edifice, and twenty-one interior doors, without counting those of the dependencies to the temple and that of the khalif's private passage, nineteen in the façade of the courtyard, and two which led to the women's part of the building.

All the outer doors were for the most part rectangular, formed by arched lintels set into ornamented horseshoe arches, their keystones were either white, or of alternate colours, the white being richly decorated with stucco ornaments in relief, and the coloured with beautiful mosaic of red and yellow brick, cut into tiny pieces. The horseshoe arch is set in a beautiful frame, richly ornamented as are the tympana between the arch and the lintel, the facias and the little windows of perforated alabaster, which, now enclosed in arches resting on little marble pillars and grouped in graceful pairs, flank the door. Some of these have projecting cornices forming a parapet with small dentalated towers, which give the sacred building the appearance of a fortress, and recall the warlike origin of the Mohammedan religion. All the outer gates have inscriptions, with invocations and verses taken from the Koran.

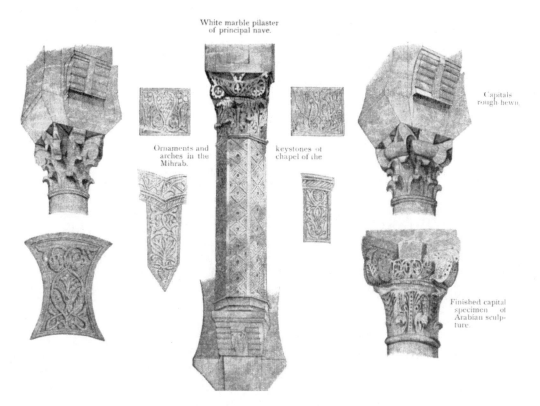

Plate 11. White marble pilaster of principal nave. Ornaments and arches in the Mihrab. keystones of chapel of the Capitals rough-hewn. Finished capital specimen of Arabian sculpture.

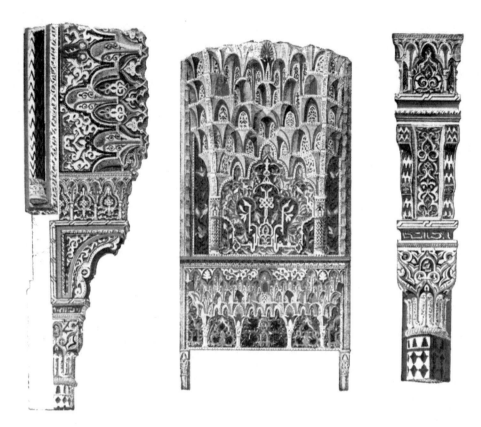

Plate 22. Cordova. Details of Moorish Work.

Plate 23. Details, Villaviciosa Chapel and Mihrab.

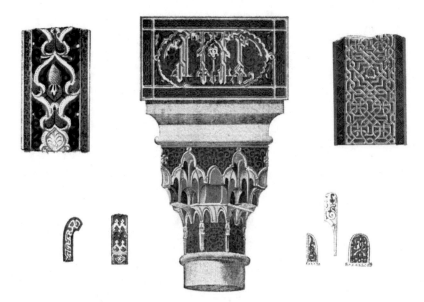

Plate 24. Details of Moorish Work.

Figure 49. Cordova. The Mosque—Dome of the Sanctuary.

Figure 50. Cordova. The Mosque. Roof of the Chapel of the Masura and St. Ferdinand.

Hakam II had an apartment constructed in the western part of the temple, which was to serve for the distribution of alms, and here any poor wanderer, who happened to be in the city without protection or means of subsistence, could obtain the wherewithal to continue his journey. For this purpose the khalif endowed the establishment in a splendid manner. It was not exactly a hostel, as its space was too limited; and, besides, Hakam had already established other places of lodging for poor travellers outside the mosque, one of these being quite near this "Dar-as-asdaca," or "Alms Chamber." Poor students, too, were looked after, and received a daily meal, and even small sums of money. The wise men received annual pensions from the treasury, according to their merit and personal circumstances.

Figure 51. Cordova. Villaviciosa Chapel.

The Alms Chamber was, properly speaking, only intended for the distribution of alms to the poor. Its beautiful door, to-day blocked up, can still be seen, both inside and out, in the wall of the mosque, and, according to El-Makkari, it was the most beautiful of the western side. It is no longer possible to form an exact idea of the aspect of the chamber as it was when Hakam II completed its decoration. He covered it with gilded and painted stucco work, which turned its walls into beautiful filigree, and to-day this apartment is half forgotten, after having served as a vestibule to the first Christian cathedral of Cordova. No one would think that this place, beyond St. Michael's postern, and separated from the body of the building by a wretched partition and a door of pine-wood, is the ancient "Dar-as-asdaca." For many years it was used as a Chapter Hall, and the archives of the extinct music-school, with its choir books, were kept here.

Figure 52. Cordova. The Mosque—Detail of the Hall of Chocolate.

The actual dimensions of the mosque varied at different periods, and are difficult to establish. One authority says, that in length from north to south the mosque measured six hundred and forty-two feet, in width four hundred and sixty-two feet. Mr. Waring, in his *Notes of an Architect in Spain*, describes the mosque as an oblong of three hundred and ninety-four feet by three hundred and sixty feet. The famous Orange Court is in length two hundred and twenty feet, and, being within the boundary walls of the mosque, it is probably included in the former measurement.

It is also impossible to fix, with any degree of certainty, the number of columns contained in the mosque during the time of Mohammedan supremacy. Ambrosio de Morales, and the Infante Don Juan Manuel, both of whom described the mosque before the columns were reduced in number by the alterations to which the building has been subjected, estimate the figures at one thousand and twelve, but it is only too certain that when the mosque was converted into a Christian church very many were removed to make room for altars and chapels.

No less than one hundred columns were comprised within the "maksurrah," which was further provided with three doors of exquisite workmanship, one of which was covered with plates of pure gold, as were the walls of the "mihrab." The floor of the "maksurrah," it is said, was paved with silver, and the pavements adjacent to it were covered with "sofeysafa."

Figure 53. Cordova. Entrance to the Vestibule of the Mihrab.

Figure 54. Cordova. Mihrab or Sanctuary of the Mosque.

The ceiling of the mosque was formerly covered with oval cartouches, bearing appropriate monitory inscriptions and pious sentences—such as, "Be not one of the negligent," "Felicity," "Blessing," "There is no God but God, to whom all beings address themselves in their need"—thus inciting the minds of the faithful to contemplation and prayer. Some few of the cartouches are still remaining; but the inscriptions were, for the most part, carefully effaced when the mosque was transformed into a Christian temple. Those in the "mihrab," and in the angles near the tower, may yet be seen.

Figure 55. Cordova. The Mosque—Arch And Front of the Abd-Er-Rahman and Mihrab Chapels.

Figure 56. Cordova. Entrance to the Chapel of the Mihrab.

The number of brazen chandeliers of different sizes in the mosque is computed at upwards of two hundred, and the number of cups attached, and containing oil, at upwards of seven thousand. Some of the oil-reservoirs for the great lamps were Christian bells, deprived of their clappers; inverted, and suspended from the roof. It is known that in the many expeditions against the Christian, bells were frequently removed from the churches and brought to Cordova. Sometimes the metal of the bells was recast into forms more in accordance with the Moorish style of ornament.

The following rites had to be observed in the service of the mosque: The ornaments were to consist only of brass, silver or glass lamps, which were lighted at night when the doors were opened for prayer. Some striking design was painted on the west wall, in order that the faithful should look in that direction. There was only one pulpit, which was on wheels, as the sermon was preached from any spot the Talvi wished.

The courts of the mosque were paved with porcelain tiles, over which pure water could flow. Those who did not wash themselves at home were obliged to do so in the Court of Ablutions before entering the sacred precincts. All shoes had to be left at the door of the mosque, and no buildings, such as inns and hostelries, and disreputable houses, were allowed in the neighbourhood. No Jews were allowed to pass before it. Women were not permitted to enter some mosques, because they were not circumcised, the sultana alone having an oratory, where she prayed for all women.

At midnight a mezzin mounted the minaret, and cried out: "God is great, to pray is better than to sleep"; at two o'clock in the morning he said the same; at four o'clock he placed a lantern at the end of a rod and said, "Day is breaking, let us praise God"; at the fourth prayer he hoisted a white flag, which was lowered at one o'clock, saying, "God is great." Friday was their feast day, and a blue banner was hoisted at dawn, and left floating till half-past ten. The fifth prayer was at four o'clock in the afternoon, in winter at three; when the evening star appeared, the sixth prayer was called out; and at nine o'clock the last prayer of the day was said. Sand glasses were employed to mark the passage of the hours.

The state of Cordova died with Almanzor; and the races, who alternately took possession of the throne, did not leave the least trace in the mosque. Finally, St. Ferdinand, King of Castile and Toledo, completely routed the Moors, and the mezquita was purified and dedicated to Our Lady of the Assumption. The following is an extract from the archives of the cathedral: "Let it be known that I, Ferdinand, by the grace of God, King of Castile, with the consent and approval of Dona Berenguele, my Mother, and of Dona Juana, the Queen my wife, and of my children, Alfonso, Frederico, and Ferdinand, make a deed of gift to God of the Cathedral Church of Santa Maria of Cordova, and to you, Master Lope, my beloved chosen Bishop of the same, from now on, and to your successors, and the Chapter of Canons, &c. November 12th, 1238." This pious monarch founded a chapel dedicated to St. Clement, which was erected against the south wall, embracing the space occupied by three naves from east to west, and by four transverse naves from north to south. This space was shut in with walls, leaving the two Arab arches inside intact, the altar dedicated to the saint being placed against the east wall. Many nobles followed the king's example, and founded chapels, amongst them being that of St. Inez, erected by Piedro Diaz de Haro, in 1250, in the tenth principal nave, counting from the west wall, also against the south wall, and only occupying two transverse naves. St. Ferdinand endowed the cathedral so richly that on his death its benefices were very considerable.

Figure 57. Cordova. View of the Interior of the Mihrab Chapel.

He was succeeded by his son, Alfonso X., who showed the same religious spirit as his father, giving large grants to the funds of the cathedral; and, in the year 1258, erecting the grand chapel, conceding many privileges to the work and the fabric. The donations made by other Christians up to this time had been of a very modest nature; and, as the

Jews of Cordova were expending great sums on the erection of a synagogue, it seems as though the Christians were shamed into greater generosity to the cathedral, for at the same time the famous commander, Domingo Muñoz, erected the chapel of St. Bartholomew, and the chapter and the king decided to turn the mosque into a real Christian cathedral in developing Western architecture. The commander made his chapel in the angle formed by the inner south wall and the west side of the vestibule, or "maksurrah," of Hakam II., taking the area of two principal and two transverse naves. As this chapel could not be lighted from outside on account of the west wing of the "mihrab," and the khalif's secret passage being behind, it was illuminated with light from the temple, a pointed door and four windows being made in the north wall.

Figure 58. Cordova. The Mosque—Details of the Interior of the Chapel of the Mihrab.

Figure 59. Cordova. The Mosque—Marble Socle in the Mihrab.

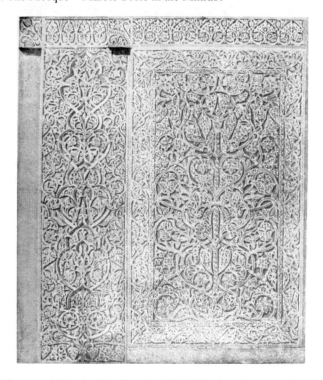

Figure 60. Cordova. Basement Panel of the Façade of the Mihrab.

Figure 61. Cordova. The Mosque—Front of the Trastamara Chapel.

The chapter set about their work with more splendour. They selected the three first transverse naves of the noble apartment, beginning at the re-inforcing wall, which marks the prolongation of Hakam, giving to the single nave that they opened a length of one hundred feet from the inner door of the Alms Chamber to the central apartment of the three enclosed in the old "maksurrah." They made the Alms Chamber into a vestibule, leaving the re-inforcing wall as it was without touching the bold ultra-semi-circular arches resting on pairs of columns; they pulled down the cadi's apartment in order to make way for the transept, and also the three transverse naves it had occupied. The three columns in front of the Arab pillars, which stood in the length from east to west, were pulled down too, and three handsomer pillars were erected in their place, fortified at right angles by walls in the manner of buttresses, which intercepted the entire width of one transverse nave. Great pointed arches sprang from pillar to pillar, corresponding with the horse-shoe arches in front; a light and graceful dome stretched from one side to the other, divided into four compartments by three great arches, of which that nearest to the sanctuary rested on high columns, and the other two on well-carved brackets, with open-work borders suspended at a regular height above the spaces. Finally, they took the central apartment of the ancient "maksurrah," where we presume the khalif sat, and erected there the Grand Chapel.

Figure 62. Cordova. General View of the Chapel of Villaviciosa.

The arrangement of this space was perfectly adapted for the purpose of a Grand Chapel; the other room adjoining to the east being converted into a sacristy. It was doubtless in the same condition as when finished by the architects of Hakam II. At the north side it had a horse-shoe arch corresponding with the re-inforcing wall of the same khalif, and on the east side it had a great arched window and two little doors at the sides, which communicated with the tribune of the "Alicama," at the south side, giving a splendid example of the rich Byzantine style of the time of Hakam, and forming a combination of segment arches crossing in space and forming crosses of undulating ribbons in the intercolumniations, the whole being similar to the decoration displayed in front of the vestibule of the "mihrab."

Figure 63. Cordova. North Angle of the Chapel of Villaviciosa.

Figure 64. Cordova. Villaviciosa Chapel.

This chapel was built at the king's expense, for which the grateful chapter resolved to celebrate the anniversary of his death, a practice which has been faithfully observed to the present day.

We do not know how the west side was decorated, where this space was united with the apartment of the cadi, which had been pulled down. In order to convert this into a Grand Chapel it was not necessary to disfigure it completely; it was sufficient to fill up the great northern arch, which in the time of the khalifs was closed by the first "maksurrah," and also to block up the great window at the east, communicating with the tribune of the "Alicama;" to leave the two little side doors open for communication with the sacristy, and to enlarge the sanctuary as much as necessary, to shut it in at the south side with glass windows, and to place the customary chancel at its opening. Perhaps no more than this was done; but who is capable to-day of saying how much respect the king's architects had for Arab-Byzantine work?

In the year 1260 Don Gonzalo Yanez, first gentleman of Aguilar, founded the Chapel of St. John the Baptist. Five years later the Bishop Fernando de Mesa built the Chapel of Santiago, in the south-east corner, near the Chapel of St. Clement. This chapel was wide and commodious, and the Arab arches in its area were not disturbed. In 1263 King Alfonso X. had the ancient aqueducts repaired, and in 1275 Prince Ferdinand gave an order for four Moors, who should be free from taxation, to be kept at work in the building operations of the cathedral. Two of these were to be carpenters, and two masons. This privilege was confirmed several times in succeeding years, and a charter exists, dated Cordova, 25th October, 1282, which orders that all the Moors living in the city, whether they were artificers or not, shall work for two days of the year in the cathedral. It was thought that these workmen would understand the repairing of Moorish work better than Christians, but the task was also meant as a humiliation. As time went on, these workmen, more or less, lost the traditions of their faith and their architecture, so that they were really of little service in preserving the original character of the edifice.

Figure 65. Cordova. The Mosque—Chapel Of Villaviciosa.

In 1278 the first statue of St. Raphael the Archangel was placed on the top of the minaret. At that time Cordova was visited by the plague, which worked terrible destruction amongst the inhabitants. It is related that St. Raphael appeared to Friar Simon de Sousa, of the Convent of Our Lady of Mercy, and told him that God was moved with compassion, and that He would take away the visitation if a statue of St. Raphael himself were placed on the tower of the Cathedral, and if his Feast were celebrated properly every year. This was done, and the plague immediately ceased. A new chapel to St. Bartholomew was erected in 1280 by Martin Muñoz, nephew of the famous commander Domingo Muñoz; and after this, the Chapel of St. Paul, which belonged to the family of the Godois. Then followed the foundation of the Chapel of St. Nicholas, by a pious Archdeacon; and of the Chapels of St. Benedict, St. Vincent, and St. Giles, and that of Our Lady of the Snow.

Figure 66. Cordova. Arab Tribune, To-Day the Chapel of Villaviciosa, Left Side.

Figure 67. Cordova. Ancient Inscription of the Time of Khalifate, Found In an Excavation.

A.

B.

Figure 68. Cordova the Mosque. A. Detail of the Trastamara Chapel. The Mosque. B. Chapel of Trastamara, South Side.

It was not thought wise to make any great efforts to introduce the art of the West into a city which could not as yet be considered sure of not falling again into the hands of the infidels. In the year 1369 Don Enrique, the Fraticide, came to the throne of Castile. He desired to carry out the wishes of his father, and to give him a place of sepulchre worthy of his high renown. For this purpose he ordered a Royal Chapel to be erected in the cathedral at the back of the Grand Chapel in the Arab Tribune, which served as a sacristy. He decided to bury here his grandfather, Don Fernando X., whose body had been laid under the grand chapel by order of his Queen, Constanza. This fabric must have taken some considerable time, for the stucco, wood and tile work are really wonderful. Mohammedan art had undergone a complete transformation; the grandiose Arab-Byzantine style had been succeeded by the effeminate Moorish school, first practised by the Almoravides, and after by the Almohades; and the Moorish architects and decorators of Cordova could not remain uninfluenced by the taste which had become general through the artificers who had renovated the Alcazar at Seville, and who had embellished the Alhambra at Granada. Nothing was more unlike the architecture of the days of Hakam II than that employed now in the construction of the Royal Chapel. Two parts are noticed—an upper and a lower. The Moorish architect who directed the work had windows with ornamented arches in the new style opened in the east and west sides, which were longer than the others. He ordered, too, that Saracen art, emancipated from the Byzantine traditions, should be stamped on the ornamentation of the four walls, and on the cupola that crowned them. These arches were given festoons with lobules, which boldly, though corruptly, hid the true object of the curves. They were also set in square compartments, forming many edges beautifully worked with hammer and chisel. The framings were crowned with beautiful little cornices of small interlaced and open-worked arches, and above them ran round all the four sides a wide facia of little pine-shaped domes, which imitated stalactites of crystallised gold, having a most surprising effect, and of a sort until then unknown in the most famous mosque of the West.

In the east and west walls, which were the longest of the rectangle, the arches with lobules, which could not be opened, were in relief; and resting on the light cornice were two tablets with lions. There were four of these lions—two on the western and two on the eastern facia, equi-distant from one another; and from each lion to that which faced him sprang a great arch, whose facing projected some feet over the lower zone, and from each lion to that by his side sprang another great arch, which did not project beyond the facing of the lower wall. These four upper arches, each one with twenty-one trefoil lobules, formed a perfect square, their four supports being at an equal distance, thanks to the ingenious method of cutting the longer sides, putting the lions perpendicularly over the great lower arches. Once this difficulty was overcome it was doubtless an easy matter to raise the cupola, which was to crown the fabric. The ancient dome must have been similar to that which has been discovered in the Chapel of Villaviciosa, but it must have seemed poor in the eyes of King Henry II., so accustomed to seeing the Moorish cupolas with stalactites; so they placed a cornice on the arches described above, and on this rested the segments of the circle, which form the elegant and strange African cupola.

A.

B.

Figure 69. Cordova. A. The Mosque. Interior of the Mihrab. B. The Mosque. Arab Arcade above the First Mihrab.

A.

B.

Figure 70. Cordova. A. The Mosque. Details, Arches of the Mihrab. B. The Mosque. Detail of the Mihrab.

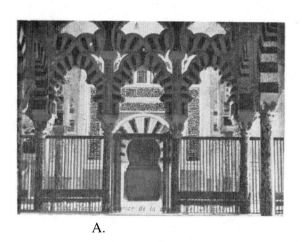 

A.   B.

Figure 71. Cordova. A. The Mosque. Exterior of the Chapel of the Mihrab. B. The Mosque. Gate of the Sultan.

A.   B.

Figure 72. Cordova. A. Principal Entrance to the Mosque. B. Detail near The Mihrab.

The following distribution is seen in the lower portion: Towards the middle of the east side there is an arch formed of little domes with stalactites, slightly pointed, sufficiently deep, enclosed in a sort of framing of gilded stucco, forming beautifully interlaced branches. The square compartment finishes at the lower end in a wide facia, which runs on both sides on a high socle of minute and beautiful tiling, and between the complicated ornaments in relief circles are formed, enclosing the arms of Castile and Leon. To the right side, on this same facia, is an ornamental arch of eleven lobules enclosed in another framing, entirely covered with tracery in relief, sustained by two very slight columns, built into the wall. Joined to this is another arch, much lower, with seven lobules, also ornamented, and sustained by columns of the same style as those just described, bearing a shield with the same arms. The left side has the same ornamentation, with the difference that both the arches have seven lobules, because the wall has more frontage on this side: and another difference was that in the north-east corner it had an ornamentation of minute open-work instead of a shield. The wall opposite had the same distribution with a deep central arch and small arches at the side, with little columns in the Gothic style, which show already that the style is no longer purely Moorish, but a sort of base mixture of the decorative art of the East and the West. Perhaps we may consider this the true concession of the Moorish artificers to the art preferred by the Court, and as their final abandonment of the pure style, which had been traditional with them.

In 1521 the Bishop Don Alonso Manrique obtained permission from the Emperor Charles V. to erect the Gothic cathedral, which is in existence to-day. Three years later, when he visited the buildings, the Emperor repented having given his permission. Indeed the Christian work appears cold and pallid by the side of that of the Arabs.

As Amados de los Rios, a great Spanish antiquary and Orientalist, sings in his mournful requiem over the departed glories of the mosque: "Neither the sumptuous Christian fabric that to-day rises in the midst of those countless columns, nor all the treasures of art lavished upon it by the celebrated artists of the sixteenth century who erected it, nor that interminable series of chapels of every epoch which, resting against the walls of the mosque disfigure it; nor the clumsy angels that seem to suspend their flight to shed glory over the Divine service, nor the words of the Evangelist sounding from the seat of the Holy Spirit, can dispel or banish, in the slightest degree, the majesty of those wandering shades that in vain seek in the sanctuary the sacred volume whose leaves, according to tradition, were enamelled with the blood of the Khalif Othman, martyr to the faith. A world of souvenirs here enthrals the mind of the traveler as he gazes with a feeling of sorrow upon these profanations—works dedicated by the intolerant, yet sincere, faith of our ancestors; impelled by the desire of banishing forever from that spot, consecrated to the law of Jesus, the spirit of Mohammed and the ghosts of his slaves that haunt it, and will forever haunt it while it exists. For, in spite of the mutilations it has endured, and of the changes it has undergone, there is impressed upon it, by a superior ineradicable law, the seal of the art that inspired it, and the character of the people by whom it was planned and erected."

Don Amados is not alone in his eloquent, if unavailing, protest. When Charles V. observed St. Peter's Chapel rising out of the very centre of the mosque, he rebuked the Bishop, Alonso Manriquez, who had erected the incongruous edifice, in no measured terms. "You have built here," said the king, "what you or anyone might have built elsewhere; but you have spoilt what was unique in the world." Alas! the monarch had forgotten, or did not choose to remember, that the reprimand came with a very bad grace from one who, for his never-completed palace at Granada, had torn down whole courts and halls of the Alhambra.

A.   B.

Figure 73. Cordova. A. The Gates of Pardon. B. the Bishop's Gate.

The mosque of Cordova is still to-day, by universal consent, the most beautiful Mussulman temple, and one of the most wonderful architectural monuments in the world. The susceptible Italian author, Edmondo de Amicis, has given us a vividly picturesque description of his first impression of the interior of the building. "Imagine a forest," he says, "fancy yourself in the thickest portion of it, and that you can see nothing but the trunks of trees. So, in this mosque, on whatever side you look, the eye loses itself among the columns. It is a forest of marble, whose confines one cannot discover. You follow with your eye, one by one, the very long rows of columns that interlace at every step with numberless other rows, and you reach a semi-obscure background, in which other columns seem to be gleaming. There are nineteen aisles, which extend from north to south, traversed by thirty-three others, supported (among them all) by more than nine hundred columns of porphyry, jasper, breccia, and marbles of every colour. Each column upholds a small pilaster, and between them runs an arch, and a second one extends from pilaster to pilaster, the latter placed above the former, and both of them in the form of a horseshoe; so that in imagining the columns to be the trunks of so many trees, the arches represent the branches, and the similitude of the mosque to a forest is complete. The middle aisle, much broader than the others, ends in front of the "maksurrah," which is the most sacred part of the temple, where the Koran was worshipped.

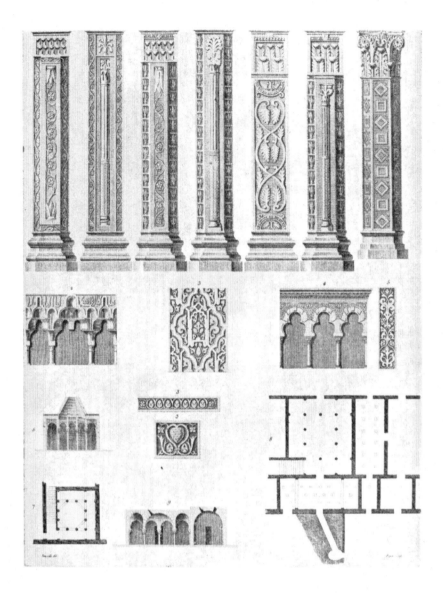

Figure 74. Cordova. The Mosque—Pilasters and Arabian Baths.

Here, from the windows in the ceiling, falls a pale ray of light that illuminates a row of columns; there is a dark spot; farther on falls a second ray, which lights another aisle. It is impossible to express the feeling of mysterious surprise which that spectacle arouses in your soul. It is like the sudden revelation of an unknown religion, nature, and life, which bears away your imagination to the delight of that paradise, full of love and voluptuousness, where the blessed, seated under the shade of leafy palm trees and thornless rose bushes, drink from crystal vases the wine, sparkling like pearls, mixed by immortal children, and take their repose in the arms of charming black-eyed virgins! All the pictures of eternal pleasure, which the Koran promises to the faithful, present themselves to your bright mind, gleaming and vivid, at the first sight of the mosque, and cause you a sweet momentary intoxication, which leaves in your heart an indescribable sort of melancholy! A brief tumult of the mind, and a spark of fire rushes through your brain—such is the first sensation one experiences upon entering the cathedral of Cordova."

Listen again to the musings of this same impressionable writer, as he gazes at the ceiling and walls of the principal chapel, the only part of the mosque that is quite intact. "It is," he says, "a dazzling gleam of crystals of a thousand colours, a network of arabesques, which puzzles the mind, and a complication of bas-reliefs, gildings, ornaments, minutiæ of design and colouring, of a delicacy, grace and perfection sufficient to drive the most patient painter distracted. It is impossible to retain any of the pretentious work in the mind. You might turn a hundred times to look at it, and it would only seem to you, in thinking it over, a mingling of blue, red, green, gilded, and luminous points, or a very intricate embroidery, changing continually, with the greatest rapidity, both design and colouring. Only from the fiery and indefatigable imagination of the Arabs could such a perfect miracle of art emanate."

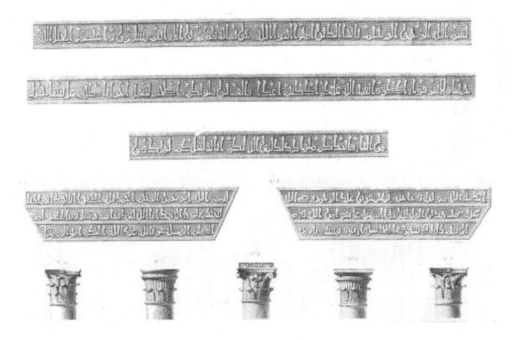

Figure 75. Cordova. Inscriptions and Arabian Chapters.

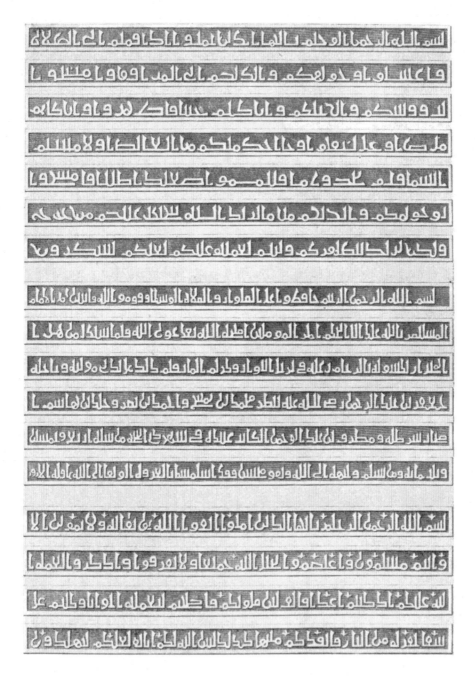

Figure 76. Cordova. The Mosque—A Cufic Inscription in the Place Appropriated to the Performance of Ablutions.

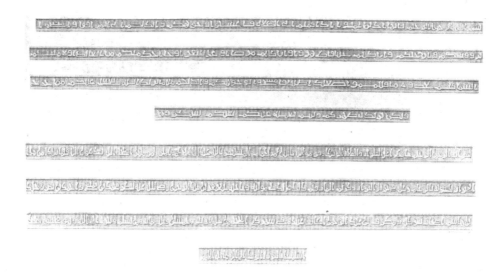

Figure 77. Cordova. Arabic Inscriptions.

Figure 78. Cordova. A Cufic Inscription on the Additions Made to the Mosque, By Order of the Khalif Al-Hakam.

But if the mere shell of this majestic edifice, this voiceless testimony to the glory of a world-power that has gone the way of all temporal empires is still eloquent in decay, and still a force to stir the imagination, what must it have been when the spirit of Moslemism filled its courts, and the temple resounded with praise and devotion? We can get some idea of the impressiveness of a Mohammedan service in the pages of Frederick Schack's *Poetry and Art of the Arabs in Spain and Sicily*. The following vivid passage is a description of the mosque of Cordova on a solemn fête day: "On both sides of the pulpit wave two standards to signify that Islam has triumphed over Judaism and Christianity, and that the Koran has conquered the Old and New Testaments. The 'Almnedian' climb upon the gallery of the high minaret and intone the 'salam' or salutation to the Prophet. Then the nave of the mosque fills with believers, who, clothed in white and wearing a festive aspect, gather for the oration. In a few moments, throughout the edifice nothing is to be seen but kneeling people. By the secret way which joins the temple to the alcazar, comes the khalif, who seats himself in his elevated place. A reader of the Koran reads a Sura on the reading-desk of the Tribune. The voice of the Muezzin sounds again, inviting people to the noon-day prayers. All the faithful rise and murmur their prayers, making obeisances. A servant of the mosque opens the doors of the pulpit and seizes a sword, with which, turning towards Mecca, he admonishes all to praise Mohammed, while the Prophet's name is being celebrated from the Tribune by the singing of the 'mubaliges.' After this the preacher ascends the pulpit, taking from the hand of the servant the sword, which recalls and symbolises the subjection of Spain to the power of Islam. It is the day on which 'Djihad,' or the holy war, is to be proclaimed, the call for all able-bodied men to descend into the battle-field against the Christians. The multitude listen with silent devotion to the discourse (woven from the head of the Koran) which begins like this:

"'Praised be God, who has increased the glory of Islam, thanks to the sword of the champion of the Faith, and who, in his Holy Book, has promised aid and victory to the believer.

'''Allah scatters his benefits over the world.

'''If he did not impel men to dash armed against each other, the earth would be lost.

'''Allah has ordered that the people be fought against until they know there is but one God.

'''The flame of war will not be extinguished until the end of the world.

'''The Divine benediction will fall upon the mane of the war-horse until the Day of Judgment.

'''Be you armed from head to foot, or only lightly armed, rise, and take your departure.

'''O, believers! what will become of you if, when you are called to battle, you remain with your face turned toward the ground?

'''Do you prefer the life of this world to that of the future?

'''Believe me: the gates of paradise stand in the shadow of the sword.

'''He who dies in battle for the cause of God, washes with the blood he sheds all the stains of his sins.

Figure 79. Cordova. The Bridge across the Guadelquivir, With a View of the Cathedral (Mezquita). The Scene As It Appeared in 1780. From Antigüedades Arabes de España. Madrid, 1780, fol.

Figure 80. Cordova. View of Cordova Cathedral (Mezquita), As It Appeared In 1780. From *Antigüedades Arabes de España*. Madrid, 1780. fol.

Figure 81. Cordova. Wall of the Mosque.

"'His body will not be washed like the other bodies, because in the Day of Judgment his wounds will send out a fragrance like musk.

"'When the warriors shall present themselves at the Gates of Paradise, a voice from within will ask: "What have you done during your life?"

"'And they will reply: "We have brandished the sword in the struggle for the cause of God."

"'Then the eternal Gates will open, and the warriors will enter forty years before the others.

"'Up, then, O believers! Abandon women, children, brothers, and worldly possessions, and go forth to the holy war!

"'And thou, O God, Lord of the present and future world, fight for the armies of those who recognise thy Unity! Destroy the incredulous, idolaters, and enemies of thy holy faith! Overthrow their standards, and give them, with all they possess, as booty to the Mussulmans!'"

Figure 82. Cordova. Façade of the Mihrab.

The preacher, when he has finished his discourse, exclaims, turning towards the congregation: "Ask of God!" and prays in silence. All the faithful, touching the ground with their foreheads, follow his example. The "mubaliges" sing: "Amen! Amen, O Lord of all beings!" Like the intense heat which precedes the tempest, the enthusiasm of the multitude (restrained, up to this time, in a marvellous silence) breaks out in loud murmurs, which, rising like the waves of the sea, and inundating the temple, finally make the echo of a thousand united voices resound through the naves, chapels, and vaults in one single shout: "There is no God but Allah!"

Abd-er-Rahman I was old when he commenced the building of the Mosque, and experienced in every description of architecture. His passion for building was as eager as that of his predecessors of the house of Omeyyad, who had made Damascus the envy of the world; and, during the frequent periods of peace, he had turned all his thoughts to the adornment of his capital by works which he had himself superintended. One of his first undertakings was to supply Cordova with water by means of an aqueduct, which came from the distant hills, and the vestiges of which are visible to this day.

Figure 83. Cordova. The Mosque—Arch of One of the Gates.

Figure 84. Cordova. The Mosque—Lattice.

The water thus brought from the mountains was conveyed to the palace, and thence carried to every quarter of the city by means of conduits, from which it flowed into basins, as well as into lakes, enormous tanks, reservoirs and fountains. The sultan then planted a most delightful garden, to which he gave the name of Munyat-Arrissafah, in remembrance of a country seat near Damascus, which his grandfather, the Khalif Hisham, had built, and where he himself had spent the earliest years of his life. Finding the spot a very charming one, he erected in the middle of it a magnificent palace; and, moreover, made it his residence in preference to the old palace, inhabited by the former governors of Andalus. Having an ardent love of horticulture, he commissioned a botanist to procure for him in the East fruits and plants that could be easily naturalised in Andalus; and, in this manner, it is said, Abd-er-Rahman introduced the peach, and the particular kind of pomegranate, called "Safari," into Spain. It is believed that this best species of pomegranate obtained its name from having been sent to Abd-er-Rahman by his sister, then residing in the East, and was called "Safari," or "the Traveller," from this circumstance. Other derivations of the name are given, all plausible enough. One thing is certain, the fruit is called to this day in Spain, "Granada Zafari," and is considered the best of its kind in point of flavour, smallness of seed, and abundance of juice. Abd-er-Rahman II carried on the work of beautifying Cordova with gardens, palaces, and bridges, but it was the third sovereign of his name, the Great Khalif, Abd-er-Rahman III., who restored the Moslem supremacy in Spain, and won for himself the title of En-Nasir li-dini-llah ("The Defender of the Faith of God"), who placed the crown on Cordova's beauty and splendour. Byzantium, perhaps, compared with it in the loveliness of her buildings, and the luxury and refinement of her life, but no other city of Europe could approach the "Bride of Andalusia." "To her," sang the old Arab writer, "belong all the beauty and the ornament that delight the eye and dazzle the sight. Her long line of Sultans form her crown of glory; her necklace is strung with the pearls which her poets have gathered from the ocean of language; her dress is of the canvas of learning well knit together by her men of science; and the masters of every art and industry are the hem of her garments."

"The inhabitants of Cordova," says Ahmed-El-Makkari, the great Arab historian, "are famous for their courteous and polished manners, their superior intelligence, their exquisite taste and magnificence in their meals, dress, and horses. There thou wouldst see doctors, shining with all sorts of learning; lords, distinguished by their virtue and generosity; warriors, renowned for their expeditions into the country of the infidels; and officers, experienced in all kinds of warfare. To Cordova came from all parts of the world students eager to cultivate poetry, to study the sciences, or to be instructed in divinity or law; so that it became the meeting-place of the eminent in all matters, the abode of the learned, and the place of resort for the studious; its interior was always filled with the eminent and the noble of all countries, its literary men and soldiers were continually vying with each other to gain renown, and its precincts never ceased to be the arena of the distinguished, the retreat of scholars, the halting place of the noble, and the repository of the true and virtuous. Cordova was to Andalus what the head is to the body, or what the breast is to the lion."

To-day there is nothing left in Cordova but the mosque, the bridge, and the ruins of the alcazar to mark the spot where, in the time of Abd-er-Rahman III., a city, ten miles in length, lined the banks of the Guadelquivir with mosques and gardens and marble palaces. The royal palaces of the Great Khalif included the Palace of Lovers, the Palace of Flowers, the Palace of Contentment, the Palace of the Diadem, and the palace which the Sultan named Damascus, of which the Moorish poet sang, "All palaces in the world are nothing compared to Damascus, for not only has it gardens with the most delicious fruits and sweet-smelling flowers, beautiful prospects, and limpid running waters, clouds pregnant with aromatic dew, and lofty buildings; but its night is always perfumed, for morning pours on it her gray amber, and night her black musk." The city contained over fifty thousand palaces of the nobles, and twice that number of houses of the common people, while seven hundred mosques and nine hundred public baths had close companionship among a community who made cleanliness co-ordinate with godliness.

But perhaps the greatest monument of Moorish architecture that was ever created in Spain, the most wonderful city and palace that has ever been constructed, is to-day a name and a memory of which not a trace is in existence. That marvellous suburb of Cordova, called Ez-Zahra, "the Fairest," which was built at the suggestion of the favourite mistress of Abd-er-Rahman III, and was forty years in the making, has been entirely obliterated. At the foot of the "Hill of the Bridge," at a distance of three miles from Cordova, the foundation of the city was laid in A.D. 936. A third of the royal income was expended every year in the prosecution of the work. Ten thousand labourers and three thousand beasts of burden were employed continually, and six thousand blocks of stone were cut and polished each day for building purposes. Many of its four thousand columns came from Rome, Constantinople, and Carthage; its fifteen thousand doors were coated with iron and polished brass; the walls and roof in the Hall of the Khalif were constructed of marble and gold. A marble statue of Ez-Zahra, "the Fairest," was erected over the principal gateway.

Figure 85. Cordova. The Mosque—Ornamental Arched Window.

Figure 86. Cordova. The Mosque—Capitals of the Entrance Arch.

Figure 87. Cordova. Details of the Frieze.

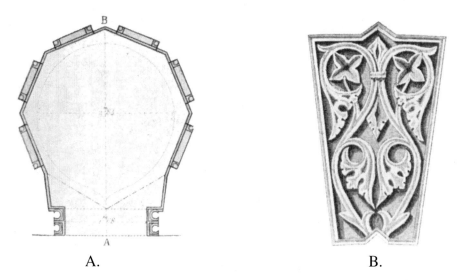

Figure 88. Cordova. A. Plan. B. Keystone of Ornamental Arch.

Figure 89. Detail of the Cornice.

Figure 90. Detail of the Cornice.

Arabian chroniclers have exhausted their eloquence in attempting to do justice to the wonders of Medinat-Ez-Zahra, and the result is so monotonous a surfeit of superlatives that even the beauty that inspired them can scarcely reconcile us to the repetition. But the historians occasionally drop into prose in recounting the marvels of the palace, and then we learn that "the number of male servants employed by the khalif has been estimated at thirteen thousand seven hundred and fifty, to whom the daily allowance of flesh meat, exclusive of fowls and fish, was thirteen thousand pounds; the number of women of various kinds and classes, comprising the harem of the sultan or waiting upon them, is said to have amounted to six thousand three hundred and fourteen. The Slav pages and eunuchs were three thousand three hundred and fifty, to whom thirteen thousand pounds of flesh meat were distributed daily, some receiving ten pounds each, and some less, according to their rank and station, exclusive of fowls, partridges, and birds of other sorts, game, and fish. The daily allowance of bread for the fish in the pond of Ez-Zahra was twelve thousand loaves, besides six measures of black pulse, which were every day macerated in the waters." It is small wonder that travellers from distant lands, men of all ranks and professions in life, following various religions—princes, ambassadors, merchants, pilgrims, theologians, and poets—all agreed that they had never seen in the course of their travels anything that could be compared to it.

"Indeed," writes one Moorish chronicler, "had this palace possessed nothing more than the terrace of polished marble overhanging the matchless gardens, with the golden hall and the circular pavilion, and the works of art of every sort and description—had it nothing else to boast of but the masterly workmanship of the structure, the boldness of the design, the beauty of the proportions, the elegance of the ornaments, hangings, and decorations, whether of shining marble or glittering gold, the columns that seemed from their symmetry and smoothness as if they had been turned by lathes, the paintings that resembled the choicest landscapes, the artificial lake so solidly constructed, the cistern perpetually filled with clear and limpid water, and the amazing fountains, with figures of living beings—no imagination, however fertile, could have formed an idea of it." So at least it struck the Moorish author, and the sight inspired him to ejaculate: "Praise be to God Most High for allowing His humble creatures to design and build such enchanting palaces as this, and who permitted them to inhabit them as a sort of recompense in this world; and in order that the faithful might be encouraged to follow the path of virtue, by the reflection that, delightful as were these pleasures, they were still far below those reserved for the true believer in the celestial Paradise!"

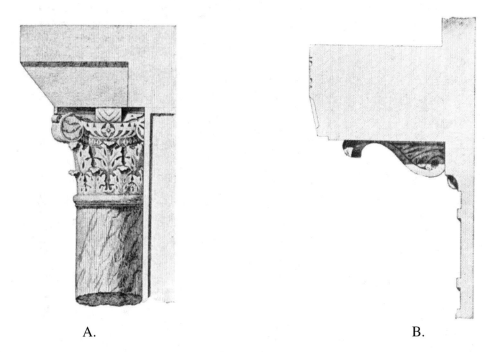

Figure 91. Cordova. A. Capital of Arch. B. Side View of the Cornice.

Figure 92. Bases.

 The effect of all this massed splendour upon the mind, even of those whose position and duties made familiar with the treasures of Abd-er-Rahman's palaces, is illustrated by one of the ambassadors of the Greek Emperor. The khalif received Constantine's emissaries in the great hall of the palace of Ez-Zahra, which was specially arranged for the occasion. The richest carpets and rugs, and the most gorgeous silk awnings, covered the floor, and veiled the doors and arches, and in the midst of the apartment was set up the royal throne, overlaid with gold, and glittering with precious stones. On the right and left of the throne stood the khalif's sons, beside them were the viziers, and behind them, in the order of their rank, were ranged the chamberlains, the nobles, and officers of the household. The ambassadors were awed and amazed by the magnificence of the scene, and the orator, charged with the office of delivering the speech of welcome, was literally struck dumb by the splendour of the spectacle. With wide, staring eyes and speechless lips he stood spellbound, caught in a maze of wonder. This man, who had grown accustomed to superb beauty, who had seen splendour piled upon splendour under the directing hand of his master, was paralysed by the effect it produced. His brain reeled, and, without uttering a word, he fell senseless to the ground. A second orator took the embossed scroll, and faced the august assemblage, but the witchery of the scene hypnotised his senses, and he, too, hesitated, faltered, and broke down.

Figure 93. East Façade, Without the Portico.

The mere outward and visible aspect of this "brightest splendour of the world," as the nun Hroswitha described it, fired the imagination of man, and deprived the practised orators of speech. But the mind of Cordova at this period of its history was as beautiful as its frame. It was the fountain-head of learning, the well-spring of art, the scientific centre of Europe. Literature became the study of every class, poetry was the common language of the people. The potters, the silk weavers, the glass blowers, the jewellers, swordmakers, and brass workers of Cordova were renowned throughout Europe—in all that appertained to art she was acknowledged to stand pre-eminent. The greatest doctors, the most skilled surgeons, had their homes in Cordova; and astronomers, geographers, chemists, philosophers, and scientists of every kind resorted thither to study and prosecute their researches.

Under Hakam II., the Royal library at Cordova became the largest and most celebrated collection of books in the world; and under Almanzor, the powerful minister who ruled Spain for the Khalif Hisham, the beauty of the Imperial city was jealously maintained. But the end of the Omeyyad dynasty was even then in sight, the sun of Cordova's glory was already commencing to set. After the death of Almanzor

> "Sultan after Sultan with his pomp
> Abode his destin'd hour and went his way,"

the puppet khalifs were enthroned and deposed at the will of successive prevailing factions. Anarchy had broken out again, the mob was Sultan, and the work of pillage and plunder was begun. The overthrow of the Almanzor order was followed by the wrecking of the Almanzor palace, which was ransacked and burned to the ground. For four days the work of riot, robbery, and massacre went on unchecked. Palace after palace was reduced to ruins, gardens were devastated, the public squares ran with blood. The brutal, savage Berbers captured the beautiful city of Ez-Zahra (A.D. 1010) by treachery, and put its garrisons to the sword, while the flying inhabitants were chased into the sacred precincts of the mosque and butchered without mercy.

Ez-Zahra, "the city of the fairest," was pillaged; its palaces and mosques were thrown down, and the walls were given to the flames. To-day its site alone remains, and its glories exist only in name.

Chapter 2

SEVILLE

The beginning of the history of Seville is buried, with the date of its foundation, in oblivion. It has its place in mythology as the creation of Hercules; its origin being more reasonably credited to the Phœnicians, who colonised the mineral-yielding region of Andalusia, which is watered by the Guadalquivir, and called it Tartessii. Strabo states that they built the town of Tartessus; and some authorities favour the conclusion that Seville stands on the site of that Phœnician stronghold. In 237 B.C. Hamilcar Barca conquered Andalusia, and his son-in-law founded Carthagena, which was seized by Publius Cornelius Scipio, or Scipio Africanus, during the second Punic War. Scipio founded Italica, which was to serve as a sanatorium for his invalided soldiers, and for awhile its importance eclipsed that of the neighbouring city of Seville. Honoured by the gifts of three Roman emperors born within its walls, and adorned with the splendid edifices raised by Trajan, Adrian, and Theodosius, Italica was advanced to the first rank among the Roman cities of the Peninsula. Julius Cæsar restored the balance of power to Seville in 45 B.C., when he made it his capital, and changed its name to Julia Romula. The city was fortified and protected by walls, which have been variously described as from five to ten miles in length. To-day the remains of the great aqueduct, the two high granite columns in the Alameda de Hercules, and the beautiful fragments of capitals and statues in the Museo Arqælogico, are the only existing relics of the Roman sway in Seville, while on the opposite bank of the Guadalquivir a ruined, grass-grown amphitheatre is all that is left of the once mighty town of Italica. In 584 Leovigild repaired the walls of Italica when he was beseiging Seville, and less than two centuries later those walls were greatly injured by the Moors, who further fortified and enlarged Seville with the stones brought from Italica.

In 711 Tarik captured Cordova, and in the following year Musa, the Governor of Africa, appeared before Seville with an army of 18,000 warriors. In a few weeks the city had fallen, and for 536 years the "Pearl of Andalusia" remained in the possession of the

Moors. The conquerors abandoned Italica to its fate, or, rather, they used the remains of the city as a quarry, while some of the sculpture of the deserted capital, which appealed to the Arabs by its surpassing beauty, was removed to Seville. Despite the injunctions contained in the Koran, the sculptures were not destroyed, and a statue of Venus was long preserved in one of the public baths of the city. El-Makkari, writing in the sixteenth century, and quoting from an early Moorish manuscript, records that "there was once found a marble statue of a woman with a boy, so admirably executed that both looked as if they were alive; such perfection human eyes never beheld. Indeed, some Sevillians were so much struck with its beauty as to become deeply enamoured of it." An anonymous poet, a native of Seville, made a set of verses about it, which have been translated by Don Pascual de Gayangos as follows:

"Look at that marble statue, beautiful in its proportions,
surpassing everything in transparency and smoothness.
"She has with her a son, it is true, but who her husband
was I cannot tell, neither was she ever in labour.
"Thou knowest her to be but a stone, but yet thou canst
not look at her, for there is in her eyes something that
fascinates and confounds the beholder."

It has been said that the Sevillians pretend to regard Hercules as the builder of the city, and the *Puerta de la Carne* is inscribed with the following distich:

"Condidit Alcides—renovavit Julius urbem, Restituit Christo Fernandus tertius heros."

This has been paraphrased in an inscription over the Puerta de Xerex:

"Hercules me edificó
Julio Cesar me cercó
De muros y torres altas;
Un Rey godo me perdió,
El Rey Santo me ganó,
Con Garci Perez de Vargas."

Hercules built me; Julius Cæsar encircled me with walls and lofty towers; a Gothic king (Roderick) lost me; a saint-like king (St. Ferdinand), assisted by Garci Perez de Vargas, regained me.

The inscription might well have included the name of the brother of Garci Perez, Diego de Vargas, surnamed "El Machuca," or "the Pounder," who performed prodigies of valour at the breaking of the Moorish bridge of boats across the Guadalquivir, when the destruction of that gallantly-defended means of access to the city led to the capture of Seville by the Christians in 1248. These two brothers are the heroes of Spanish ballads, and were greatly distinguished by St. Ferdinand; the grateful monarch freely acknowledging their prowess by the bestowal of houses and lands wrested from the Moors. A curious "Repartimiento," or Domesday Book of Seville, is still extant, and many families can trace their actual possessions back to this original partition.

Musa appointed his son, Abdelasis, a brave soldier and a humane ruler, to be governor of Seville. That he was a successful general, that he married Egilona, the widow of the unfortunate King Roderick, and was murdered by the order of Suleyman, brother and heir of the Khalif of Damascus, is all that history records of him. A malignant rumour, that he was scheming to make himself sole ruler of the Berber dominion in Spain, reached Damascus. Suleyman immediately sent emissaries to Seville with secret instructions that Abdelasis should be put to death, adding as an incentive to swift compliance with his order, that whoever among them executed the deed, should be appointed his successor as Amir of Seville. The delegates were armed with friendly letters to Abdelasis, who received them cordially, and entertained them in accordance with his exalted position as an amir under the khalif. It appears, according to the tradition, that the scheme was revealed to 'Abdullah Ibn, "who was the most eminent and most conspicuous officer in the army." 'Abdullah, however, would have no hand in the projected assassination, but, on the contrary, endeavoured to dissuade the conspirators from their purpose, saying to them: "You know the hand of Musa has conferred benefits on every one of you: if the Commander of the Faithful has been informed as you represent, he has been told a lie. Abdelasis has never raised his hand in disobedience to his master, nor dreamt of revolting against him." Suleyman's emissaries, however, disregarded his words, and decided on the murder. One morn they stood among the rest at the gates of the palace, waiting till the governor should go to the mosque, and, when he appeared, followed him to prayer. Scarcely had he entered the "kiblah," and begun to read the Koran, than one of the conspirators rushed upon the governor and stabbed him. Abdelasis, leaving the "kiblah," took refuge in the body of the mosque, whither he was followed and slain. When the news spread through the city, the inhabitants were roused to fury. The assassins produced the letters and commands of the khalif, but to no purpose; the people refused to abide by the sultan's behests, and chose 'Abdullah to be his successor. 'Abdullah was, however, quickly displaced by Ayub, Suleyman's nominee, and the conspirators then departed to make their report at Damascus, carrying with them the head of the unfortunate Abdelasis.

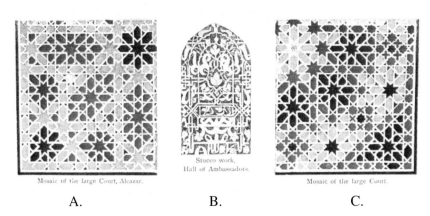

Plate 25. Seville. Frieze in the Hall of Ambassadors. A. Mosaic of the large Court, Alcazar. B. Stucco work, Hall of Ambassadors. C. Mosaic of the large Court.

Figure 94. Seville. Façade of the Alcazar.

Figure 95. Seville. Alcazar—Gates of the Principal Entrance.

The author of the tradition, Mohammed Ibn, says that when these emissaries arrived at Damascus and produced the head of Abdelasis before Suleyman, he sent immediately for Musa. Upon his appearance, Suleyman, pointing to the head, said: "Dost thou know whose head that is?" "Yes," answered Musa, "it is the head of my son Commander of the Faithful, the head of Abdelasis (may Allah show him mercy) is before thee, but by the life of Allah there was never a Moslem who less deserved such unjust treatment; for he passed his days in fasting, and his nights in prayer; no man ever performed greater deeds to serve the cause of the Almighty, or His messenger Mohammed; no man was more firm in his obedience to thee. None of thy predecessors would have served him thus. Thou even wouldest never have done what thou hast to him, had there been justice in thee." Suleyman retorted, "Thou liest, O Musa, thy son was not as thou hast represented him; he was impious and forgetful of our religion, he was the persecutor of the Moslems, and the sworn enemy of his sovereign, the Commander of the Faithful. Such was thy son, O doting, foolish, fond old man!" Musa replied, "By Allah! I am no dotard, nor would I deviate from truth, wert thou to answer my words with the blows of death. I speak as the honest slave should speak to his master, but I place my confidence in God, whose help I implore. Grant me his head, O Commander of the Faithful, that I may close his eyes." And Suleyman said: "Thou mayest take it." As Musa was leaving the Hall of Audience one who was present wished to interfere with him, but Suleyman said: "Let Musa alone, he has been sorely punished;" and added: "The old man's spirit is still unbroken." But the old man, whose name had once stood for the symbol of conquest, whose initiative had won Spain for the Moor, had received his death sentence. Grief, which could not bend his spirit, seized upon his frame. The old man fell sick of grief and shame, and in a little while he was dead.

Suleyman's treachery had its first result in the removal of the seat of Moorish rule in Spain to Cordova. Ayub, the successor of Abdelasis, recognising the insecurity of his tenure in Seville, forsook "the Pearl of Andalusia" with all speed, and when in 777, Abd-er-Rahman proclaimed himself sole ruler of Spain, it was from his palace at Cordova that the fiat was sent forth to the world. Seville, the first and the natural capital of the South, dropped into second place among the cities of the Peninsula, and it was not until 1078 that it re-established its claim as the Moorish metropolis. For three hundred and fifty years the Moslems were faithful to the sovereignty of Cordova; and although Seville came, by reason of its beautiful palaces, gardens, and baths, to be regarded as one of the fairest cities of earth; the alcazar and the lordly mosque, which now bear evidence of its former grandeur, are of a later Moorish period. And Seville grew in beauty under, and in spite of, the destructive influence of strife and conflict.

Plate 26. Seville. Alcazar. Hall of Ambassadors. Details.

While Abd-er-Rahman was cultivating the graces of Cordova, Seville was being desolated by many assaults. Yusuf, and, after his death, his three sons, made attacks upon Seville, and Hixem ben Adri el Fehri, who had stirred the Toledans to insurrection, was subsequently defeated at the gates of Seville by the Governor, Abdelmelic. At a later

date, Cassim, the son of Abdelmelic, fled with his army before the advance of the Wali of Mequinez, and was stabbed to death by his father for cowardice. Abdelmelic, who threw himself upon the invaders, was overcome and wounded in a night battle on the banks of the Guadalquivir; but, despite his hurt and his defeat, he rallied his soldiers, and drove the hitherto victorious Wali through the streets of Seville, and out again into the open country, where he was captured and killed.
'

Figure 96. Seville. Façade of the Alcazar.

Under the shifty and opportunist rule of Abdallah, who had caused his brother Mundhir to be murdered to make his way to the throne of Cordova in 888, Andalusia was split up into a number of independent principalities. The turbulent Ibn-Hafsun had made himself virtual King of Granada, the governors of Lorca and Zaragoza rendered but nominal homage to the khalif, the walls of Toledo rattled with the crash of contending revolutionary factions, and in Seville Ibrahim Ibn-Hajjaj treated with the King of Cordova on equal terms. In the time of Ibn-Hajjaj Seville was the most orderly and best-governed city in the Peninsula. The poets of Cordova, the singers of Baghdad, and the lawyers of Medina were attracted to the court of Ibn-Hajjaj, of whom it was sung, "In all the West I find no right noble man save Ibrahim, but he is nobility itself. When one has known the delight of living with him, to dwell in any other land would be a misery." Yet in 912-13, Ibrahim Ibn-Hajjaj, who kept his state like an Emperor, opened the gates of Seville to the masterful and gallant Abd-er-Rahman III., and the city became once more subject to the self-proclaimed Khalif of Cordova. It was Abd-er-Rahman who planted

Seville with palm trees, beautified her gardens, increased the number of her palaces, and made the Guadal quivir navigable by narrowing the river's channel. Ibrahim "the Magnificent" received the Great Khalif with the homage which a feudal lord offers to his king, and the independence of Seville was at an end.

Figure 97. Seville. Chief Entrance to the Alcazar, Moorish Style, Built Under Don Pedro I. The Cruel, 1369-1379.

But Seville at this period was the rival of Cordova in intellectual eminence, and much of the Moorish thought and research which was destined to influence Spain in future ages was pondered, and practised, and published from the former city. Abu Omar Ahmed Ben Abdallah, called "El Begi," "the Sage," and unquestionably one of the most learned men of his time, was a native of Seville, and here he wrote his encyclopædia of the sciences. It was said that there was no man who could surpass him in knowledge of arts and sciences, and "even in his earliest youth," says Condé, "the cadi very frequently consulted him in affairs of the highest importance." Chemists, philosophers, astronomers, and men famous in every branch of science, resorted to "the Pearl of Andalusia;" while art was fostered in silk and leather manufactures, and the joy of life found expression in music, poetry, and the dance.

The victorious expeditions of Alfonso VI. found the Moors demoralised from the massacres of Cordova and Ez-Zahra, and the whole of Andalusia in a state of ferment, anarchy, and military unpreparedness. In every town of importance in the South a new independent dynasty sprang into existence, and the Abbadites exercised kingly sway over the so-called republic of Seville. Some of these usurpers and pretenders, as Mr. Lane-Poole has pointed out, were good rulers; most of them were sanguinary tyrants, but (curiously) not the less polished gentlemen, who delighted to do honour to learning and letters, and made their courts the homes of poets and musicians. Mo'temid of Seville, for instance, was a patron of the arts, and a prince of many attainments, yet he kept a garden of heads cut off his enemies' shoulders, which he regarded with great pride and delight. Yet Seville was secure and peaceful under these barbarous rulers until the menace of Alfonso's inroads made Mo'temid silence the fears of his court with the reflection, "Better be a camel-driver in African deserts than a swine-herd in Castile." So they fled from the danger of the Castilians to the succour that Africa was waiting to send them. A conference of Moorish rulers was held in Seville, and a message imploring assistance was despatched to Yusuf, the Almoravide king.

Plate 27. Seville. Details in Hall of Ambassadors.

Figure 98. Seville. Alcazar—Principal Façade.

Figure 99. Seville. Interior Court of the Alcazar.

Yusuf defeated the army of Alfonso near Badajoz in 1086. Four years later the King of Seville again besought the help of Yusuf against the Christians of the North. This time he came with a force of twenty thousand men at his back, and before the end of 1091 the leader of the Almoravides had captured Seville and established a dynasty which was to last until its overthrow by the Almohades in 1147.

The Almoravide rule, which was distinguished in the beginning by piety and a love of honest warfare, ended in tyranny and corruption, and the Almoravides gave place to a race more pious and fanatical than the demoralised followers of Yusuf had ever been. For a hundred and one years the Almohades remained masters of Seville. The monuments of their devotion and artistic genius are extant in the mosque and the alcazar, and we know that under Abu Yakub Yusuf a new era of commercial prosperity set in for Seville, and a new light arose to illumine the fast deepening shadows which fell over the vanishing glory of Cordova. The thunder of the blows which had reduced "the City of the Fairest" to a heap of ruins still echoed in the air, and mixed with the noise of the builders and artificers who were re-moulding Seville "nearer to the heart's desire."

The remains of Moorish architecture which we find in Cordova, in Seville, and in Granada, enable us to realise that the civilisation and art of the Spanish Moslems were progressive, and that each stage developed its varied and singular characteristics. "The monuments of Seville," says Contreras in his *Monuments Arabes*, "produce quite a peculiar effect on the mind, a sublime reminiscence of ancient and profound social transformations, which only the inartistic aspect of bad restorations can dissipate—a vandalism inspired by the desire to see the building shining with colour and gold, and which impelled people to restore it without paying the smallest heed to the most elementary principles of archæology. The alcazar of Seville is not a classic work; we do not find in it the stamp of originality, and the ineffaceable character that one admires in ancient works like the Parthenon, and in more modern ones like the Escurial; the first on account of their splendid simplicity, and the latter for their great size and taciturn grandeur. In the alcazar of Yakub Yusuf, the prestige of a heroic generation has disappeared, and the existence of Christian kings, who have lived there and enriched it with a thousand pages of our glorious history, is perfectly represented there. The Almohades who left the purest African souvenirs there, and Jalubi who followed Almehdi to the conquest of Africa, left on the walls Roman remains, taken from the vanquished people. St. Ferdinand, who conquered it; Don Pedro I., who re-built it; Don Juan II., who restored the most beautiful halls; the Catholic monarchs, who built chapels and oratories within its precincts; Charles V., who added more than half, with the moderated style of this epoch of sublime renaissance; Philip III., and Philip V., who further increased it by erecting edifices in the surrounding gardens; all these, and many other princes and great lords, who inhabited it for six centuries, changed its original construction in such a degree that it no longer resembles, to-day, the original Oriental monument, although we have covered it with arabesques, and embellished it with mosaics and gilding."

Figure 100. Seville. Alcazar—Arcade in the Principal Court.

Figure 101. Seville. Alcazar—View of the Interior.

All that succeeding generations have constructed in the alcazar has contributed to deprive it of its Mohammedan character. Transformed into a lordly mansion of more modern epochs, one no longer sees there the voluptuous saloons of the harem, nor the silent spaces reserved for prayer, nor the baths, nor the fountains, nor the strong ramparts, supporting the galleries, which, by circular paths, communicated with the rich sleeping apartments, situated in the square towers. It is not that Arab art is in a different form here to that seen in other parts of Spain; but while the Moors always built palaces in close proximity to fortified places, they here combined the two, and for that reason they sacrificed the exterior decoration to the works of fortification and defence. On approaching the palace, one finds marks of grandeur, but one must not look for them in the structure, but rather in the numerous reparations and additions which have been made there, and also in the solid walls, dominating the ruins of those castles, which seem to protest eternally against the cold indifference with which so many generations have passed over them. And if, on the one hand, there is no doubt that this is the old wall or the ancient tower, on the other hand, the traveller, greedy for impressions left by a past world, finds nothing but square enclosures, gardens and rectangular saloons of the mansions of the 16th century. Here there is nothing so majestic as the Giralda; nothing so essentially Oriental as the mosque of Cordova; nothing so fantastic and so picturesque as the alcazar of Granada. One only sees here the chronicle of an art, carried out by a thousand artists, obeying different beliefs, and which presents rather the appearance of a game played by children who had invaded the spot where the most valued works of their ancestors were preserved, rather than the passionate conception of the terrible descendants of Hagar, who in fifty years invaded half the globe. But one still catches something of the spirit of an art that was almost a religion, as one lingers in the quiet gardens of the alcazar; the deep impress of the Moor will never be entirely obliterated from the courts and saloons of this palace of dreams. As Mr. W. M. Gallichan writes: "The nightingales still sing among the odorous orange bloom, and in the tangle of roses, birds build their nests. Fountains tinkle beneath gently waving palms; the savour of Orientalism clings to the spot. Here wise men discussed in the cool of summer nights, when the moon stood high over the Giralda, and white beams fell through the spreading boughs of lemon trees, and shivered upon the tiled pavements. In this garden the musicians played, and the tawny dancers writhed and curved their lissom bodies in dramatic Eastern dances."

Ichabod! The moody potentate, bowed down with the cares of high office, no longer treads the dim corridor, or lingers in the shade of the palm trees. No sound of gaiety reverberates in the deserted courts, no voice of orator is heard in the Hall of Justice. The green lizards bask on the deserted benches of the gardens. Rose petals strew the paved paths. One's footsteps echo in the gorgeous patios, whose walls have witnessed many a scene of pomp, tragedy, and pathos. The spell of the past holds one; and, before the imagination, troops a long procession of illustrious sovereigns, courtiers, counsellors, and warriors.

This wonderful monument, which has moved generations of artists and poets to rhapsody and praise, and inspired that picturesque Italian author, De Amicis, to people the gardens of the alcazar with Mo'temid and his beautiful favourite, Itamad, who had been dead nearly a century before the alcazar was erected, failed to create any impression in the mind of Mr. John Lomas, whose strictures upon the place in his *Sketches of Spain* must ever be a standing reproof to those who dare to see Oriental beauty in this Sevillian castle. "Greater far," says Mr. Lomas, "is the alcazar in reputation than in intrinsic worth. Like the Mother Church, it forms a sort of sightseers' goal, and it shares equally in the good fortune of so entirely satisfying the requirements of superficial observers, that it is esteemed a kind of heresy to take exception to its noble rank as a typical piece of Moorish work. Yet it is just a great house, of southern and somewhat ancient construction—say the fifteenth century—with a number of square rooms and courts, arranged and decorated after Arab models as far as was possible in the case of a building designed to fulfil the requirements of Western civilisation. Nothing else. Of course, if the courts and towers of the Alhambra have not been seen—or are not to be compassed— there will be found here an infinity of fresh loveliness in design and colouring, together with a vast amount of detail which will repay study. But even then it must all be looked upon as an exceedingly clever reproduction of beautiful and artful forms, not as their best possible setting forth, or type. There are dark winding passages—evidently dictated by the exigencies of the work—but they yield none of the delicate surprises which form so great a charm of the old Moorish monuments. There is any amount of rich decoration and Moresque detail; but never the notion of the luxury and voluptuousness of Eastern life, or a suggestion of its thousand-and-one adjuncts. There are, here and there, indubitable traces of the original Eleventh Century alcazar of Yakub Yusuf" (it was not built until the latter part of the twelfth century) "but there is nothing either distinctive or precious about them, and the rest is a record rather of Christian than Arab ways."

Plate 28. Seville. Alcazar. Details of Hall of Ambassadors.

Mr. Lomas is perfectly correct in suggesting that the alcazar of Seville is, in great measure, a reproduction of the delights of the Alhambra, a reproduction due, without any doubt, to that school of architecture which embellished the sumptuous palace of Granada for the kings of the second Nazarite dynasty. In it we see the record of the ingenious almizates, of its gates and ceilings, of those stalactited domes, which dazzle and confuse, of those wall-facings encrusted with rich ornamentation, of those graceful Byzantine and Moorish geometrical designs, which even to-day are the despair of perspective painters, of those enchanting saloons where the genius of harmony seems to rest, and of those balmy gardens which invite repose, meditation, and melancholy.

Figure 102. Seville. Alcazar—Court of the Dolls.

While it is generally accepted that the city of Seville possessed no alcazar of striking importance until the declining power of the khalifate of Cordova made Seville the capital of an independent kingdom, there is substantial reason for believing that in the foundations of the present superb edifice there are unmistakable relics of an earlier work of truly Arab architecture. The Almohades so thoroughly effaced and distorted the magnificence of their predecessors' work that it would be impossible to point with certainty to any of the original remains of this many-times-restored palace. The ultra-semi-circular arches which are seen in the Hall of the Ambassadors, those graceful arches which carry the mind from Seville to the graceful arcades of the mosque of Cordova, incline one to regard this apartment as a relic of Abbadite antiquity, while the rich columns with their gilded capitals of the Corinthian style appears to contain authentic proof of their Arabic-Byzantine origin. Señor Pedro de Madrazo, whilst admitting the difficulty of determining the period to which the various parts of the alcazar belong, disregards the conclusions of Señores José Amador de los Rios and his son Rodrigo, who resolutely denied the antiquity of these ultra-semi-circular arches, and declares the Hall of Ambassadors to be an example of Abbadite architecture. He further attributes to the same epoch, the showy ascending arcade of the narrow staircase which leads from the entrance court to the upper gallery, and rises near the balcony or choir of the chapel, and the three beautiful arches, sustained by exquisite capitals, which remain as the sole relic of the decoration of the abandoned apartment situated close to the "Princes' Saloon."

Figure 103. Seville. Alcazar—Court of the Dolls, Moorish Style, Built 1369-1379.

In his work on "Sevilla," the same authority distinguishes between the art of the Mudejare, or transition artificers, and that of the Almohado Moors. "The latter art," he observes, "is less simple, less select in its ornamentation, discloses less rational regularity, and is, generally speaking, more affected."

Plate 29. Blank Window.

Figure 104. Seville. Alcazar—The Court of the Dolls.

Figure 105. Seville. Alcazar—Right Angle of the Court of the Dolls.

These differences may be seen in a comparison between the Moorish Giralda of Seville and the beautiful creation of artists of the Arab-Andalusian period which are to be studied in the ornamental parts of the Alhambra. The Almohade architecture displays a base taste, which imitates rather than feels, and creates forms by exaggerations which are unsuitable to the design, and thus differs in æsthetic principles from the Mudejaren-Moorish work of the 13th, 14th, and 15th centuries, which reveals an instinctive feeling for the beautiful in ornamentation, which never loses sight of the elegant, the graceful, and the bold, and consequently never falls into aberration. The Almohade period, in short, discloses at once the force of the barbarous spirit civilised by conquest, while the latter offers the enduring character of cultured taste and wisdom in all the epochs of prosperous or adverse fortune; both are the faithful expression of people of different ages, origins, and aptitudes. "It is certain," declares Señor de Madrazo, "that the innovations which characterise Mussulman architecture in Spain in the 11th and 12th centuries, cannot be explained as a natural mutation from the Arab art of the khalifate, or as a preparation or transition to the art of Granada, because there is very little similarity between the style called secondary or Moorish and the Arab-Byzantine and Andalusian, while on the other hand it is evident that the Saracen monuments of Fez and Morocco, of the reigns of Yusuf ben Texpin, Abdel-ben-Ali, Elmansur and Nasser, bear the principal character of the ornamentation which the Almohades made general in Spain."

Plate 30. Soffit of Arch.

It must always be remembered when approaching the forbidding exterior of the alcazar, that it was erected to serve the purpose of a fortress as well as a palace. Yusuf is supposed to have used a Roman prætorium as the foundation of his castle, and there are parts of the wall which date back to Roman times. But the principal gateway which gives entrance to the palace is of Arab origin, and it is evident that all the upper part, from the frieze with the Gothic inscription, is purely Mohammedan, according to the Persic style, very much used in the entrances to mosques of the first period, in Asia. The two pilasters, in their entire height, as well as the sculptured framing of the lower part, are of the Arab style; but the balconies with arches, and Byzantine columns, the Roman capitals, the lintels of the doors and windows with Gothic springs, are indications, which prove the reconstruction of the time of Don Pedro. The later restorations have not completely changed the primitive form, but have only modified it. On entering the palace one finds other works less Arab than these, the ornaments do not form an integral part of the decoration, and one can observe that in order to place them it was necessary to remove inscriptions and Mohammedan shields which filled the little spaces.

Figure 106. Seville. Alcazar—Court of the Dolls.

But in passing this square entrance, whose form recalls Egypt, and which began to be used when the horseshoe arch was no longer in vogue, we find ourselves in the chief courtyard of the alcazar, which makes a slight detour in order not to be overlooked from the street, and which offers an extravagant assemblage of lines without departing from exactness. The actual lines of this superb edifice, mentioning principally the two types of architecture which prevail, are the Moorish of the works erected from 1353 to 1364, and the Renaissance, in the works carried out under the monarchs of the house of Austria.

Figure 107. Seville. Alcazar—Upper Part of the Court of the Dolls.

It is curious that while the Alhambra was allowed to fall into decay, and suffered periods of neglect that could be reckoned by scores of years at a stretch, the alcazar has seldom been free from the hands of the restorers. The fact accounts, of course, for the splendid state of preservation in which it is to be found to-day, but it also owes to it the weird incongruity of style and decoration which lovers of pure Moorish art deplore. After Pedro had almost entirely reconstructed the palace—and to him the alcazar owes many of its best portions—it came under the restoring influence of Juan II., that weak but artistic monarch, whose handiwork is seen in some of the chief apartments. The arch-vandal, Charles V., whose palace in the Alhambra would be a work of art anywhere save on the spot on which he chose to erect it, could not be expected to spare the alcazar. Under his direction the greater portion of the Renaissance additions were made, and the portraits of Spanish kings hung in the Hall of Ambassadors were introduced by his successor. In the 17th century this favourite residence of the kings of Spain attained to the zenith of its magnificence; and then for a whole century the palace was allowed, for the first and only time, to fall into a state of disrepair. Spain was passing through troublous times, and its rulers had weightier matters to absorb their attention. The alcazar, stricken by neglect, shrank to something like its original proportions, and its beauties fell into decay. In the middle of the 19th century Queen Isabella II. rescued the ancient structure from the ravages of time, and the present order and distinction which it now enjoys is largely due to her timely efforts.

After the restorations made by Don Pedro were finished, the alcazar had various entrances, but the principal were the two opened in the old Arab wall, which lead to the courts called the "Banderas y de la Monteria." The delicate pointed arches which composed them were almost hidden between the massive towers of the neighbouring minaret; nothing externally reveals the dazzling beauty which is to be seen behind these walls.

In the courtyard one sees very fine ornaments placed hap-hazard, which had been left over from the last restorations of the palace of Granada, and which were sent here without any consideration for period or style. That this system prevailed can be proved by reference to the archives of the royal patrimony, where there is a document requesting, on the part of the keeper of the alcazar, that some of the "best" arabesques, which were being used for the restorations at Granada, should be sent to Seville. These ornaments, of different epochs and styles, can be seen on the walls of the alcazar, face to face with others corresponding to the infancy of the art. The Alhambra does not suffer from these incongruities, because it has not suffered a great transformation similar to that which the alcazar underwent at the hands of Don Pedro. It has not been altered to suit the requirements of a Christian court, and it has never been occupied by great personages, with large revenues at their disposal, to reconstruct it according to their caprice.

Figure 108. Seville. Alcazar—Upper Portions of the Court of the Dolls.

Figure 109. Seville. Alcazar—Court of the Dolls.

The ornaments of the ceilings of the alcazar are magnificent, because, as Contreras points out, the Moorish workmen were beginning to understand all the majesty and grandeur that Christian art stamped upon the complicated and minute assemblage of Mussulman edifices; they began to make rich coverings, with bolts or stays with apertures, and with hollows in the form of an arch, and keystones imitating rhombus, stars, and bow ornaments. The famous Gothic roofs and ceilings of the Bretonne buildings of the ninth century have never been able to equal this one, because here one finds more beautiful specimens than in the other edifices, when the vaults with little stalactites had not yet acquired their complete development. The perfectly-worked and carved designs of the doors give a great relief to the palace. One remarks here that the ceilings are less magnificent or luxurious, when the ornamentation is less classic, and, as at Fez, the walls were covered with hangings instead of reliefs in plaster; and then they used more gold in the cornices, in the friezes, in the domes, in the lintels, and in the crownings, whilst the walls remained bare, as in the Moz-Arabian constructions. There was here such a mixture of styles, such a confusion of ideas, and such a number of little quadrangular windows, which interrupt the general line of the ornamentation, as one does not see anywhere else. One sees, too, walls covered with arabesques, stretching like pieces of tapestry or coverings of bright colours, and which produce a rich effect, beautiful and varied, thought-out and elegant—but not at all simple—which is the chief condition of art in the epochs of great culture.

In going through this alcazar one sees nothing but square saloons, one following the other, of the same shape and dimensions, occasionally varied by the composition of the arabesques traced there. Symmetry has been sacrificed to convenience, and the central arches to the alignment of the doors. In the time of the Arabs the alcazar constituted a series of constructions, flanked by the walls and the towers, which surrounded the town, which had not the symmetrical form of the rectangular plan of the buildings of the Renaissance. Neither does it resemble the palaces of Egypt or of Syria. These quays, placed side by side, give this edifice the appearance of a Christian house of the fifteenth century; and one can only confidently give the name "Arab" to the Court of the Damsels, the Hall of Ambassadors, and the apartments immediately adjoining it.

The Court of the Banners, and of the Hunters, lead to the Court of the Principal Façade, where one sees the first specimen of Mussulman decoration! In all these divisions the monument is only revealed by the vestiges of battlements of the towers and of the walls, in which the original doors were opened, and where the sultans had the chambers for judging the quarrels of their subjects,—a custom perpetrated by the Christian monarchs. In the Court of the Hunters one can still see the apartment named the Hall of Justice, where all writers suppose that the audiences were held. Here Don Pedro held his tribunal; and the traveller, Don Antonio Ponz, asserts that he saw one of the columns of the memorable seat occupied by the monarch when he held those famous audiences, which were an imitation of the judgments of the East and of the feudal lords of the West, and which magnified the idea of justice in the eyes of foolish and irreflective people, but which were held by men of good sense to be a mere pretence of equity, with which to mask his tyranny. The place where justice was administered in the time of the Almohadan kings was in the Court of the Monteria—a vast and beautiful apartment, one of the oldest constructions in the alcazar, and of a more purely Moorish style.

Figure 110. Seville. Alcazar—The Little Court.

Figure 111. Seville. Alcazar—View in the Little Court.

The Court of the Hunters leads to another larger court, known as the Princes' Hall. This is more regular in form, and in it rises the chief entrance, dazzling and richly ornamented with painting and gilding, from its twin windows to the topmost moulding of its projecting eaves, of the purest Almohadan style. How can one describe it? Not only the entrance, but the whole façade is of precious marbles, the capitals of the columns being in the most exquisite Moorish taste; and the facia of interlaced arches above the doorway display the escutcheons of Castile and Leon; while round another facia, running between the brackets over the twin windows of the principal floor, there is a legend in

Gothic characters, which says: "The very high, and very noble, and very powerful, and very victorious Don Pedro, King of Castile and Leon, commanded these alcazars, and these palaces, and these doorways to be made, which was done in the era of one thousand four hundred and two." The cupola of the Princes' Hall rises above this façade, its outer walls being adorned with little arches and blue tile work, in imitation of a pyramid, and bearing at its summit, in the Oriental fashion, a weather-cock with gilded spheres.

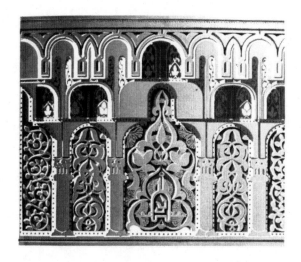

Plate 31. Cornice at Springing of Arch of Doorway at one of the Entrances.

On entering the vestibule, one sees first the result of unfortunate modern reformations, little rooms or recesses to right and left, now almost stripped of their ancient ornamentation. On taking the corridor, which is at the back of a sort of ante-chamber, nearly square, one arrives at the chief inner court called the Court of the Damsels. There is an unfounded tradition which says this court derives its name from the disgraceful tribute of one hundred damsels levied by Mauregato, and paid to the khalifs of Cordova, it being supposed that the throne upon which the Moorish king sat when receiving this tribute was situated in this court. In point of fact, as Pedro de Medrazo reminds us, there were no Moorish kings in Spain, and neither was Seville the capital of the Andalusian khalifate, nor can it be asserted that there was a Saracen palace there before the eleventh century. Without any doubt this court was part of the great restorations of the fourteenth century. Its plan is a rectangle, with galleries of marble columns in couples and pointed mitred arches; the central arches of each side are higher than the rest, and instead of resting, as these do on the columns, they are supported by small square pillars, which appear to be held up by the capitals. These small pillars have beautiful little columns at their angles, which at first sight seem to be a prelude to the caprices of the Renaissance, which loved so much to surmount one style by another; but here it is really an accident very characteristic of the Arabic-Granadian architecture, such as is often to be noticed in the Courts of the Alhambra.

These arches are only seen in the façade here, in the House of Pilate, and in the buildings of the eighth century in the East. One could not explain them unless there were hanging decorations, such as tapestries attached to the walls, which were neither seen nor guessed in the intercolumniations. It is a strange shape, which is elegant on account of the lobules, the point, and the horseshoe-formed span, which at a later period regulated the arches of the palaces of Fez, of Tunis, and of Cairo.

Figure 112. Seville. Alcazar—View of the Hall of Ambassadors from the Little Court.

Figure 113. Seville. Alcazar—Hall of Ambassadors.

The second gallery of the Court of the Damsels, added to the ancient construction, is an addition of little importance; but it is a fine court, if one considers the modifications of its style, its socles showing beautiful panels of decorated porcelain of admirable delicacy. Different doors lead to the saloon of Charles V., to that of the Ambassadors, and to those of the "Caracol," or of Don Maria de Padilla. They have scarfs cut into polygons, which cover them on both sides, but this fine work has been badly restored with stucco barbarously painted.

The Hall of Ambassadors is a square apartment of a solemn aspect, with four frontages composed of high arches, which enclose twin windows, placed on slender columns, whose little arches are more than semi-circular, without having the characteristic form of the horse-shoe,—a curve which marks the decadent transition. The capitals are degenerate Greco-Roman; but the great decorative arch with running knots, although it has an Arab curve, has not the two squares in height from the floor of the hall, and that deprives it of elegance in its ornamentation. The spaces, or triangles, are not original, the work is interrupted, as in the inner side of the wall of the frontage, by shutters which open, as though escaping from the tympan of the twin windows. A wide frieze of windows, or painted transparencies, stretches above, in an admirable manner, and higher still there is a geometrical band of ornaments in the form of knots, and then come architraves and supports on which the roof rests. The sub-basements of porcelain are adorned with arabesques, and the connecting doors are decorated with almost exaggerated profusion. The open balconies, with the eagles on their consols, are an eternal affront for him who had them made; and we may say the same thing of the portraits with Gothic frames, placed under the arch-like hollows of the walls, and also of the gilding, which has not the fine ornamentation of blue, red, and black, which renders these little vaults more graceful, when they are done by Arabs. The spherical cupola, with rafters with arabesques forming stars of symmetrical polygons, may have been constructed for stained glass windows at a higher light, but later it was ineffectively decorated with little mirrors. The mosaics have been restored with pieces larger than the originals, and the jasper columns seem to be Roman and not Arab, as do many others of the decadence; and the capitals too, without uniformity, and unsuited to the columns, appear to be Moz-Arabian work, which is seen in many of the Saracen mosques.

The type of the African inscriptions in the alcazar is not as fine or as pure as are those in the Hall of Comares at Granada; but on the other hand the classic character of the cufic inscriptions here is more uniform and more simple. The ornaments, in the shape of leaves, of pine cones, and of palms interlaced with ribbons, with geometrical outlines, is a style that is no longer seen after the beginning of the Thirteenth Century. The little windows, in parallelograms above the doors, the Roman imposts, the Gothic carvings, and the escutcheons with broken chiselings shown in this palace, are the work of several generations who were wanting in the consciousness of art.

Yet the Hall of Ambassadors is beyond dispute the most splendid and beautiful apartment of all the palaces of Moorish architecture belonging to the Crown in Spain. The painting and gilding of arabesques, the lovely carved wooden ceilings, now shaped like inverted bowls, now like sections of a sphere, and now like capricious many-sided figures, which reflect the light and shade with a marvellous effect; the inscriptions in African characters; the rich doors of marquetry, surrounded by Arabic invocations (a beautiful work done by artificers of Toledo); the columns of various marbles with capitals of exquisite cut, now primitive, now Almohadan, now Moorish; the variegated marble of the pavement, the perforated stucco of the partitions, the ingenious work, with birds introduced in the doorways; and finally this strange combination of five different styles, which in theory is so impossible, and in practice so harmonious—Arabic, Almohadan, Gothic, Granadian, and Renaissance—to be seen in so many apartments of the alcazar, but more especially in this hall, are things which the pen could never describe satisfactorily, and which must be left to the impression produced by a sight of the original, or to a contemplation of its pictured representation. For this reason one may not endeavour to describe, either technically or minutely, this magnificent hall, to the gradual architectural composition of which overseers and workmen of so many different times contributed. The Abbaditas made the bold horse-shoe arches of the lower part; the Almohadans, and afterwards the school of Christians of Granada which arose, carried out the work of ornamenting the walls with the ornamental arches, the perforated windows, the facias of little interlaced arches, and the inscriptions; and they covered the hall with the marvellous dome shaped like an inverted bowl. It is probable that the architects of the Catholic monarchs constructed the third body in the pointed style, forming a series of corrupted trefoils bordered with lilies, in whose centres the portraits of the kings of Spain, from Chindasvinto, are reproduced; and, finally, the kings of the House of Austria added the third body of the decoration, four balconies, of great projection, which doubt less formerly were twin windows (ajimeces) with one or more columns, supported by griffons gilded, and of bold outline.

Figure 114. Seville. Alcazar—Interior of the Hall of Ambassadors.

Figure 115. Seville. Alcazar—Hall of Ambassadors.

It was probably in this saloon that the ceremonious and perfidious reception of Abu Said, King of Granada, by Don Pedro took place. The usurper of the Throne of Granada presented himself to the owner of the alcazar, thinking he had ensured his personal safety by the gifts he had forwarded, and by his complete submission to the wishes of his host. But after being entertained at a splendid supper, he was rewarded with prison, and death, accompanied with the most horrible mockeries. Amongst the jewels, with which the unhappy Abu Said is supposed to have hoped to win the heart of his faithless enemy, was the immense ruby, which to-day shines in the royal crown of Edward VII. It was given by Don Pedro to the Black Prince; it later came into the possession of Queen Mary Stuart of Scotland, and through her son, James I., returned once more to England.

If the Hall of Ambassadors is rich, the Court of the Dolls is not less so in its own style. This, with some other saloons, constituted one of the remaining splendours of the alcazar which are associated with Don Fadrique, Master of the Order of Santiago, the timid son of Alonso XI. We cannot tell from what source this court has received its modern denomination. In the old chronicles there is no trace of such a name; but they, and tradition, have handed us down copious notes, all of which make this part of the alcazar the theatre of that sanguinary drama of the Fourteenth Century. After reading these chronicles and romances, one imagines the ghosts of the actors moving about the apartments; one sees Don Pedro, who has already planned his execrable plot, receiving, with false expressions of interest, his half-brother Don Fadrique; one sees the lovely Padilla, sad and terrified in her room, in the "caracol" apartments, wishing to reveal the danger which awaits him to the Master, but not daring to do so; and one also seems to feel the impending doom of the eccentric prince, when he is deprived of the help of his servants, whom the porters force to leave the courtyard with their mules, where they were waiting for their lord.

A. B.

Figure 116. Seville. A. Alcazar—Throne of Justice. B. Alcazar—Hall of Ambassadors.

And finally we see the return of Don Fadrique to the presence of the irritated monarch, who has called him, and who has ordered that his companions shall be detained outside the doors, whilst the stewards of the king kill his unfortunate brother. Fadrique, after a desperate struggle, manages to escape from the murderers and to reach the court, looking for the postern of the corral, which he fancies is open—all the time making unavailing efforts to draw his sword, the handle of which has become entangled in the cords of his sash—and there at last he falls, his head being crushed by a blow of a club. Other accounts declare that when Fadrique returned to Don Pedro's apartment, after paying a courtesy visit to Maria de Padilla, he was met with the sentence, shouted in the king's voice, "Kill the Master of Santiago!" Don Fadrique drew his sword and made a valorous defence, but was overpowered and struck down by blows on the head. Seeing that his half-brother was still breathing, the king handed his own drawn dagger to an attendant and commanded him to kill the Master outright.

Figure 117. Seville. Alcazar—Façade of the Court of the Virgins.

Plate 32. Borders of Arches.

To-day we cannot say positively which was the "Palacio del Yeso," or "Palace of stucco or lime," where Don Pedro received his unhappy half-brother, nor yet which were the apartments of the "caracol." It is thought the court which has the chief façade of the alcazar was that which in the chronicle is called the "caracol," and that the "postern" was that which led from this court to that of the "banderas." It is true that tradition persists in pointing out the Court of the Dolls and the Hall of Ambassadors as the theatre of this horrible fraticide, without taking into account the notes of the historian, who relates that Don Fadrique, pursued by his murderers, ran in the direction of the postern, where he had been warned that he could make a stand, but found that all his escort had been driven out.

The King Don Pedro fills with his grand sinister figure the apartments which he occupied, and even those added by later monarchs, just as the whole gloomy pile of the Escurial seems to be haunted by the ambiguous personality of Philip II. Sad privilege of despots; the terror which they inspire in life, survives them, freezing the smile of happiness on the lips of generations, who are free from their malevolent actions, even in the very chambers which they dedicate to their pleasures.

The architecture of the Court of the Dolls is purely in the style of Granada. The surface of the arches is covered with minute mosaic work, and they rest upon beautiful brick pillars, sustained by marble columns with delicate capitals, while the double partitions, covered with perforated work, are of brick, wood, and stucco. Delicate tints cover the ornamentation with a beautiful veil, which is like a lovely Persian tapestry. This court is a rectangle with unequal sides; there is a great arch in those looking towards the Hall of Ambassadors, somewhat pear-shaped, between two smaller arches of the same form; in the other two sides there is a large arch and a smaller one, all resting upon graceful columns of different colours, in the capitals of which (believed to belong to the primitive epoch, on account of their resemblance with those of the primitive part of the Mosque of Cordova) there is a freshness and delicacy of line which holds the imagination captive. The entablatures, which are borne by the columns, are finely decorated with vertical borders, formed by inscriptions in cufic characters. The upper part of this lovely court has been spoilt by bad restorations.

The Hall of Ambassadors, as well as the Court of the Dolls, is surrounded by beautiful saloons, starting from the chief façade of the alcazar, running round the north-east angle of the building, and forming a series of mysterious and voluptuous rooms adjoining the galleries of the "Gardens" of the "Princes" of the "Grotto" and of the "Dance," till they terminate at the other south-west corner of the Court of the Damsels where the chapel used to be, and where it is believed the luxurious apartments of the "caracol" stood. According to tradition they were at the eastern side of the Court of the Damsels where the lower chapel stands to-day; this space adjoins at its north-east corner the baths, which still bear the name of the unhappy favourite, more worthy of pity than of hatred; and they also lead, by a narrow and almost hidden staircase,—the oldest in the alcazar,—to the bedroom of Don Pedro, situated in the story above. Nothing remains of the dwelling which the enamoured king prepared for the woman he loved most in his distracted and changeful life.

Figure 118. Seville. Alcazar—Interior of the Court of the Virgins, Moorish Style, Built 1369—1379.

The entrance to the famous and regal baths of Doña Maria de Padilla is in the garden of the "Dance," below the saloons constructed in the time of Charles V. It is supposed they were used by the sultanas, whilst the Saracen court was at Seville. They are surrounded by orange and lemon trees, and not enclosed by those massive walls which give the appearance of a gloomy dungeon. At the eastern extremity of the garden of the "Dance" there is a tank or fountain. It is said that one day the king, being much preoccupied with the choice of a judge to whom to confide a very complicated and obscure case, drew near this tank, and cutting an orange in two, threw one half on the surface of the water, where it floated. He then sent for one of his judges and asked him what he saw floating on the water. "An orange, Sire," was the reply. He received the same answer from several other judges whom he summoned; but finally came one who, when asked the question, broke off a branch of one of the trees near by, and with it drew the fruit floating on the water to the edge, when he answered, "Half an orange, Sire." Whereupon the monarch decided to entrust him with the conduct of the case.

Figure 119. Seville. Alcazar—General View of the Court of the Hundred Virgins.

The strange character of Don Pedro, and his manner of administering justice, take us now to the upper floor of the alcazar, to the south-east corner, where, at the end of a series of saloons of little interest, with rich bowl-shaped ceilings and cornices of mosaic, there is the king's sleeping chamber, whose walls still preserve the high socle of inlaid tile work, the stucco ornaments with borders of inscriptions in African characters, and the recessed windows with shutters, the frieze with stalactites, the ceiling of good design and beautiful gilding, and an alcove with a mosaic arch. Near one of the corners there is a bas-relief in one of the walls, representing a man seated with his body twisted towards the entrance door, and his head turned upwards, as though contemplating the skull which is to be seen above the facia of African characters.

It appears that this horrible emblem was placed there by order of Don Pedro, in order to perpetuate the memory of his summary punishment of some deceitful judges.

The Princes' Hall and the Oratory are the only upper apartments, prior to the Renaissance, which are left for us to examine,—a fire in the year 1762 having destroyed many of the rooms of the upper story. But we must first take note of the external objects which surround us. Don Pedro's bedroom looks on the south over the gardens; the Princes' Hall looks north, and occupies the upper floor of the chief façade, whose elegant "ajimeces" illuminate it. The oratory is in the east wall. In the bedroom there is a balcony, which leads to a wide gallery, with other little balconies, with seats running round them, at the end of which there is a sort of turret, with three semi-circular arches, supported by pairs of marble columns, with capitals of the purest Arab style. The spacious gardens stretch at our feet, forming a delightful spectacle. From the Princes' Hall one can perceive, above the watch-towers of the alcazar, the innumerable perforated weather-cocks of the cathedral; and, towering over all, like a gigantic sentinel, the Giralda, crowned with the sacred sign of the conversion to the faith of Christ.

Figure 120. Seville. Alcazar—Court of the Hundred Virgins.

Figure 121. Seville. Alcazar—Court of the Virgins.

In the Princes' Hall and in the Oratory the influence of the pointed style of architecture is very noticeable; and yet in studying the arches of the Oratory and the little pillars, which surmount the columns in the centre, the influence of Moorish architecture on the Gothic or pointed architecture of the third period is most striking. The columns of the Princes' Hall, and of the other adjoining apartments, are of marble, with very rich capitals. According to Jeronimo Zurita, these columns were in the royal palace of Valencia, and were removed after the defeat of Don Pedro, King of Aragon, by the King of Castile. There are luxurious divans all round the hall, and everything is rich except the ceiling, now destroyed, and the floor, which is poor and in very bad repair. The Oratory was built by order of the Catholic monarchs in 1504; its altar screen has a picture in the centre, representing the Visitation, with the signature, "Niculoso Francisco Italiano," *me fecit*, which is notable for the mixture of the pure Italian school, and the realistic Dutch school in its design. The blue tile plaques of this oratory are purely Italian, and perhaps they are the most beautiful examples of this class of Christian ornamentation in Andalusia.

Ford says that the Emperor, Charles V., married Doña Isabella of Portugal in this oratory, but the statement is not correct. Sandoval, better informed, describes the happy event in the following words:—"Eight days after the empress entered Seville, the emperor entered, being greeted with the same ceremonies. He went direct to the principal church, and from there passed to the alcazar, where the empress awaited him, accompanied by the Duchess of Medina-Sidonia, Doña Ana of Aragon, and the Marchioness of Cenete, wife of the Count of Nassau, and by other great ladies; the empress and her ladies being all most richly dressed. Afterwards the emperor arrived; they were married that same night by the Cardinal Legate, in the great room which is called the "half orange" (the Hall of Ambassadors), in the presence of all the prelates and grandees assembled there. The empress appeared to all present one of the most beautiful women in the world, as is testified to by those who saw her, and by her portraits. The hour of supper came, and the emperor and empress retired to their apartments; and after midnight, the emperor wishing it thus for religious reasons, an altar was erected in one of the apartments of the alcazar, and the Archbishop of Toledo, who had remained for the purpose, said mass there."

This marriage, as M. de Latour rightly says, was the last memorable page in the history of the alcazar; and the works completed by the emperor are the last notable improvements made in the monument. The architects, Louis and Gaspar de Vaga, were responsible for important works in the alcazar, the high gallery of the Court of the Damsels, and those looking south over the gardens and over the baths of Doña Maria de Padilla. New habitations were then erected, which shone with the art of the Renaissance, intertwined with the Arab adornments of the style called "plateresco." But the emperor did not confine himself to restoring, re-building, and to erecting fresh works in the old alcazar; nor were the above-mentioned architects the only ones who worked, but he also enlarged and embellished the gardens, and in that which is called the "Lion Garden," he had built by a certain Juan Hernandez, in the year 1540, an elegant dining hall, of singular architecture—half Italian, half Moorish—which, without doubt, is a worthy dwelling place for a fairy princess of the days of chivalry. This supper hall, or pavilion, has a square plan, and measures ten steps in each frontage; a gallery of five arches surrounds it on each side, which rest on graceful pillars of the rarest marbles with capitals in the Moorish style. A frieze is seen, externally made of arabesques, forming ribbons, cutting each other at angles, and making stars; all the lower part is faced with blue tiles of Triana, with the outlines of the designs in bold relief. Inside there is another frieze in the "plateresque" style, cleverly perforated, and a socle of blue tiles with a border, in which shine the arms of Castile and the imperial eagles. In the centre rises a beautiful fountain with a white marble basin. A facia of blue tiles, in imitation of inlaid tile work, runs around, and between the work one can read the date of its construction and the abbreviated name of the artificer. The dome is of a decadent taste.

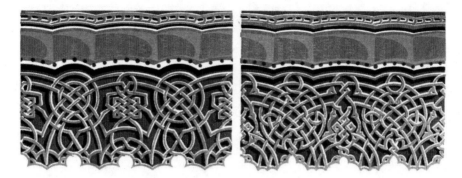

Plate 33. Borders of Arches.

Figure 122. Seville. Alcazar—Gallery in the Court of the Hundred Virgins.

Figure 123. Seville. Alcazar—The Sultana's Apartment and Court of the Virgins.

The wall which encloses these gardens to the west is decorated in the style called "vignolesque," with stout pilasters, and a frontispiece of two bodies above the pond in the garden of the "Dance," and light arches which form a long "loggia" of beautiful effect.

The works carried out under Philip III., and Philip V., and Ferdinand VI are not worthy of close attention. They constructed the parts which face the gateway of the "banderas," containing the "apeadero" and the "armeria." The "apeadero" is a portico thirty-eight yards long and fifteen wide, with two rows of marble columns in pairs. The "armeria," or armoury, is a spacious apartment above, destined for the object indicated by its name. The epoch of the construction of both is testified to by a stone set in the façade, which bears the following inscription: "Reigning in Spain Philip III., he erected this work in the year MDCVII; Philip V. enlarged and repaired it, and destined it for the royal armoury in the year MDCCXXVIII."

Ferdinand VI only constructed the offices above the baths of Doña Maria de Padilla, repairing the damage caused by the terrible earthquake of 1755.

The greater part of the halls on the upper story looking on the gardens perished in the dreadful fire of 1762; and the Government doubtless fearing the expense which would be incurred by a regular restoration in the original style, ordered all the roofs and ceilings destroyed by the fire to be repaired in the "modern manner." The unhappy result of this order was to make the ceiling of many of the apartments much too low, and to scrape away many of the ancient arabesques from the walls. In the year 1805 the unhappy idea was conceived of changing the principal entrance, and of white-washing with hideous lime the magnificent stucco work in the Princes' Hall, and of other ancient apartments. The unfortunate reformation even went so far as to substitute a plaster ceiling, which makes one shudder, for the beautiful Arab bowl-shaped one, and to put modern windows in the hall over the principal façade, called the Hall of the Princes, near the Court of the Dolls; and also to spoil the ceiling of the Hall of Ambassadors with heavy beams and supports, quite ruining the beauty of this enamelled half-orange. One is curious to know who it was who first tried to repair in a measure the harm done by these so-called "restorations." In 1833 a rational restoration of the Court of the Dolls, and of the hall near it to the north, was begun with laudible zeal by the Don Joaquin Cortes, professor of painting, and the intelligent overseer, Antonio Raso, and the official, Manuel Cortes. The real work of restoration commenced about the year 1842, thanks to the praiseworthy efforts of Don Domingo de Alcega, administrator of the royal patrimony, and to those who helped him in his difficult task, the distinguished artist, Don Joaquin Dominguez Becquer, and the master artificer, José Gutierrez y Lopez. Señor Becquer designed the Arab cornice which to-day decorates the outer part of the edifice defining the dome of the Hall of Ambassadors, which had been half destroyed in 1805, and he never ceased to devote his genius to the restoration, now in part and again general, of the most precious monument of Moorish art of the fourteenth century. During the years 1852 and 1853 the alcalde of the royal palaces completed the work of replacing some of the stucco ornaments in various apartments. Afterwards the vice-alcalde, Don Alonso Nuñez de Prado, assisted by Señor Becquer, brought a complete restoration to a successful end, which, though it may not be faultless in the eyes of a modern critic, is still worthy of praise, considering the period in which it was undertaken. In 1855 the administrator of the alcazar invited the Queen, Doña Isabella II., to interest herself in the works, with the result that he was able to cover the Court of the Dolls with glass, and to re-build the thirty-six arches of the Court of the Damsels.

Plate 34. Border of Arches.

Figure 124. Seville. Alcazar—Entrance to the Sleeping Saloon of the Moorish Kings.

Figure 125. Seville. Alcazar—Dormitory of the Kings.

There is no inscription in the alcazar which offers a real historical or literary interest to the archæologist. One does not find here the fragments of poems on the walls which in the Alhambra rest the eye and speak to the intelligence in praising the heroic deeds of warriors and the beauties of the sumptuous habitations. In the alcazar one reads the Koran with its repeated salutations and some praises of Don Pedro, in which the praises of the Mohammedan sultans have been suppressed, also the word, Islamism; but we must draw attention to the fact that the greater number of the inscriptions are the same as those employed in the alcazar of Granada, repeated a thousand times, and it would be tedious and tiresome to accompany the artistic description with the same verse, repeated a hundred times, which is to be found in the different apartments, and interrupted a hundred times also by others put in at the time of the restorations. As the persons who were charged with the work of restoring the inscriptions did not know the ancient language, they very often placed the inscriptions upside down.

Figure 126. Seville. Alcazar—The Dormitory.

On the façade, and over the principal entrance of the alcazar, around the twin windows, one reads the well-known verses: "Glory to our Lord the Sultan;" "Eternal Glory for Allah, the perpetual empire for Allah;" "Lasting happiness;" "Benediction;" "The kingdom of God, the power of God, glory to God;" "Happiness and peace, and the glory and generosity of perpetual felicity;" "In prosperous fortune this palace is the only one." The inscription, "There is no conqueror but God," placed above and below the wide frieze of painted porcelain, in cufic characters, in our opinion, must be the work of an artist from Granada.

A.   B

Figure 127. Seville. A. Alcazar. Front of the Sleeping Saloon of the Moorish Kings. B. Alcazar. Sleeping Saloon of the Moorish Kings.

Then comes the vestibule, where one sees almost the same inscriptions. The African characters are changed into cufic, or neskis. These are what are in the frieze:

> "Happiness and prosperity are the benefits of God;" and after: "Glory to our Lord the Sultan Don Pedro, may his victories be magnificent."

In the Court of the Damsels we find very much the same thing: "Praise to God, on account of His benefits."

It must be remarked that, in all the inscriptions mentioned above, the word "Islamism" has been suppressed, which proves that the artists were the same Arabs who, under the Christian dominion, took advantage of the traditional formulas in effacing the religious part of the verse.

On a frieze of the same court:

> "Glory to our Sultan Don Pedro, may God lend him His aid and make him victorious," &c., &c.

Then follow a number of inscriptions of no importance, where one sees repeated: "Happiness, Praise, Grandeur; God is Unique, the Fulfilment of Hopes;" and this one, more worthy of notice, "God is Unique, He does not Beget, He was not Begotten, He has no Companion." This inscription is also found at Granada on the Charcoal Gateway, in cufic characters, and it proves that it could not have been constructed under the Christian dominion, because it is completely contrary to the religion of Christ; and, consequently, that Don Pedro profited by the work of Yusuf as much as was possible. Amador do los Rios, the well-known *savant*, supposes that artists were brought from Toledo to construct this alcazar; but this is not exact, they only did the repairs and restorations.

On one of the doors, which like all the rest in this edifice has undergone many restorations, the most interesting legend is found: "The Sultan our Lord, the exalted, noble Don Pedro, King of Castile and of Leon—may God perpetuate his happiness— ordered Jalabi, his architect, to make the doors of worked wood for this magnificent portal of happiness; he ordered this in honour of the Ambassadors. Joy broke out for their construction and dazzling embellishment. The chiselings are the work of artists from Toledo, and it was done in the year of grace 1404.

"Similar to the twilight of the evening, and very similar to the light at dawn of day, this work is dazzling on account of its brilliant colours and the intensity of its splendours, from which abundance of felicity flows for the happy town where the palaces were built, and these habitations, which are for our Lord and Master, the only one who communicates life to his splendour, the pious Sultan, who is also severe, had it built in the town of Seville, with the aid of his intercessor, in honour of God."

One sees the same inscriptions repeated in the Hall of Ambassadors, and in the room to the left one reads:

"Oh! entrance to the habitation newly dazzling and noble, Lord of protection, of magnificence, and of virtues."

In the Court of the Dolls, and round the entrance arch, one reads:

"There is no protection if it is not Allah, in whom I trust, for I shall return to him." "All that thou dost possess comes from God," &c., &c. And in the same court (cufic): "Oh! incomparable Master, issue of a royal race, protect it." "Praise God for His benefits." "God, my Master."

In the sleeping apartment, called that of the Moorish kings, amongst other known inscriptions this one is found: "Oh! illustrious new dwelling, thy splendid happiness has progressively increased on account of the lasting brilliancy of the greatest beauty. Thou wert chosen for the place where the feasts should be celebrated. He is the support and the rule for all good, source of benefits, and food of courage! For thee...."

Plate 35. Ornament in Panels on the Wall.

We left the story of Seville somewhat abruptly to deal in detail with the alcazar. Under Almohade rule, and while the alcazar and the mosque were in course of construction, the city knew peace, and its commerce flourished. But the days of its security were limited; the end of the Moslem domination in Seville was drawing to its close. The revived prosperity of the Mohammedans spurred the Christian Spaniards to renewed efforts to encompass the overthrow of the infidels. Pope Innocent III. declared a crusade, and numbers of adventurous French and English free-lances travelled to Spain in answer to the call. But in 1195 the Christians were defeated at Alarcos, near Badajoz, and again the ambitious projects of San Fernando were temporarily frustrated. In 1212 the Almohade army, it is said to the number of 600,000 men, was almost destroyed on the disastrous field of Las Navas, and the work of the expulsion of the Moors from Spain was begun. City after city was captured by the soldiers of Fernando III., Cordova fell in 1235, and the conqueror, with the help of the King of Granada, who had sworn allegiance to the Christian monarch, marched against Seville.

The army brought by the holy king to Seville was the most brilliant and numerous ever seen in Christian or Mohammedan Spain. No smaller force would have been sufficient for the taking of a city which contained 12,000 Mussulman families divided into twenty-four tribes, and which had been in the hands of the followers of Islam for more than five centuries. In the spring of the year 1235 the army was moved from Cordova and divided into two parts, one under the command of the Prince of Molina and the Master of Santiago, which was to march to the Ajarafe; and the other under the direction of the King of Granada and the Master of Calatrava, which was to harass the country near Jerez. The attack on Seville and its territories commenced immediately, and a series of uninterrupted victories prefaced the happy termination which was to crown the constant and generous efforts of the Christian warriors.

Figure 128. Seville. Alcazar—Room of the Infanta.

Figure 129. Seville. Alcazar—Columns Where Don Fadrique Was Murdered.

Seville, at this period the court and seat of the Islamite empire, was a city calculated to defy the strategy of the most skilful generals, the valour of the most devoted men at arms. In form it would resemble a shield, stretching from north-east to south-west. Its head and right side were formed by the walls with its towers, defended by a barbican and a moat, with eight gates and a narrow side entrance. These gates were veritable fortresses. They were defended by towers and bastions. Their exits were narrow, and never in front; the exterior passages to the city had angles and turnings, and very often the first turning opened into a square armed place, with narrow doorways at both sides. "The gates of Seville," says Morgado, "were constructed of planks of iron, fastened on to strong hides with steel bolts. And because it was best defended on its west side by the river Guadalquivir, which protected more than half the city, with the six gates in that side, it was thought well to place the strongest walls and the best fortified towers, with as many barbicans, and the widest and deepest moats on the other side."

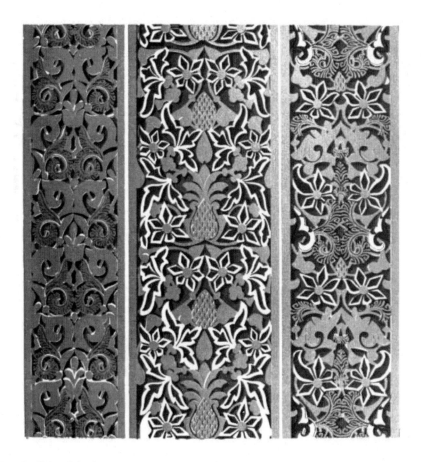

Plate 36. Bands, Side of Arches.

The left side of the shield boasted the majestic curve of the river, the arsenal, and another series of walls and gates; but at this part, there were no moats nor false entrances, because it had the strong towers of the Ajarafe opposite to defend it. There were four gates on this side, not counting that of Bib-Ragel, which occupied the north angle of the city; and, in addition to these, it is believed there was a small postern, afterwards called the "atarazanas," through which it is supposed that Axataf, or "Sakkáf" his Moorish name, went out to receive King Ferdinand, and to deliver up the keys of Seville. The old wharf of Saracen Seville came as far as this; and in all the space, which to-day is called El Barrio de los Humeros, or the Chimney Quarter, the Mohammedans had their arsenal and shipbuilding yard, while the sailors and fishermen of the Guadalquivir were also housed in this district. The Gate of the Triana must have been in the vicinity; and the Gate of Hercules was directly opposite the Ajarafe, which was also called the Garden of

Hercules. With the gardens and orchards of the Macarena, which adorned it to the north, the plains and woods of Tablada, which supplied it with corn and wood to the east and south, with an abundant supply of fresh water brought from Carmona by the aqueduct, with the river which was its principal commercial artery to the west, with the castles on the opposite side of the Guadalquivir, protecting the river and its bridge, and occupying all the heights from Azalfarache nearly as far as Italica, Seville was one of the best situated, best supplied, best defended, and most prosperous cities of the Mussulman empire in Andalusia. To attack her she must be cut off from the Ajarafe, and her bridge of boats must be taken. It would have been useless to descend to Italica and be exposed to the assaults of the city and of Triana, as long as the bridge existed, and this task was thought to be beyond the power and ingenuity of any enemy.

The bridge of boats, protected by a great wooden chain, linked by iron rings, kept the communication open between the city and the Ajarafe, that vast and fertile district from which the Sevillians received all sorts of supplies, and where the Saracen magnates had their country villas. This delightful Garden of Hercules, in whose praise many Arab writers have exhausted the treasure of their rich and exalted imagination, has been described in the following manner by an anonymous poet, in some verses dedicated to the Abbadite Sultan Almutamed: "Seville is a young widow, her husband is Abbad, her diadem the Aljarafe, her collar the winding river."

A.   B.

Figure 130. Seville. A. Alcazar. Gate of the Hall of San Fernando. B. Alcazar. Gallery of the Hall of San Fernando.

Figure 131. Seville. Alcazar—Hall In Which King San Fernando Died.

 Indeed, says the poet Ibn Saffar, "the Aljarafe surpasses in beauty and fertility all the lands of the world, the oil of its olives goes even to far Alexandria, its farms and orchards are superior to those of other countries on account of their extension and convenience; and, always white and pure, they seem to be so many stars in a sky of olive gardens." Travelled Arab historians recall with pleasure the delights of Andalus; preferring Seville to either Baghdad or Cairo, saying: "The Aljarafe is a luxuriant wilderness without wild beasts, and its Guadalquivir is a Nile without crocodiles." One of the authors, quoted by El-Makkari, gives the following exact description of the Aljarafe: "It is an immense district, measuring forty miles long, and almost as many broad, formed of pleasing hills of reddish earth, on which there are woods of olive and fig-trees, which offer a delicious shade to the traveller in the hours of the mid-day heat. This district contains a numerous population, scattered in beautiful farms or collected in villages, none of which are wanting for markets, clean baths, fine buildings, and other conveniences, such as are usually only to be found in cities of the first order."

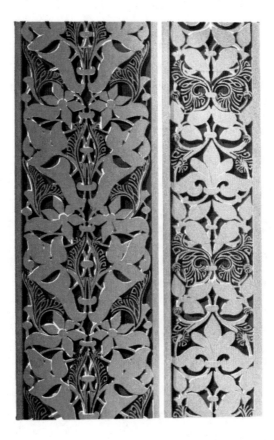

Plate 37. Bands. Side of Arches.

This fertile territory, which the Saracens called the "Orchard of Hercules," rose gradually to the west of Seville, after stretching along the right bank of the river.

Its heights were covered with farmhouses and hamlets, as the Arab writer indicates, which formed, as it were, a continuous population, rich in provisions, from which Seville usually received abundant supplies of all necessaries. There were four principal villages: Aznalfarche (to-day, San Juan de Alfarache), Aznalcazar, Aznalcollar, and Solucar de Albayda, strong walled places, where the Mohammedans collected the revenues of the district. The fringe, formed by the heights of the Aljarafe, was given the name of "Mountain of Mercies" (Jebl arrahmah) by the Mohammedans, on account of its extraordinary fertility, a surprising abundance of figs, known as "Al-kuiti" and "Ash-shari," being produced there.

The Sevillians faced the Christian attack with boldness, bred of confidence, and a determination to strain every nerve, and exhaust every resource, in repelling the invaders. They were engaging upon their last throw for the sovereignty of Andalusia. Fernando's warships encountered the Moorish fleet at the mouth of the Guadalquivir, and drove them from their position, and the infidels collected their forces to make a last stand on land. But their stubborn front was broken by the Christian host, and the war-worn remnant of the Moorish army prepared to withstand a siege. Even when the bridge of boats was destroyed, and all communications with the suburb of Triana and the surrounding country was cut off, the Moors still fought on within the city walls, and it was not until fifteen months had elapsed that Seville was starved into submission. On the 23rd February, 1235, Fernando entered the city, and Abdul Hassan, rejecting the king's invitation to become a dependent officer of the Spanish Crown, retired with thousands of his vanquished Almohades to Africa.

Figure 132. Seville. Alcazar—Room of the Prince.

Figure 133. Seville. Alcazar—View of the Gallery from the Second Floor.

Fernando's first act was to have the mosque purified for the celebration of a high and imposing Mass; he took up his quarters in the alcazar; divided the Moorish possessions among his knights, and rested his army after their long and arduous campaign. Four years later he died of dropsy. He was succeeded by Alfonso X., who founded the University of Seville, devoted his leisure to the study of poetry, history, and ancient laws, and merited the title of "El Sabio," "the Learned." But although the beautiful alcazar appealed to the studious temperament of "El Sabio," the fortress-palace is more closely associated with his son, Pedro I., Pedro, "the Cruel," the most renowned of all the Christian sovereigns who ruled Andalusia from Seville.

Figure 134. Seville. Tower of the Giralda.

Pedro's character has been made the study of many biographers and historians, and he has not been without his literary whitewashers, but the "incidents" which illuminate his career do not place him in a favourable light. His Bohemianism endeared him to the people, and a certain sense of justice, in cases in which his own interests were not concerned, has gained for him the title of "The Justiciary." It may be that the plottings of Albuquerque, his father's chancellor, and the perfidious behaviour of his relatives, including his own mother, served to warp and embitter his nature; but he had no sooner, at the instigation of his mistress, Maria de Padilla, taken up the reigns of government, than he revealed the cruelty and malignity of his character. Leonora de Guzmar, the mother of Alfonso's illegitimate son, Enrique, was done to death in his prisons; Abu

Said, the King of Granada, was seized by treachery, robbed, and executed; Urraca Osorio, for refusing Pedro's addresses, was burned to death in the market-square of Seville; his wife, Blanche of Bourbon, was mysteriously murdered; Don Fadrique, his half-brother, was assassinated with Pedro's dagger; and he himself was eventually defeated in battle by the troops of his brother Henry and Bertrand du Guesclin, and killed in single combat by Henry.

Figure 135. Seville. Details of the Giralda Tower.

Pedro wearied of his first wife, Blanche of Bourbon, in forty-eight hours; and, having had his marriage annulled, he espoused the handsome Juaña de Castro, only to desert her a few days later to return to his beautiful mistress, Maria de Padilla. This woman appears to have been the only person who inspired Pedro with more than a transitory passion, and the courtiers testified to the power she wielded by chivalrously drinking the waters of her bath in El Jardin del Crucero. But Pedro's passion for his mistress, though lasting, was not monopolising, and his amours supply us with an incident which reveals at once the king's ferocity, his humour, and his alleged respect for justice. It was his custom at night to muffle himself in a cloak and adventure alone into the city in quest of entertainment. On one of these excursions he encountered a hidalgo serenading a lady, whose favours he himself coveted. Cloaked by the dim light, and made secure by the emptiness of the street, the king fought and slew his rival, in defiance of his own order, which made street fighting punishable upon the officers of the city when they failed to bring the disturbers of the peace to justice. He had not bargained for the noise to disturb the rest of an old lady in the vicinity; he had not observed a venerable head protruding through an upper window. Believing the incident to be "wrapped in mystery," he summoned the alcade of the city to his presence, acquainted him with the fact that the body of a hidalgo, pierced to the heart, had been found in the street, and gave him the option of discovering the murderer within forty-eight hours, or of being hanged in his stead.

Plate 38. Ornaments on Panels.

Figure 136. Seville. Court of the House of Pilatos.

And hanged he doubtless would have been but for the timely confidence of the old lady who had witnessed the fight. The alcade came again to the king with the news that the murderer had been found, and would be on view upon the gallows within the time specified by Pedro. Curious to see who had been secured to expiate his sin, or eager to fasten a new dereliction of duty upon the alcade, the king went to the place of execution and found, suspended from the gallows, an effigy of himself. "Good," said the king, "justice has been done! I am satisfied." There is a street in Seville which is called the Calle della Cabeza del Rey Don Pedro, to commemorate the duel; and the alley from which the old lady observed the issue is known as the Calle del Candilejo, "the street of the candlestick."

The alcazar extends along the river as far as the Golden Tower, built during the reign of Yusuf Almotacid Ben Nasir, by the Almohadan governor Abulala. The view of Seville, from the Christina promenade, the famous thoroughfare, which extends from the palace of the Duke of Montpensier to the Golden Tower, is a spectacle of which the Sevillians never tire, and visitors are never weary of praising. The tower itself, which took its present name either from the fact that it held the gold which the Spanish ships brought from America, or because Don Pedro secreted his treasures there, is octagonal in shape, with three receding floors, crowned with battlements, and washed by the Guadalquivir. The shimmering Torre del Oro, reflecting its light upon the broad bosom of the rose-coloured river beneath the setting sun, has inspired poets and painters of every age and nationality. George Borrow believes it probable that it derived its name from the fact that the beams of the setting sun focussed upon it makes it appear to be built of pure gold; and then, carried away by the loveliness of the picture, he cries: "Cold, cold must the heart be which can remain insensible to the beauties of this magic scene, to do justice to which the pencil of Claude himself were barely equal. Often have I shed tears of rapture whilst I beheld it, and listened to the thrush and the nightingale piping forth their melodious songs in the woods, and inhaled the breeze laden with the perfume of the thousand orange gardens of Seville."

Figure 137. Seville. Court of the House of Pilatos.

Of the great mosque of Seville, which was built by Abu Yakub Yusuf in 1171, and completed by the addition of the tower in 1196 by his son, only the barest traces now remain. It is impossible to determine who really designed the famous Tower, now called the Giralda; but historians favour the claims of the renowned architect, whose name is variously spelt Gever, Hever, or Djabir, and who is erroneously supposed to have been the inventor of algebra. In its original state this structure was an immense and stately pile, planned on the model of the mosque of Cordova, and decorated with lavish magnificence. In 1235 it was dedicated to the service of God and the Virgin, but it retained all its Moorish characteristics until 1401. The Moors would have destroyed the building and the beautiful Muezzin tower before it fell into the hands of San Fernando's soldiers, and thus save their sacred temple from desecration by the "infidels," but the king's son, Alonso "el Sabio," threatened to visit such spoliation upon the garrison by sacking the city. This threat had the desired effect, and for nearly two centuries the religious spirit of Seville found expression in a temple which had been built to the glory of Allah. But at the beginning of the fifteenth century the mosque was razed to the ground, and Seville cathedral began to take that huge and splendid form which, in the words of the pious originators, was to inspire succeeding generations with the idea that its designers were mad. It was to be the greatest cathedral in Spain, and it ended in being second only to that of Cordova, but still the third largest Christian church in the world. Its area of 125,000 square feet is 35,000 square feet less than Cordova cathedral, and 105,000 square feet less than St. Peter's at Rome; but it is 15,000 square feet greater than that of Milan Cathedral, and greater by 41,000 square feet than St. Paul's in London.

The Moors, in building their mosque, employed the remains of ruined Roman and Gothic structures, and the Spaniards in 1401 used the Arab foundations in the construction of their cathedral, while the Moorish tower was preserved to do duty as a spire. In its original form the Giralda was only 250 feet high, the additional 100 feet which forms the belfry being added by Fernando Ruiz in 1567. In 1506 the cathedral was completed. Five years later the dome collapsed, and was re-erected by Juan Gil de Hontanon. Extensive restoration work was carried out in 1882, under the superintendence of Cassova; but six years after this work was completed, the dome again gave way, and workmen have been constantly employed ever since in reconstructing this part of the vast building.

Plate 39. Ornaments on Panels.

According to Contreras, the Giralda is the most expressive monument of the Mohammedan dominion; and, despite all that has been said of its Moorish structure and primitive African style, it is in his opinion a perfect work of Arab art. The construction is anterior by four centuries, at least, to that of any tower of Granadian architecture such as that which to-day belongs to the Church of St. John of the Kings, but there is not the slightest difference in the manner of their ornamentation, and the rhomboids of painted bricks, the festoons of terra cotta, the windows with double arches, following the segments of a circle, present all the variety of the alcazar of Granada.

Figure 138. Seville House of Pilatos—View in the Court by the Door of the Chapel.

Figure 139. Seville. House of Pilatos—Chapel.

"Here one sees plainly," Contreras says, "the origin of the superposed arch of the belvedere of Lindaraja of the Alhambra, of the hanging arch of the three entrances of the Lions' Court, of the festoons of the Court of the Fountain, and of all those forms, so delicate and so luxurious, that they are without equal in architecture. It is in the Giralda that one finds the beginning of truly decorative art. Built of varnished bricks, with a stout construction, as is demanded by the façade of a very high tower, it is to be regretted that such a beautiful edifice should be crowned by so strange a body as its gilded frontages and painted porcelains."

With the exception of the Giralda, and part of the lower portions of the walls, the Moorish remains that are to be recognised in the cathedral are few and not remarkable. The Puerta del Perdon in the Calle de Alemanes was reconstructed by Alfonso XI., after the victory of Salado, and the plateresque ornamentations were added by Bartolome Lopez about 1522. But although the bronze-covered doors have been disfigured by paint, their Moorish character is still distinctly traceable. Through the gateway we enter the old Moorish courtyard, the Patio de los Naranjas (Court of Oranges), robbed of its former grandeur, but still distinguished by its beautiful Arabic fountain, with an octagonal basin, which occupies the centre of the court. From this spot we get a splendid view of the cathedral and the massive yet delicate Giralda tower, which has been declared to be even more to Seville than Giotto's Campanile is to Florence, or that of St. Mark's to Venice. "Long before the traveller reaches the city," writes an imaginative admirer, "the Giralda seems to beckon him onwards to his promised land; during all his peregrinations through the intricate streets and lanes it is his trusted guide, always ready to serve him, soaring as it does far above all surroundings, it is a thing of unfailing beauty and interest as day by day he passes and repasses it, or wanders about its precincts; it tells him even afar off, how the day moves on, and how the night; and it dwells in his thoughts the fairest memory of his sojournings in the queen of the Southern cities."

From the Court of Oranges to the Giralda the way leads through the Capilla de la Granada of the cathedral. A solitary horseshoe arch reminds us of the Moorish origin of the building; and the huge elephant's tusk suspended from the roof, a bridle that tradition declares belonged to the Cid's steed, and a stuffed crocodile, are Oriental rather than Christian relics. And the Giralda, in spite of its added belfry—its surmounting figure symbolic of the Christian faith—and the fact that it is under the special patronage of the two Santas Justa and Rufina, "who are much revered at Seville," is still a Moorish monument. At its base the tower is a square of fifty feet, and it rises by a series of stages, or cuerpos, which are named after the architecture, decoration or use for which they are designed. At the Cuerpo de Campanas is hung a peal of bells, of which the largest, Santa Maria, eighteen tons in weight, and referred to in the vernacular as "the plump," was set up in 1588 by the order of the Archbishop Don Gonzola de Mena, at a cost of ten thousand ducats. Above, we come to the cuerpo of the Azucenas, or white lilies, with which it is embellished; and, going still higher, we reach El Cuerpo del Reloj, the clock-tower, in which was erected, in 1400, the first tower-clock ever made in Spain. Portions of this old timepiece were employed by the Monk Jose Cordero in making, in 1765, the clock which is working to this day. The belfry, which is the home of a colony of pigeons and hawks, is girdled with a motto from the proverb, "Nomen Domini fortissima turris"—("The name of the Lord is a strong tower.")

Figure 140. Seville. Gallery of the House of Pilatos.

The Moorish summit was crowned with four brazen balls, so large that in order to get them into the building it was necessary to remove the keystone of a door called the Gate of the Muezzin, leading from the mosque to the interior of the tower. The iron bar, which supported the balls, weighed about ten cwt., and the whole was cast by a celebrated alchemist, a Sicilian, named Abu Leyth, at a cost of £50,000 sterling. These particulars were set down by a Mohammedan writer of the period, and their accuracy was proved in 1395 (157 years after the overthrow of the Arab dominion), when the earthquake threw the entire mechanism, balls and supports, to the ground, where they were weighed, and the figures were found to be absolutely correct. The figure of La Fé, "The Faith," which now tops the Giralda, was cast by Bartolomé Morel in 1568. It stands fourteen feet high, and weighs twenty-five cwts., yet so wonderful is the workmanship that it turns with every breath of the wind. The head of the female figure is crowned with a Roman helmet, the right hand bears the Labaro, or banner, of Constantine, and in the left it holds out a palm branch, symbolical of conquest.

Figure 141. Seville. Gallery of the Court of the House of Pilatos.

But when we return from this "strange composite fane," with its Christian summit surmounting a Moslem tower, which again has its foundations in a Roman temple, when we re-cross the Court of Oranges, with its Moorish fountain, flanked by a Christian pulpit, and enter the cathedral, the mind is transported at a bound from the fairy-like beauties of Morisco ornamentation to the sombre, awe-inspiring majesty, which prompted Theophile Gautier to the reflection that "the most extravagant and monstrously prodigious Hindoo pagodas are not to be mentioned in the same century as the Cathedral of Seville. It is a mountain scooped out, a valley turned topsy-turvy; Notre Dame, at Paris, might walk erect in the middle nave, which is of frightful height; pillars as large round as towers, and which appear so slender that they make you shudder, rise out of the ground, or descend from the vaulted roof, like stalactites in a giant's grotto."

Seville

Plate 40. Ornaments on Panels.

Plate 41. Ornaments on Panels.

Figure 142. Seville. Court of the Palace of Medina-Cœli.

Lomas, who finds the exterior of the cathedral "simply beneath criticism," and deplores that "age after age a great band of glorifiers of self, through self's handiwork, should have been employed in producing what they determined should be a world's marvel," is compelled to admit that "the first view of the interior is one of the supreme moments of a lifetime. The glory and majesty of it are almost terrible. No other building, surely, is so fortunate as this in what may be called its presence." Even George Borrow, who thought more of his beloved testaments than of Spanish monuments erected to "the spiritual tyranny of the Court of Rome," was feign to declare that it is impossible to wander through the cathedral of Seville "without experiencing sensations of sacred awe and deep astonishment"; and Caveda describes the general effect as "truly majestic."

The Italian rhapsodist, Edmondo de Amicis, who always succeeds in conveying a strikingly convincing impression of the spectacles that fascinate his sensitive mind, is at his best in his description of Seville cathedral. "At your first entrance," he says, "you are bewildered, you feel as if you are wandering in an abyss, and for several moments you do nothing but glance around you in that immense space, almost as if to assure yourself that your eyes are not deceiving you, nor your fancy playing you some trick. Then you approach one of the pillars, measure it, and look at the more distant ones, which, though as large as towers, appear so slender that it makes you tremble to think that the building is resting upon them. You traverse them with a glance from floor to ceiling, and it seems as if you could almost count the moments it would take for the eye to climb them. There are five aisles, each one of which might form a church. In the centre one, another cathedral, with its cupola and bell tower, could easily stand. All of them together form sixty-eight bold vaulted ceilings, which seem to expand and rise slowly as you look at them. Every thing is enormous in this cathedral. The principal chapel, placed in the centre of the great nave, and almost high enough to touch the ceiling, looks like a chapel built for giant priests, to whose knees the ordinary altars would not reach. The paschal candle seems like the mast of a ship, and the bronze candlestick which holds it, like the pillars of a church. The choir is a museum of sculpture and chiselling. The chapels are worthy of the church, for they contain the masterpieces of sixty-seven sculptors and thirty-eight painters.... The chapel of San Ferdinand, which contains the sepulchres of this king and his wife Beatrice, of Alonso the Wise, the celebrated minister, Florida Blanca, and other illustrious personages, is one of the richest and most beautiful of all. The body of Ferdinand, who redeemed Seville from the dominion of the Arabs, clothed in his uniform, with crown and mantle, rests in a crystal casket, covered with a veil. On one side, is his sword which he carried on the day of his entrance into Seville; on the other, a staff of cane, an emblem of command. In that same chapel is preserved a little ivory Virgin, which the holy king carried to war with him, and other relics of great value." And here also, although De Amicis makes no mention of them, are the keys of Seville which Abdul Hassan handed to Ferdinand at the surrender of the city. One key is of silver, and bears the inscription, "May Allah grant that Islam may rule for ever in this city." The other key is made of iron gilt, and is of Mudejar workmanship. It is inscribed, "The King of Kings will open; the King of the Earth will enter."

In its churches and its old houses, Seville is rich in Moorish influences, and exhibits abundant traces of Morisco art, which prevailed against the material dominancy of the Christian conquerors. The reconciled Arabs who remained as subjects of Ferdinand became the chief of the most lavishly-remunerated artisans of the city. They pursued their craft in the dwellings of the rich; and in the churches of the "infidel." Untrammelled by religion and uninspired by faith, they worked for art's sake, and the substantial pecuniary award that sweetened their labours. The church of San Marco has a beautiful Moorish tower built in imitation of the Giralda, and second only to the minaret tower of the cathedral in point of height; San Gil is a Christianised Mezquita; Santa Catalina reveals the survival of Moorish art in its façade, while its principal chapel is Gothic. In nearly all the sacred edifices of antiquity the combination of Moorish and Renaissance architecture betrays an incongruity of style and sentiment which is only to be found among the Christian churches of Spain. And if the Catholic kings, who were sworn to the extirpation of the Moslems, allowed the Moors to build their churches in the style of temples devoted to Allah, it is not surprising that many of the finest private residences of the city retain a Moorish design, and possess a distinctly Oriental atmosphere.

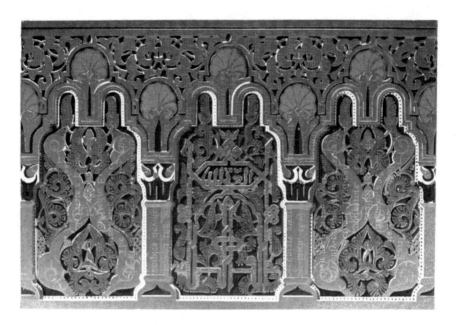

Plate 42. Frieze in the Upper Chamber, House of Sanchez.

The Casa de Pilatos, which has been pronounced the fourth great monument of older Seville, was commenced in 1500 by Don Pedro Enriquez, in the then popular decadent Saracenic style, and was completed by his son, Fadrique, in imitation of Pilate's palace at Jerusalem. In accordance with this scheme, he fashioned a reception-hall, called the Prætorium, erected an upright column—a gift of Pope Pius V.—copied from the pillar at which Christ was scourged, and made a replica of the basin into which the thirty pieces of silver were counted. When the house came into the possession of the first Duke of Alcalá, he was acting as the Spanish viceroy at Naples, and he filled the rooms and corridors with Roman busts and statuary, gathered from Italy and the ruins of Italica. On every side the art treasures of the Romans adorn the perfect Moorish colonnades, and the shadows of Roman sculptures are thrown upon diapered marble pavements from light that enters through Arab lattices and ajimez windows. It has been described as a great curiosity shop, but to the art lover it is a treasure house of almost infinite beauty and variety.

The Moorish palace of the Duke de Alba, in the Calle de las Dueñas, once consisted of eleven courtyards, nine fountains, and more than a hundred marble pillars, and was surrounded by a garden, which is a forest of orange trees and myrtles. In Seville one wanders through streets which are redolent of Arabia, and peep into countless Oriental patios, cool with fountains, and shaded by palms and Eastern canopies. One "feels the East a-calling"—the colour, the scent, the witchery of it gets into one's blood—and one recognises the truth that inspired the old Spanish saying: "To whom God loves He gives a house in Seville."

Chapter 3

TOLEDO

Toledan history proper, as distinguished from the mixture of fable and tradition which are associated with the story of this ancient and royal city, dates from the invasion of the Goths. Toledo was old when Euric successfully scaled its seven rocks and stormed its battlements—how old, cannot be determined. Legend claims that the town was in existence when God made the sun; less exalted imagination dates its foundation no further back than the days of Tubal, the grandson of Noah. Alphonsus, "the Learned," and Diego Mossem Valera, the historian of Isabel the Catholic, agree that it was built by Pyrrhus, the son-in-law of King Hispan, and a captain of the army of Cyrus. Hercules has been claimed as the father of Toledo by Rufo Festo Avieno, and Ferecio, one of the companions of Ulysses, is held by some to have retreated to this spot to escape the blood-vengeance of that little band of Greek adventurers. Other legends declare the city to be of Jewish origin; and its builders, the Judians, who fled from Jerusalem before the victorious hosts of Nebuchadnezzar. Don Rodrigo Jimenez de Rada discovers the founders of Toledo in Tolemon and Brutus, two Roman consuls in the reign of Ptolemy Evergetes, and more reasonable supposition favours the theory that it was first settled by nomadic Celtic shepherds, who forsook their flocks to erect walls and fortifications on the rocky eminence above the Tagus. The little that is known of the origin and beginning of Toledo; the very mystery and obscurity of its earliest days, is accepted by the old historian, Alcocer, as a proof of its antiquity and nobility. Rais, the Moorish writer, says that Tago, at Toledo, was one of the eleven governors of Carpetania. Tago was foully murdered by Hasdrubal, the successor of Hamilcar, and the assassination of Hasdrubal was followed by so determined an insurrection that even Hannibal was forced to retreat before the infuriated Carpetanians. But Hannibal retreated, only to return with a reinforced army, and break Carpetania beneath the might of Carthagenian rule. In 191 B.C., after the fall of Carthage, Hilermo surrendered Toledo to the Roman forces, under Marcus Fulvius Nobilior. But Toledo held itself sullenly and haughtily aloof from the affairs of Rome.

Viriate and Caius Plancius might cut each other's throats on the banks of the Tagus; Sertorius might nurse his hates within the city; Cæsar and Pompey might be locked in a death struggle—those things mattered nothing to the contemptuous and independent Toledans. The Goth was the first real conqueror of Toledo; and the city, outwearing the scars of Rome, and throwing off the marks of the Moors, is, to-day, as insistently Gothic as Cordova and Seville are unmistakably Moorish.

Plate 43. Cornice at Springing of Arches in a Window.

One sees Toledo from the distance, from the bridges, and from the heart of the city, and recognises that it is as it has always been—that it will go down into the tomb of the centuries unchanged. It grew "out of the night of ages"—its rocky throne has defied the ravages of time and the transforming ingenuity of man. Maurice Barrès, who has felt the majesty and melancholy of this gaunt monument of mediævalism, writes: "The landscape of Toledo, and the banks of the Tagus, are amongst the saddest and most ardent things of this world. Whoever lives here has no need to consider the grave youth, the 'Penseroso,' of the Medicis Chapel; he may also do without the biography and the 'Pensées' of Blaise Pascal. With the very sentiment realised by these great solitary works he will be filled, if he but give himself up to the tragic fierceness of the magnificences in ruins upon these high rocks. Toledo, on its hillside, with the tiny half circle of the Tagus at its feet, has the colour, the roughness, the haughty poverty of the sierra on which it is built, and whose strong articulations from the very first produce an impression of energy and passion. It is less a town, a noisy affair yielding to the commodities of life, than a significant spot for the soul. Beneath a crude illumination, which gives to each line of its ruins a vigour, a clearness, by which the least energetic characters acquire backbone, at the same time it is mysterious, with its cathedral springing towards the sky, its alcazars and palaces, that only take sight from their invisible patios. Thus, secret and inflexible, in this harsh, overheated land, Toledo appears like an image of exaltation in solitude, a cry in the desert."

Figure 143. Toledo. Santa Maria La Blanca—Interior, 1100-1156.

Grim, austere, and forbidding is the general type of the Gothic character; the history of their kings in Spain is a long story of menace, bloodshed, and persecution; and that history covers Toledo as with a suit of battered mail. Christianity without the practice of the Christian virtues, valour divorced from mercy, power disjoined from justice—the religion, the might and majesty of the Gothic sovereigns, is a record of gloomy and revengeful despotism. Hermengildo, the Gothic saint, used his religion as an excuse for attempting to wrest the throne of Toledo from his father, Leovigildo, whom he denounced as a minister of the devil; Recaredo, who has been painted by historians as a model of all the Christian virtues, practiced a rigorous system of cruelty and vindictive bigotry; and his successors were notorious for their queer morality, and their persecution of the Jews. Yet San Ildephonso, the most famous archbishop of Toledo under the Goths, has enriched the history of Spain with many splendid fables of heavenly manifestations; and the piece he cut from the veil of a visiting saint, and the chasuble, with which the Virgin invested him with her own hands, are still displayed among the treasures of Toledo cathedral. The figures of Wamba and Rodrigo—the warrior king who was offered the alternative of the crown of Toledo, or the thrust of a Toledan dagger, and "the Last of the Goths"—stand out with dominating prominence on the stage of Gothic history, on which warriors and priests are the principal actors.

Plate 44. Panels on Walls.

The doctrine of the Gothic priesthood has been described as the "hardest, meanest, and brutallest imaginable," and the Gothic warriors as men who were never other than savage tyrants, who "aped a culture which they could not understand, and with whose aims and tendencies their inmost character was powerless to sympathise." These are the people who gave Toledo its character, a character which the art-adoring Arabs were unable to change or even to greatly modify. It is so important to understand the influence which was at work in the creation of the Toledan character, the atmosphere in which it was reared, and the discipline under which it developed, that I make no excuse for quoting the following illuminating appreciation of the Gothic nature from Mr. Leonard Williams' chapter on Toledo: "Originally barbaric in their ferocity, the Goths became as their domination approached its inevitable end, barbaric in their effeminacy. So, too, with their religious beliefs. Excepting the clergy, who were men of some education and unlimited unscrupulousness, the Christian Visigoth was every whit as barbaric as the heathen; barbaric, either in his violent fanaticism, or else in his total lack of individuality, and idiotic acquiesence in the schemes of a designing priesthood. An intermediate type was wholly, or almost wholly, wanting, and there is little to choose between Leovigildo, the ignorant and cruel desperado, and his meek successor, Recaredo, the unresisting prey of the ambitious metropolitan of Toledo.... The morals of the Visigoths were on a par with their refinement and their mode of living. Serfdom was the distinguishing mark of the commons; arrogance of the nobility; avarice and ambition of temporal power of the clergy; regicide and tumult of the Crown. It is clear that a people, disunited in this manner, could never have exercised a long supremacy in any case; and destiny, or chance, precipitated their downfall by the arrival of the one-eyed Tarik and his host, and the defeat of 'the Last of the Goths,' beside the memory-haunted osiers of the Guadalete."

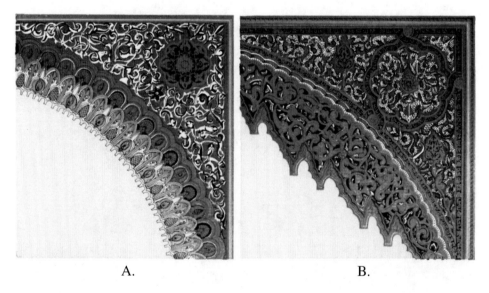

Plate 45. A. From one of the centre arches. Spandrils of Arches. B. From the entrance to the Divan.

Arrogance, avarice, ambition, regicide, tumult—here we have the distinguishing qualities of the nobles, the priests, and the kings of Toledo under the Gothic rule. The sovereigns and the nobles stamped their personality upon the city, and were themselves moulded and dominated by the priests. The priestly influence in Spain has ever been for austerity and heartless magnificence; it has ever sought to impress by fear and superstition. In the time of the Goths, Christianity developed through the increasing power of the bishops. The Church was terrible and forbidding; the nobility was arrogant and cruel; the monarchy was tyrannical and despotic. Hallam dismisses the consideration of the Visigoths in a sentence: "I hold," he says, "the annals of barbarians so unworthy of remembrance that I will not detain the reader by naming one sovereign of that obscure race." But, under those sovereigns, and by the hands of that obscure race, Toledo was established upon its rocky eminence, and it bears its character on its face to-day, as it did in the opening quarter of the eighth century, when the one-eyed Tarik entered its melancholy, deserted streets.

Figure 144. Toledo. The Gate of Blood.

The plunder that fell to the Moorish invader is variously reported, but all accounts are agreed that it was beyond calculation. According to the learned Mohammedan author, Al-leyth Ibn Said, the spoils were so abundant that the rank and file of the army all shared in the rewards, and it was a common thing for the humblest bowmen to be possessed of costly robes, magnificent gold chains of exquisite workmanship, and strings of matchless pearls, rubies, and emeralds. So great, in many instances, was the greed for plunder, and so grossly ignorant were the Berbers of the value of the spoil, that whenever a party of them happened upon a rich fabric, they did not hesitate to cut it up between them, without regard to its worth or workmanship. It is recorded that two Berbers secured a superb carpet, composed of the most splendid embroidery, interwoven with gold, and ornamented with filigree work of the purest gold, with pearls and other gems. The men carried it for awhile between them, but, finding this method of conveyance cumbersome, they carved the gem-encrusted fabric in twain with their swords. In this fashion, masterpieces of art were heedlessly destroyed for the sake of the raw material of which they were composed.

Among the precious objects seized in the palace and church of Toledo were twenty-five golden and jewelled crowns—the crowns of the different Gothic kings who had reigned in Spain—the psalms of David, written upon gold leaf in water made of dissolved rubies, vases filled with precious stones, quantities of robes of cloth of gold and tissue, tunics of every variety of costly skirts and satins, magnificent suits of chain armour and mail inlaid with jewels, and jewel-studded swords and daggers, weapons of every description, and Solomon's emerald table, wrought in burnished silver and gold. "This table," says the Arabian chronicler, "was the most beautiful thing ever seen, with its golden vases and plates of a precious green stone, and three collars of rubies, emeralds, and pearls." Other Arabian historians have claimed that it was composed of a solid emerald, and they are practically agreed that it was brought to Toledo after the sacking of Jerusalem, and that it was valued in Damascus at a hundred thousand dinars—about £50,000. Washington Irving, who invariably goes the whole hog when dealing with legendary history, says that this "inestimable table" was composed "of one single and entire emerald, and possessed talismanic powers; for tradition affirms that it was the work of genii, and had been wrought by them for King Solomon the Wise, the son of David. This marvellous relic was carefully preserved by Tarik, as the most precious of all his spoils, being intended by him as a present to the khalif; and, in commemoration of it, the city was called by the Arabs, Medina Almeyda; that is to say, 'The City of the Table.'"

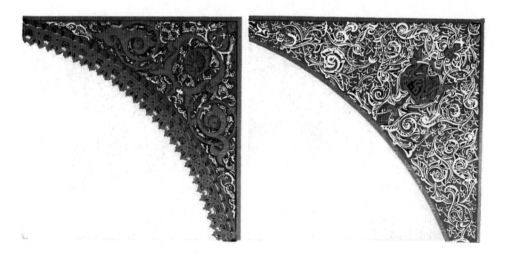

Plate 46. Spandrils of Arches.

But the historian, Ibnu Hayyau, the greatly trusted authority of El-Makkari, gives, in the translation of Don Pascual de Gayangos, the following account of the origin of this article of virtue: "The celebrated table which Tarik found at Toledo, although attributed to Solomon, and named after him, never belonged to the poet-king. According to the barbarian authors, it was customary for the nobles and men in estimation of the Gothic Court, to bequeath a portion of their property to the Church. From the money so amassed the priests caused tables to be made of pure gold and silver, gorgeous thrones and stands on which to carry the gospels in public processions, or to ornament the altars on great festivals. The so-called Solomon's table was originally wrought with money derived from this source, and was subsequently emulously increased and embellished by successive kings of Toledo, the latest always anxious to surpass his predecessors in magnificence, until it became the most splendid and costly gem ever made for such a purpose. The fabric was of pure gold, set with the most precious pearls, rubies, and emeralds. Its circumference was encrusted with three rows of these valuable stones, and the whole table displayed jewels so large and refulgent that never did human eye behold anything comparable with it.... When the Moslems entered Toledo it was found on the great altar of the Christian church, and the fact of such a treasure having been discovered soon became public and notorious."

The history here assigned to the table is, it must be confessed, somewhat less improbable than the supposition of Gibbon, who is under the impression that if it ever existed it may have been carried away by Titus at the sacking of Jerusalem, and, later, to have fallen into the hands of the Goths at the taking of Rome by Alaric. Don Pascual, however, asks, very pertinently, whether it is likely that Bishop Sindered, and those who accompanied him in his flight, would have left behind them so valuable an object. And the conundrum still remains as to the present whereabouts of the table. It has been asserted that it forms part of the inestimable treasures of the Vatican, but as the devout Moslem would say, "Allah alone knoweth."

Tarik, who perceived in Musa's haste to join him in Toledo and take possession of the spoils, an indication of the governor's envy, decided to conceal one of the feet of the table against future emergencies. Musa, who met Tarik with savage upbraidings for exceeding his instructions—and some go so far as to say that he supplemented his speech with strokes of his whip—demanded the production of Solomon's table, and questioned Tarik as to the absence of the missing fourth foot. The wily general declared that he had found it in that condition, and Musa had the missing emerald supplied by a foot of gold. Subsequently Musa had Tarik cast into prison, and, it is said, that he would have encompassed his death but for the prompt intervention of the khalif, who sent peremptory commands that the successful campaigner should be restored to his command of the Moorish army. Thereupon Musa professed to restore Tarik to his confidence and friendship; but he must have regretted that he had not executed his original purpose, when, on the occasion of his presenting the famous table as his own discovery to the khalif at Damascus, Tarik proclaimed himself to be the discoverer, and, as proof of his contention, produced the missing emerald foot.

Figure 145. Toledo. Interior of Santa Maria La Blanca.

The Moorish conquerors recognised the importance of Toledo as the capital of the Gothic empire, but these art-adoring, sun-worshipping warriors, who found their Eden in Andalusia, lavished their affection and culture on Cordova and Seville, and, for a time, Toledo became a secondary town. Musa's son, Abdelasis, or Balacin, as Rasis el Moro calls him, married the widow of King Roderick, who has been variously styled Egilona, Exilona, and Blanche, and insisted upon every noble of the Moorish Court paying her extravagant homage; but the sultan held his Court at Cordova, and the Toledans never forgave this affront to their honour and dignity.

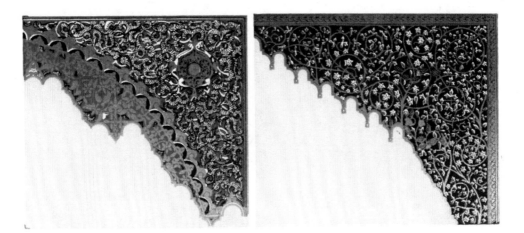

Plate 47. Spandrils of Arches.

They brooded in their stormy sullenness and independence. Their revolutionary instincts were never crushed; their discontent was never appeased through the three and a-half centuries of the Arab occupation of the city. Cassin, the Moorish ruler, became impregnated with the principles of independence, and threw off the yoke of Cordova, only to be betrayed in his turn by the Toledans, who, wearied of his tyranny, welcomed Abd-er-Rahman to the city, and submitted their allegiance to his throne. But throughout his reign the turbulent Toledans proved uncertain and prone to revolution, and his son, Hakam, who succeeded him, sought to conciliate them by appointing as governor a renegade Christian, one Amron, of Huesca. "By a condescension which proves our extreme solicitude for your interests," the sultan wrote to his disaffected subjects, "instead of sending you one of our own subjects, we have chosen one of your compatriots." Hakam's error of judgment resulted in one of the most terrible deeds in the history of Toledo, perhaps the most disgraceful blot on the Moslem domination of Spain. Amron was entrusted with the mission of humbling his fellow countrymen to the rule of the sultan, and he achieved his object by the practice of a fiendish policy of perfidious cunning.

By affecting an aversion to the sultan, and preaching the gospel of the independence of Toledo, he won the confidence of the nobles, and concerted with them in plots to reconquer the city. In furtherance of their plans, the people consented to have soldiers quartered upon them; they welcomed the building of a fortress commanded by a strong guard at the extremity of the city; and it was at their own suggestion that a castle was erected in the middle of the town as a stronghold for the valiant governor. Then, having fortified himself with the trust of the people, and packed the city with troops, Amron secretly advised the sultan that the Toledans were ready for the lesson that was to be read to them. Abd-er-Rahman, the son of Hakam, advanced towards the city at the head of a great army. The governor proposed that the nobles should go out to meet the young prince, and historians record that these implacable Gothic revolutionists were infatuated by the courtesy and cordiality with which they were received.

Figure 146. Toledo. Gate of the Sun.

The future sultan conquered their aversion by his grace and charm, and they loudly applauded Amron's suggestion that he should be invited to accept the hospitality of the city. Abd-er-Rahman, instated in the castle of the governor, invited the nobles and representative men of Toledo to a great feast. They came in crowds, they were admitted to the castle singly, and not a single invited guest returned to his home. As each man crossed the courtyard of the castle he walked past an executioner, who stood in the shadow with uplifted blade awaiting his approach. No guest passed him. The nobles entered, the blade fell, and ready hands rolled the body into a ditch. In Spanish history that bloody day is known as the "Day of the Foss." "Only conceive," writes Hannah Lynch, "the horrible picture in all its brutal nakedness! The gaily-apparelled guest, scented, jewelled, smiling, alights from his carriage, looking forward to pleasure in varied forms, brilliant lights, delicate viands, exquisite wines, lute, song, flowers, sparkling speech. Then the quick entrance into a dim courtyard, a step forward, perhaps in the act of unclasping a silken mantle, the soundless movement of a fatal arm in the shadowy silence, the invisible executioner's form probably hidden by a profusion of tall plants or an Oriental bush, and body after body, head upon head, roll into the common grave till the ditch is filled with nigh upon five thousand corpses. Not even the famous St. Bartholomew can compete with this, in horror, in gruesomeness. Compared with it, that night of Paris was honourable and open warfare. It is the stillness of the hour, the quickness of doing, the unflinching and awful personality of the executioners, who so remarkably struck down life as ever it advanced with smiling lips and brightly-glancing eye, that lend this scene its matchless colours of cruelty and savagery. Beside it, few shocking hours in history will seem deprived of all sense of mitigation and humanity."

Only a people rebellious by blood, by training, and by every tradition of their implacable race, could have thrown off the prostration that followed this terrible blow, and risen from their stupor with renewed determination to seize their independence. Yet Toledo survived this blow, and many others, which, if not so sudden and appalling, were sufficient to crush the spirit and deaden the aspiration of a more vincible nation. It is impossible to determine whether Abd-er-Rahman was an accessory to this deed of butchery, or to say if Amron planned the massacre in the belief that it was necessary to the maintenance of Moslem rule, to terrorise the Toledans into submission, or if the deed was inspired by the more subtle and diabolical intention of making the Moors more odious in the sight of the unmanageable citizens. When the people were sufficiently recovered from the horror of the atrocity to concoct a scheme of revenge, they acted with ferocious promptness. The cry for vengeance spread from the Zocodover into the surrounding country, and the people, hastily summoned into the city, surrounded the castle of Amron, and burnt the hateful fortress and its inmates to the ground. There, for the time, the insurrectionary movement stopped. An Arab governor was appointed, and the people, Christians and Jews as well as Moors, entered upon a new state of material prosperity. Under Aben Magot ben Ibraham the Moorish artistic influence began to make itself felt. The architecture bore the imprint of the governing race, beautiful gardens were laid out along the Vega, Arabian palaces sprang into being, and on the ruins of Amron's castle there was built a new alcazar.

A. B.

Figure 147. Toledo. A. Door of the Hall of Mesa. B. Exterior of the Chapel of Cristo De La Vega.

But the respite from open tumult was only temporary. The Wali, finding the merchants increasing in riches, raised their tribute to the state, and smouldering discontent was immediately fanned into a flame. Led by a wealthy young Toledan, named Hacam, who subsequently earned the affix of "El Durrete"—"The Striker of Blows"—the people murdered the Moorish officials and captured the alcazar. The Moslem troops retaliated by recapturing that stronghold and routing the revolutionists. Hacam went into retirement until the Moors, lulled into security, relaxed their vigilance in the guardianship of the city, and then, striking swiftly through the neglected gates, he recovered the city between sunset and morning. The greater part of the upper town was burnt, the troops sent by Abd-er-Rahman II were repulsed; and, although the Toledans were incidentally routed by the renegade Spaniard, Maisara, Toledo was not then retaken. In 873 the city was besieged for a whole year, and only surrendered when famine had rendered the citizens too weak to further resist the assaults of the Moorish troops.

The next firebrand to project itself into the inflammatory fabric of Toledan discontent was the fanatical martyr, Eulogius. In Cordova this frenzied religionist had fired the Christians into reviling Mohammed, and thereby exasperating the Moslems into persecution. To the tolerant and broad-minded Moors, religious observances were prejudices to be respected. They permitted, to Christians and Jews, the fullest licence in the matter of worship; they only demanded that a similar respect should be observed towards their own faith. The Christians were not asked to reverence the Prophet of Islam, but the Moslems could not allow him to be openly blasphemed by the infidels. It was against the articles of their creed, and it was contrary to human nature. To-day the Christian who rebelled against such a reasonable restriction would be accounted a bigot, undeserving of sympathy; in the days of Eulogius, the revilers of Moorish religious

176   Albert F. Calvert

prejudices were regarded as saints. Toledo jumped at their rulers' resentment of the Christians' wanton insult to their faith as an excuse for an outburst of religious indignation, and Sindola seized the city and declared war against the khalifate by way of protesting against the execution of Eulogius's disciples. Ordoño, king of Leon, sent reinforcements to Sindola, and the allied armies were caught in an ambush by the Moors, who struck off 8,000 Christian heads for public exhibition in the various disaffected towns. This reverse had the desired effect, and the Toledans made no further move until the death of Wistremir afforded them an opportunity of exasperating the sultan Mohammed by electing Eulogius to the vacant archbishopric of Toledo. The sultan, who retaliated by investing the city, had the bridge undermined while it was in the occupation of his troops, and, by making a feigned retreat, enticed the impetuous Spaniards to give chase. The depleted structure collapsed beneath the sudden burden of the pursuing army, and hundreds of men met their death in the sullen depths of the Tagus.

But neither massacre nor misfortune could shake the dogged Toledans from their purpose. With the king of Leon at their back, they put forth new efforts, and in 873 they forced Mohammed to acknowledge their independence as a Republic in return for the payment of an annual tribute. The treaty made with Mohammed was ratified by his successors, Mundhir and Abdallah. Even the Great Khalif, Abd-er-Rahman, was at first content to send from Cordova a royal proclamation, commanding Toledo to surrender her independence to the khalifate, and acknowledge him as liege lord, and it was not until 930, or eighteen years after he had ascended the throne, that he went up with his army against the arrogant and rebellious city. The siege of Toledo by Abd-er-Rahman lasted for eight years. The Moorish king built the city, which he called "Victory," on a mountain commanding Toledo, and here he quartered his troops until famine and privation should open the gates for him. The long years of waiting culminated in a swift assault, and, at the close of a day's fighting, the emaciated heads of the insurgent chiefs were impaled on spears to keep their last sightless watch from the walls of the city they had defended with such heroic fortitude.

After the death of the Great Khalif, and, thenceforth until the Christian conquest, Toledo maintained a partial independence, tolerating the rule of Moslem princes, but paying no allegiance to Cordova. And in the end she was recovered to the Christians by a piece of picturesque treachery. Alfonso of Leon (Alfonso VI.) had fled from the monastery of Sagahun, and sought the protection of King Almamon of Toledo, from whom he received the most generous hospitality, including gifts of palaces, farms, and orchards, and the government of the Christian section of the inhabitants. The Moorish king demanded only the subscription of his guest's allegiance, and, in return, he gave a sincere affection, and promises of faithful protection. Almamon, whose one vague but ever present concern was the possibility of Toledo ever falling again into the hands of the Christians, was discussing the subject one day with his courtiers in the garden of Alfonso's palace, and engrossed in the consideration of the possible misfortune, he described minutely the only plan by which, in his opinion, the city might be taken. Alfonso, who was one of the company, affected to be asleep while this dissertation was in progress, and the courtiers, who were unable to restrain the eloquence of the king, endeavoured to obtain Almamon's consent to the execution of his Christian guest. But the king refused to listen to this inhospitable proposition, and on the death of Sancho of Castile (who was murdered by Bellido, under the walls of Zamora), his brother, Alfonso of Leon, returned to his own kingdom, loaded with honours, and carrying with him the secret of Toledo's vincibility. Before he departed the two kings swore eternal amity, and entered into an offensive and defensive alliance against the enemies of either, and the enemies of Almamon's son, Yahya. But after the death of Almamon, Alfonso, forgetting his oath to his friend, and remembering only the plan of siege he had overheard in the garden of Toledo, adopted the principles invented by the Moorish theorist, and, in 1085, entered the city as its conqueror.

Figure 148. Toledo. Ancient Gate of Visagra.

What has Toledo to show to-day for the three and a-half centuries of the artistic influence of Morisco culture and influence? Surprisingly little! And yet it would be an even greater surprise if she had more to show. The village that climbs the bosom of a mountain does not alter the contour of its impassive resting-place; the etchings traced upon a Toledo blade does not affect the temper of the steel. The city is still "Moorish in appearance," to employ the guide-book phrase, but it is gradually divesting itself of the marks which at one time, and then only in part, disguised its Gothic ancestry. Since Alfonso, the tyrant of the Galicians, seized the town of Toledo, "that pearl of the necklace, that highest tower of the empire in this Peninsula" (to quote Abon I Hasan), the Moorish bridge, near Santa Leocadia, and the other, which crossed the old Roman waterway, have disappeared, and the legendary Palace of Galiana is let out in miserable tenements to the lowest class of peasants.

Figure 149. Castle of St. Servando.

Moratin has immortalised Galiana de Toledo, "most beautiful and marvellous," and Calderon has written of the palace built for her by her father, Galafre, who ruled over Toledo for Abd-er-Rahman I. Galafre took the old Visigoth shell, and transformed the edifice, by the witchery of Moorish windows and arches and staircases, into a palace of delight. He devoted his knowledge of hydraulics to the unkempt Toledan Vega, and made of it a paradise of leaf and bloom and rill. In the fairy garden, Charlemagne, according to tradition, found the "most beautiful and marvellous" Galiana, and carried her away from the unwelcome addresses of her Moorish admirer, Prince Bradamante, to reign over France as his queen. The arms of the Guzmans, into whose possession the palace passed under Castillian rule, may still be descried upon its dismantled front.

The wonderful clepsydras, or water clocks of Toledo, the invention of Abou-l'-Casem, Abdo-er-Rahman, or Az-Zarcal, as he is more usually styled, are quaintly and vaguely described in the following Moorish document: "One of the greatest towns of

Spain is Toledo, and Toledo is a large and well-populated city. On all sides it is washed by a splendid river, called the Tagus.... Among the rare and notable things of Toledo is that wheat may be kept more than seventy years without rotting, which is a great advantage, as all the land abounds in grain and seed of all kinds. But what is still more marvellous and surprising in Toledo, and what we believe no other inhabited town of all the world has anything to equal, are some clepsydras, or water clocks. It is said that Az-Zarcal, hearing of a certain talisman, which is in the city of Arin, of Eastern India, and which, Masudi says, shows the hours by means of aspas, or hands, from the time the sun rises till it sets, determined to fabricate an artifice by means of which the people could know the hour of day or night, and calculate the day of the moon. He made two great ponds in a house on the bank of the Tagus, not far from the Gate of the Tanners, making them so that they should be filled with water or emptied according to the rise and fall of the moon."

In Babylonia, India, and Egypt, the clepsydra was used from before the dawn of history, especially in astronomical observations, and Latin and Greek writers refer to a type which resembled the modern sand glass, and was used in the courts of law to limit the length of the pleadings. The general form of the clepsydra, which Pliny ascribed to Scipio Nasica, consisted essentially of a float, which slowly rose by the tricklings of water from above through a small hole in a plate of metal. As the float rose it pointed to a scale of hours at the side of the water vessel; or, in the more elaborate forms, moved a wheel by means of a ratchet, and thus turned a hand on a dial.

The Moorish recounter of the wonders of the water clocks of Toledo tells us that its movements were regulated by the moon. As soon as the moon became visible by means of invisible conducts, the water began to flow into the ponds, and, by day rise, the ponds were four-sevenths full. At night another seventh was added, so that by day or night the ponds continued to increase in water a seventh every twenty-four hours, and were quite full by the time the moon was full. On the 14th of the month, when the moon began to fall, the ponds also fell in like proportion. On the 21st of the month they were half empty, and on the 29th completely so. The exact working of those clepsydras, however, is lost, as a bungling astronomer, who was deputed by Alfonso "the Learned" to examine them and discover the secret, broke the delicate machinery, and was forthwith dubbed a Jew by the indignant and exasperated Moors.

Beyond the walls of the city is a stretch of fertile land beside the Tagus, which is called the Garden of the King; and at the further end of it is the country palace of Galiana. This pleasure house is of a later date than the palace of the same name within the city; but, like that debased edifice, it is a ruin, its walls of extreme thickness, flanked with two massive towers, only remaining to represent what was once

"A palace lifting to eternal summer
Its marble walls, from out a glossy bower
Of coolest foliage, musical with birds."

Figure 150. Moorish Sword.

In the War of Independence the French soldiers made a ruin of the one-time magnificent Casa de Vargas, which was built by Juan de Herrera, and has been described by Antonio Ponz as one of the architectural splendours of Toledo. Ponz tells us that "the façade is perfect Doric, of exquisite marble, with fluted columns on either side, and the pedestals have military emblems in bas-relief. The frieze consists of helmets, heads of bulls, and goblets. The coat of arms above the cornice is most beautiful, and the women's forms, seated on each side, are life-size. Nothing could be finer than the details, as well as the whole of this façade, and for sure it is the most serious, the most lovely, and most finished of all I have seen in Toledo. You enter a spacious courtyard with lofty galleries running round it above and below the lower gallery, sustained by Doric pillars and by the upper Ionic columns. The staircase is truly regal, and likewise the various inner chambers. They contain different chimney pieces, ornamented with graceful fancies executed in bas-relief; and thus, in the lower quarters, as in the principal, are other galleries with columns like those of the courtyard, with delicious views of the meadows and the Tagus."

In the most miserable quarter of the town, far up above the river, the visitor may see some huge blocks of stone, and a few broken arches—all that remains of the once magnificent Moorish palace of Henry of Aragon, lord of Villena. Henry of Aragon was an enlightened prince and erudite scholar, and the possessor of a superb collection of books, which were publicly burnt on the plea that their owner had intercourse with the devil. Don Enrique is said to have used the subterranean chambers and passages of the palace as a meeting-place for witches, and here he is supposed to have entertained his Satanic majesty. Samuel Levi, Pedro the Cruel's treasurer, turned the palace vault into a strong-room, but the prince, in a needy moment, proved stronger; and the Toledans, following the example of their king, completed the sacking of the mansion. The Duke of Escalona, in the reign of Charles Quint, burnt the palace to the ground, and fled the city with his family, rather than give house-room to the treacherous Bourbon, the Constable of France, at the bidding of his royal master.

There is in the little plaza of Santa Isabel, a half-obliterated Arabian inscription, wishing "Lasting prosperity and perpetual glory to the master of this edifice." This inscription identifies the ruin as the palace of King Pedro. The beautiful Casa de Mesa bears scarcely a trace of the exquisite Moorish workmanship which characterised the palace of the Dukes of Alva; it is impossible to determine from the dilapidated Casa de las Tormerias whether it was originally built for a Moorish palace or a mezquita; while some few scraps of Moorish inscription in the wood-work of a ruined wall still testify to the origin of the Casa de Munarriz. The alcazar, which was twice destroyed by fire, is represented by the façades, the three towers, the patio, and the enormous staircase—perhaps the only parts of the building that were not rebuilt by Charles Quint. The edifice commenced by that monarch, and completed by Philip II., was for long the most splendid and colossal palace in Spain. Staremberg's troops destroyed the building by fire in 1710; and, a century later, the French troops fired the structure which Carlos III. had recomposed out of the ashes of Charles V.'s alcazar. The Casa de Mesa, the palace of Estevan de Illan, is reduced to a single chamber of exquisite Moorish workmanship; the remaining Moorish part of the Taller del Moro is used as a common workshop; the regal staircase of the alcazar, so wide that a whole army might march up its noble steps, ends in space.

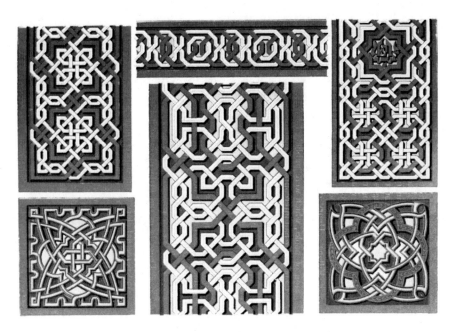

Plate 48. Plaster Ornaments, used as Upright and Horizontal Bands enclosing Panels on the Walls.

As with the palaces of Toledo, so it is with its temples—the traces of Moorish art are nearly all defaced or obliterated. The mosque, which was replaced by the church of San Roman, possesses the purest mudejar steeple of Toledo, erected by Esteban de Illan, and another, if smaller, Moorish steeple, adorns the Santa Magdalena. A monument, which ranks among the most interesting in Spain, is the Cristo de la Luz, located between the Puerta del Sol and the Puerta Bisagra—a little gem of Moorish-Byzantine architecture, which is regarded as the oldest and most perfect specimen of its kind in the Peninsula. On the walls of this church, which remains to this day a perfect mosque, the conquering Alfonso VI hung up his shield in 1035 to commemorate the first mass that was celebrated in Toledo after the defeat of the Moors. Until Tarik came to Toledo the mosque had been a Gothic temple, before which hung a cross, bearing an effigy of the crucified Christ. Legend declares that two impious Jews pricked the greatly-venerated body with a dagger, and that from the wound blood instantly gushed forth. The Jews, who attempted to evade the penalty of their folly by hiding the crucifix, were traced by the stains of blood to their house, and torn to pieces by the infuriated Christians. Tradition further asserts that the Jews planned a revenge by poisoning the feet of the restored statue, but that when a woman knelt before it the figure withdrew its foot from her kiss. Many other legends attach to the sacred relic, which was removed from before the church when the city was captured by the Moors, and secreted in a cavity in the wall, with a burning lamp placed before it. When the Moorish dominion came to an end, 370 years later, and the cavity was revealed, the unreplenished lamp was found to be still alight before the crucifix in the wall of the Moorish mosque. From this legend the church takes its name of the Christ of the Light.

This wonderful little monument, which is only twenty-two feet by twenty-five feet, possesses six short naves, which cross each other under nine vaults, and in the centre are four short, stout columns, surmounted by sculptured capitals, from which spring sixteen heavy horseshoe arches. This forest of naves and arches comprises a miniature reproduction of the mosque of Cordova. Arcades, cusped in Moorish fashion, and supported on shafts, pierce the walls; the inevitable "half orange" ceiling domes the centre, and above the principal arch is the shield of Alfonso VI., embellished with a white cross on a crimson ground, which the victorious king handed to Archbishop Bernardo to supply the place of a cross above the dismantled altar. This gem of Moorish-Byzantine architecture, so small yet so perfect, so simple yet so fantastic, conveys an impression of amazing strength, and presents an admirable example of early Arabian work.

Figure 151. Arab Fragment at Tarragona.

The nunnery of Santa Fe, which was originally a regal Moorish palace, has been shorn of nearly all its ancient beauty, which is now only traceable in the arcaded brickwork of the wall, almost obliterated by exuberant foliage. There are still the remnants of Moorish ornamentation in the convent halls and corridors of San Juan de la Penitencia, and the influence of Moorish art is also seen in some good azulejo and the artesonade ceiling of Santa Isabel.

The Alcantara bridge, which was originally a Roman structure, was repaired by the Goths in 687, and rebuilt by the Moors of 866. It was of this Moorish bridge that Rasis el Moro wrote: "It was such a rich and marvellous work, and so subtly wrought, that never man with truth could believe there was any other such fine work in Spain." Since then it has been repaired and restored wholly, or in part, no fewer than eight times; and while these alterations have changed its style and appearance, it still remains one of the finest and most picturesque monuments of Toledo. The bridge of San Martin, which compares with it in interest and beauty, was built in 1203, and is guarded at either end with a tower and gateway adorned with Moorish arches and battlements. The bridge of San Martin gives entrance to the city through the gate of the Cambron. It is no longer Moorish, as it was in the time of Alfonso VI.; but on its half-renaissance, half-classical architecture, one may still read the remains of some of those grandiloquent utterances of the Moorish spirit which prompted Ponz to style Toledo the city of magnificent inscriptions. It was a devout, if somewhat credulous, spirit which inspired the transcription of the following article of faith: "There is but one God on earth, and Mohammed is His messenger. All the faithful who believe in our prophet Mohammed, and continue to kiss the hands and feet of Murabite Muley Abda Alcadar every day, will be without sin, will not be blind, nor deaf, nor lame, nor wounded; and receiving his benediction, when the time of his death comes, will only be three days ill and dying, will go with open eyes to Paradise forgiven of all sins." Another inscription bore the following exhortation and compensatory promise: "Prayer and peace over our lord and prophet Mohammed. All the faithful, when they went to lie down in their beds, mentioning the Alfagiu Murabito Abdala, and recommending themselves to him, will enter no battle out of which they will not come victorious; and in whatever battle against Christians they may stain their lances with Christian blood, dying that same day, will go alive and whole with eyes open to Paradise, and his descendants will remain till the fourth generation forgiven."

The present Visagra Gate, rebuilt under Charles V, dates back to the Moors. It is entirely Moorish in character, with the heavy simple features, the triple horseshoe arches and upper crenellated apertures which we associate with the first period of Morisco architecture. Through this gate, which is now blocked up, Alfonso VI entered Toledo. The two graceful square towers, roofed with green and white tiles, which compose the edifice, are joined by the high turreted walls of a square courtyard, and the decorations include the Senate's dedication of the gate to Charles Quint, the sculptured arms of the emperor, a statue of St. Eugenie, two others of Gothic kings, and a life-sized angel holding an unsheathed sword. This cold, bare inventory of the ornaments of the gate convey no idea of the splendid impressiveness of the structure, the splendour and charm of which sink into comparative insignificance beside its glorious neighbour, the Gate of the Sun.

Plate 49. Blank Window.

This magnificent gate of rough stone, with its towers of brown granite, has been rightly described as one of the world's masterpieces. Yet here again the pen is powerless to do justice to its beauty; and to describe its proportions and decoration is to complicate, rather than explain, the impression that is conveyed by the camera. The square towers, with their semi-circular fronts, and the great central arch resting on two Moorish columns, and the zones of ornamental arches above the horse-shaped openings, comprise a Moorish gem against a Spanish sky, a miracle of loveliness upon a rough and naked rampart. But how, cries Hannah Lynch, to write of this Puerta del Sol, that "thing of beauty even among crowded enchantments! It is to pick one's way through superlatives and points of exclamation and call in vain on the goddess of sobriety to subdue our tendency to excess and incoherence. Put this matchless gate in the middle of the desert of Sahara; it would then be worth while making the frightful journey alone to look at it. However far you may have journeyed, you would still be for ever thankful to have seen such a masterpiece—incontestably a work of supreme art, perhaps the rarest thing of the world." Whether the writer intends her high eulogy to be applied generally to any "work of supreme art," or to the Puerta del Sol in particular, most people who have come under the witching influence of the art of the Moors, will not deny that it is well deserved.

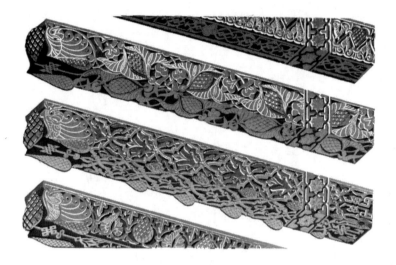

Plate 50. Rafters of a Roof over a Doorway, now destroyed, beneath the Tocador de la Reyna.

Figure 152. Ancient Arabian Baths at Palma, Majorca.

Chapter 4

MOORISH ORNAMENT

A NOTE ON THE ELEMENTS OF ARAB ART

IN art, precept is subservient; practice is supreme. The idea which may be hidden in a picture is of little moment; it is the design, fully accomplished, which is prized. Its inspiration may become a "light to shine before men," but it attains its paramount value only when realised.

Refinement of manners and acuteness of intellect have, in the East, nothing in common with what we call education. In this social state, ignorance, which, among us, condemns a man, may be the condition of great originality. The Arab tent-dweller was, and is, often, a very superior man; for the tent is a kind of school, always open, where, from contact with educated guests who have seen men and cities, was produced an intellectual movement which led the Arab, in exchanging his nomadic life for a settled habitation, to translate the tent to a more solid form; to commute the tent-pole for a slender marble column; and to transform luxurious products of the loom, which had adorned his former dwelling, to a semblance of their golden tissues on fairy-decorated diapery.

If the poetry and refinement of the South of Europe in modern times cannot be traced, as many authors would have us believe—notably Father Andres, a learned Spaniard, anxious to give to his own country the honour of imparting to the rest of Europe the first impulse of refinement after the fall of the Roman Empire—to the Arabs of Spain, much must still be allowed to their influence; for their progress in refinement was hardly less brilliant and rapid than their progress in Empire. At the period of the glory of Cordova, which began about A.D. 750, and continued to the time of its conquest by the Christians in 1236, the scholars of Spain were in a higher state of cultivation than could be found elsewhere; and if the Kingdom of Granada—the last stronghold of the Moslem—which ended in 1492, was less refined, it was perhaps more splendid and luxurious. The public schools and libraries of the Spanish Arabs were resorted to, not only by those of their own faith at home and in the East, but by Christians from different parts of Europe; and Pope Sylvester the Second (Gerbet, a Frenchman, Pope 999-1003), one of the most remarkable men of his age, is believed to have owed his elevation to the culture he absorbed in Seville and Cordova.

Plate 51. Band at Springing of Arch at the Entrance to one of the Halls.

Arab art takes its place with the arts of Greece and Japan as one of the three great schools into which all styles of ornament naturally fall. Beauty and simplicity—the restrained rhythm and order which form the essential foundation of Greek art—is as distinct from the vivacious realism and unsymmetrical, haphazard decoration of the Japanese, as from that elegance and complexity produced by geometrical involutions symmetrically constructed, which constitute the basis of Moorish art. These three styles have been compared by Monsieur J. Bourgoin, in his *Elements of Arab Art*, to the three kingdoms of Nature. Greek art he likens to the animal kingdom, the Japanese art to the vegetable kingdom, and Arabian art, from the symmetry which recalls the crystallisation of minerals in its uniformity of configuration, and its elementary structure, he compares with the mineral kingdom.

In the art of the Arabs the inspiration is completely independent of living nature. The Arab artist proceeds from within to the exterior; he sets himself problems, and transfers them by means of the compass and rule. The decorative impulse of Arab art consists of geometrical diagrams either carved into relief, or inlaid, or simply laid flat. Since the inspiration is dry, and purely abstract, the artistic development is slight and unimportant; and, since the motive is restricted, Arab decorative art has remained simple, but still of an incomparable elegance, because the harmony between inspiration and execution is perfect. By their creed Mohammedan artists were forbidden to represent living forms, yet they adopted the principles they found in Nature, and developed them with absolute fidelity. Thus, as I showed in dealing with the architecture of the Alhambra, in surface decoration by the Moors the lines flow from a parent stem; every ornament, however distant, can be traced to its branch and root. In all cases we find the lines radiating from a parent stem, as we may see exemplified in Nature by the human hand, or in a leaf. We are never offended, as in modern practice, by the random introduction of an ornament set down without a reason for its existence. However irregular the expanse they have to decorate, they always commence by dividing the field into equal areas, and round these main lines they fill in their details, which invariably return to their parent stem, a system which proves them to have been absolute masters of space.

In the introduction to my volume on the Alhambra, I emphasised this fact, that the Moors ever had regard to the first principle of architecture—to decorate construction, never to construct decoration. In Arabian architecture, not only does the decoration arise naturally out of the construction, but the constructive idea is carried out in every detail of the ornamentation of the surfaces. A superfluous or useless ornament is never found in Moorish decoration; every ornament arises naturally and inevitably from the parent design. The general forms were first laid down; they were subdivided by general lines; the interstices were then filled in with ornament, to be again subdivided and enriched for closer inspection. The principle was carried out with the greatest refinement, and the harmony and beauty of all Moorish ornamentation is derived from its observance. The highest distinction was thereby obtained; the detail never interfering with the general form. Seen at a distance, the main lines strike the eye; on nearer approach, the ornamentation comes into the composition; and a minute inspection reveals the detail on the surface of the ornaments themselves.

Monsieur A. Rhone, in his *L'Egypte à Petites Journées*, holds that, "seeing the marvellous resources which the Arabs have found in geometry for decorating surfaces, one regrets less for art that the laws of Islamism have forbidden them, as an idolatrous act, to introduce representations of animated forms. Although these laws were not so strictly observed as is generally believed, who knows, if in turning the Arabian artists away from sculpture and statuary, they have not been the means of preserving this special and almost transcendant aptitude that the Semites have for all subtle combinations, and especially for those of geometrical numbers, lines, and figures?"

Although the principles of Moorish art are so rigid and severe, the Arabs have not remained exempt from exterior influence, but have adapted and incorporated foreign feeling into their art, and modified it to their purpose. A note by the late Owen Jones greatly emphasises this fact. He says:—"When the Mohammedan religion and civilisation rose with such astonishing rapidity in the East, the Arabs, in their mosques, made use of the materials which they found ready to their hands in the ruins of old Roman buildings which they purposely destroyed; they took columns with their Corinthian capitals, etc., and adapted them to the arrangement required for their own temples. In their subsequent works they did not, as we should have done, continue to copy and reproduce the models which were at first so convenient to them; but, applying to them their own peculiar feelings, they gradually departed from the original model, to such an extent at last, that but for the intermediate steps we should be unable to discover the least analogy between them. Yet by this process the capitals of their columns can be traced back to the Corinthian order which they, in the first instance, found so abundantly for their use."

Plate 52. Panelling of a Recess.

Arab art must ever remain distinct from every other school and style, because the essential foundation of it is fixed and limited. Now, those who resign themselves to a style of art reduce themselves to formulas, to copies, or to diagrams. Greco-Roman art has its formulas of ordinance and propositions; Chino-Japanese art has its characteristic copies; and Syro-Arabian art its abstract and geometrical diagrams. The general elements of Arabian art, as applied to architecture and decoration, consist of stalactites, intertwinings, and ornaments. Stalactites, which are at the same time ornaments and members of architecture, are employed in corbelling, in coving, and in pendentives, and are modelled and superposed by tapia, or cut in wood and placed side by side, or opened into hollows by superficial casings in wire and tressing. The intertwinings which embellish the surfaces are carved and trimmed in splitboards of carpentry, or laid in compartments, or carved in open work, or engraved in stone, wood, and metal; or set in filigree, vignettes, or mosaics. The ornaments, which divide themselves into decoration by embroidery or embellishment in sections, reduce themselves to a small number of elements, or flower-work cut flat in outline. The outlines, complete in the boundary which limits them, are quite characteristic. They do not resemble in any way, except in so far as the unalterable laws of geometry decree, the outline drawn by Europeans, nor the cursive traits used by the Chinese and Japanese. All Arab ornament is by involution of lines; in short, it may be said to be *entirely* geometric.

The art of the Mohammedan, so powerful in appeal to the imagination, not only by beauty and grace, but by the doctrine of the Koran inscribed in their temples on every side in ornamented characters,—so admirably traced that they appear to form part of a perfected design proclaiming the power of Allah, and impressing upon the believer respect for the laws and the love of virtue;—produces an effect little short of magical. Still does that art accompany its religion in a lingering death. Crushed by the rapid strides which surrounding nations have made in the progress of civilization, and which have outrun and ruined it, yet do a few bright emanations appear, to show that as in religion they are faithful to their creed, so in art do their crumbling monuments preserve their shattered remains on which the observer still may see, in deep characters, the chronicles of the times.

Plate 53. Blank Window.

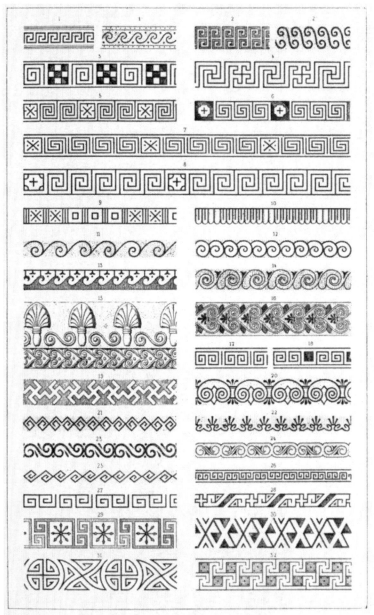

1 GREEK, RECTILINEAR.	11 CHINESE.	18 GREEK, ALTERNATING PATTERN.	25 ARABIAN.
1´ GREEK, CURVILINEAR.	12 ASSYRIAN.		26 CHINESE.
2 CHINESE, RECTILINEAR.	13 POMPEIAN.		27 CHINESE.
2´ GREEK, CURVILINEAR.	14 GREEK.	19 CHINESE.	28 PERSIAN.
3 and 4, GREEK, ALTERNATING PATTERN.	15 GREEK.	20 CHINESE.	29 POMPEIAN.
	16 GREEK.	21 ARABIAN.	30 CHINESE.
5, 6, 7, 8, 9, 10, GREEK, INTERCALARY PATTERNS.	17 CHINESE, ALTERNATING PATTERN.	22 CHINESE.	31 CHINESE.
		23 GREEK.	32 GREEK.
		24 RENAISSANCE.	

Figure 153.

Plate 54. Ornaments on the Walls, House of Sanchez.

Plate 55. Ornament in panels on the Walls.

In the illustrations which accompany these brief notes, the Arab's mastery of line in the composition of design may be studied, and its mystery revealed; but to reduce these geometrical intertwinings to their original elements demands patience, application, and very much time. At first sight these diagrams may appear monotonous, but each is constructed on a particular theme. Most of them spread throughout the Orient, and may be more particularly studied in the Moorish monuments in Spain, where they are employed indifferently in carvings, in mosaic and inlaid work, in application to chased bronze, and in compartments of decoration and embroidery.

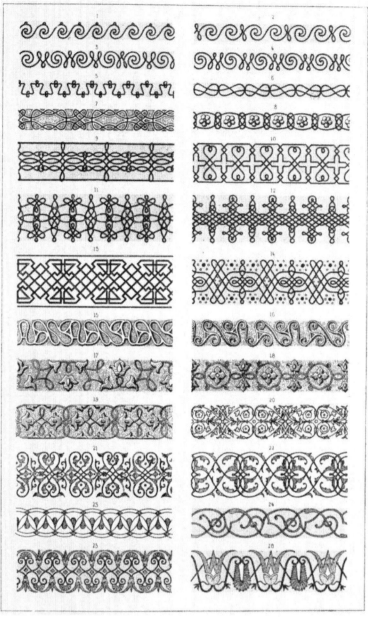

1, 2, 3, 4, GREEK AND ALBANIAN. 15, 16, GALLO-ROMAN. 23 PONDICHERY.
5, 6, 7, 8, RENAISSANCE. 17, 18, 19, ITALIAN. 24 ARABIAN.
9, 10, 11, 12, 13, 14, ITALIAN. 20 ITALIAN. 25, 26, GREEK.
21, 22, ITALIAN FAÏENCE.

Figure 154.

The infinite variety the artists are able to introduce while working on strict rules, which admit of no exception, is the result of instinct perfected by centuries of practice. That in their work was something to be learned, as well as to be felt, is evident from the

Moorish poet's exhortation to us to attentively contemplate the adornments of their palaces, and thereby reap the benefit of a commentary on decoration.

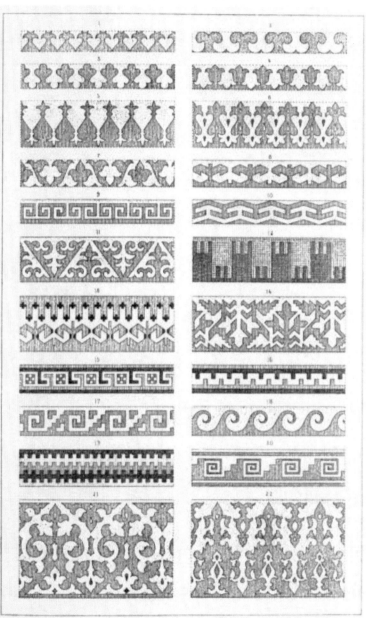

1, 2, 3, 4, 5, 6, 7, 8, 10, ARABIAN.
9 CHINESE.
11 RENAISSANCE.
12 GREEK.
13 ARABIAN.
14 ARABIAN.
15 GREEK, ALTERNATING PATTERN.
16 GREEK.
17 MEXICAN AND ARABIAN.
18 GREEK.
19 ARABIAN.
20 AMERICAN, ANCIENT POTTERY.
21, 22, ARABIAN.

Figure 155.

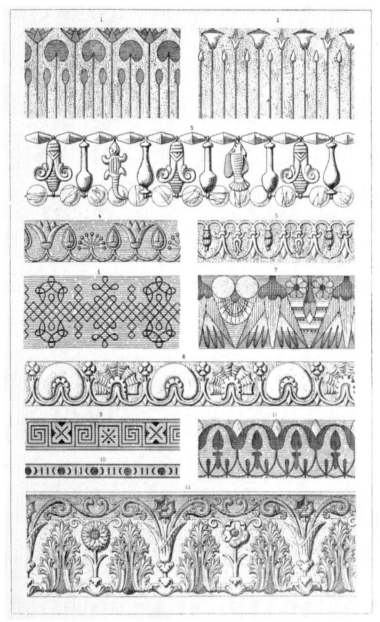

1, 2, EGYPTIAN. 7 EGYPTIAN. 11 ARABIAN.
3 EGYPTIAN NECKLACE. 8 FRIEZE. 18TH CENTURY. 12 FRIEZE. 18TH CENTURY.
4 ASSYRIAN. 9 GREEK.
5 POMPEIAN. 10 UNCERTAIN.
6 ITALIAN.

Figure 156.

It is, then, for the benefit of students who would know something more of Arabian ornamentation than can be derived from the sensation produced by broad effects, and for lovers of the fine arts who would understand the inwardness of Moorish refinement and reduce its mysteries to their primary bases, that the accompanying diagrams have been reproduced. At foot of each diagram is added a short explanatory note; but it is expedient for the student to give consideration to the *plan* which is, in every case, set out in dotted lines.

1, 2, 3, 4, FROM PAINTED VASES.
5 GREEK.
6 ORIENTAL FILIGREE.
7, 8, GREEK.
9 PERSIAN.
10 GREEK.
11 CHINESE.
12 ORIENTAL FILIGREE.
13 INDIAN.
14, 15, PERSIAN.
16 ARABIAN.
17 GREEK.
18 PERSIAN.
19 ORIENTAL CHASING.
20 ARABIAN.
21 PERSIAN.
22 TURKISH.
23 GREEK.
24 PASSEMENTERIE.
25 NEAPOLITAN.

Figure 157.

198   *Albert F. Calvert*

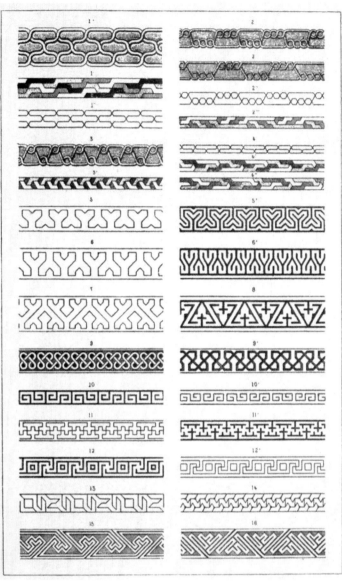

1, 1´, DAMASCENE.	4, 4´, 4´´, DAMASCENE	6, 6´, ARABIAN.	12, 12´, GREEK.
2, 2´, 2´´, 2´´´, ARABIAN.	(ANALOGOUS TO FIGS. 1´, 2´´´, 3´).	7, 8, 9, ARABIAN.	13, 14, PERSIAN.
3, 3´, ARABIAN.	5, 5´, ARABIAN.	10, 10´, 11, 11´, CHINESE.	15, 16, ANGLO-SAXON.

Figure 158.

By this means, he will discover, if he approaches his subject with a free mind, that his task will offer less difficulty than would appear at the outset. To minutely describe the construction of each diagram, and, at the same time comply with the stringent rules of geometry, would occupy much too great a space; nor would the result, perhaps, be proportioned to the labour.

Moorish Ornament

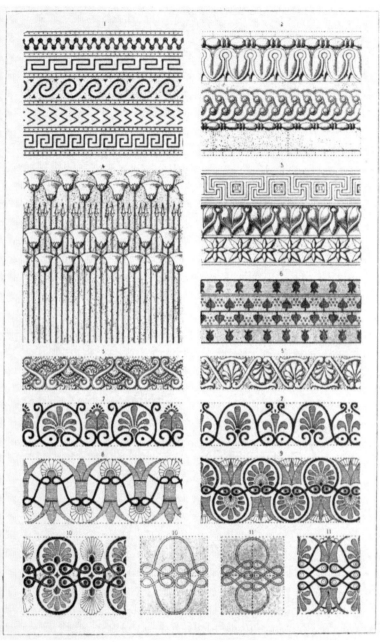

1, 2, 3, GREEK.	5 STYLE "LABROUSTE."	6 GREEK.	8, 9, 10, 10´, 11, 11´,
4 EGYPTIAN.	5´ BYZANTINE.	7, 7´, GREEK.	GREEK (PARTHENON).

Figure 159.

Figure 160. Arabian Construction. 1, 1´, One Spiral. 2, 2´, Two Spirals. 3, 3´, Three Spirals. 4 Cross Quarterly Indicating Positions Essential to the Motif Number 3. 5, 6, 7, 8, Repetitions of Motif Number 3 Variously Treated. 9, 10, 11, 12, 13, 14, Arrangements by Alternating Treatment of Motif Number 3. These Arrangements Afford Excellent Examples Of The Endless Diversity Of Geometric Forms.

Moorish Ornament

Plate 56. Ornament in spandrils of arches.

Plate 57. Centre Ornament of the Window. Mosaic Dado in a window.

The recess or divan containing these beautiful Mosaics was, doubtless, the throne of the Moorish kings. The Mosaics are as perfect as when originally executed, and seem, indeed, to be imperishable. They are formed of baked clay squeezed into moulds of the different figures, glazed on the surface.

The Mosaic Dados on the pillars present a great variety in their patterns, although the component parts are in each the same.

Figure 58. Mosaic Dados on pillars between windows.

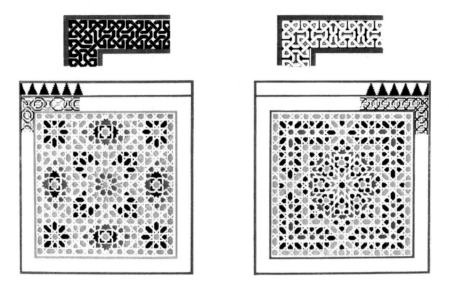

Figure 59. Mosaic Dados on pillars between windows.

These Mosaics, though in appearance so different from those of the preceding plate, will be found on examination to be composed of the same pieces differently combined.

Moorish Ornament

Plate 60. The beautiful Mosaic in the centre of this plate is part of the Dado.

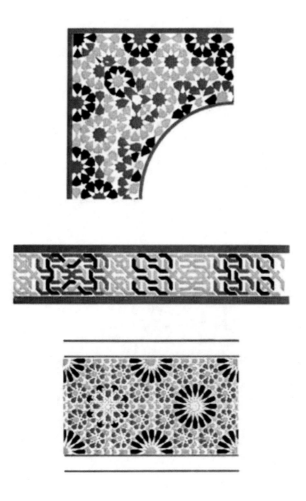

Plate 61. Pavement of the Hall of the Baths. Mosaic Dado round the internal walls of the Mosque.

Mosaics from the Mosque and the Hall of the Baths. The Mosaic Dados round the walls of the Mosque appear to be the only portions of the ancient private Mosque attached to the Palace which have been preserved intact in their original situation. The motto of the Kings of Granada, "*There is no conqueror but God*," was replaced by "*Nec plus ultra*" of Charles V., when the Mosque was converted by him into a chapel. The beautiful Mosaic at the top of the plate is placed round the fountain of the Chamber of Repose of the Baths.

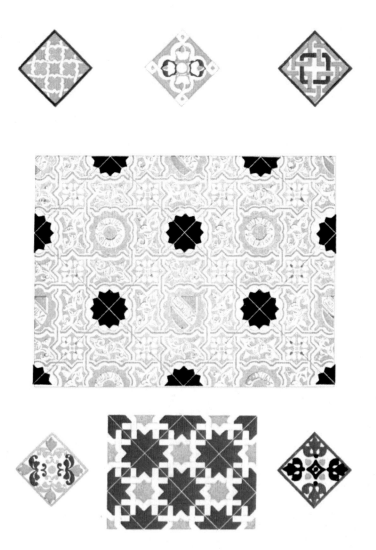

Plate 62. Azulejos. Painted Tiles.

On the floor of one of the alcoves of the Hall of Justice are to be seen the painted tiles delineated in the centre of this plate.

Moorish Ornament

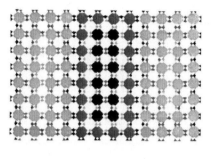

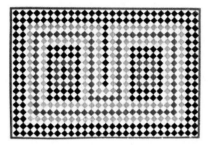

Figure 63. Mosaics in the Baths.

Figure 64. Mosaic from the portico of the Generalife.

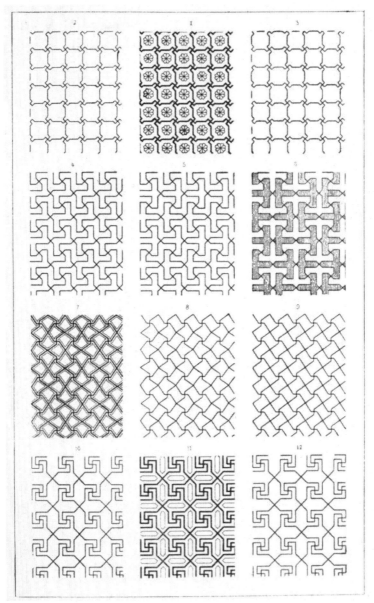

1, 2, 3, VARIATIONS ON A CHINESE *motif*. 7, 8, 9, VARIATIONS ON A *motif*, SYRO-ARABIAN.
4, 5, 6, VARIATIONS ON A *motif* HISPANO-ARABIAN. 10, 11, 12, VARIATIONS ON A *motif*, GALLO-ROMAN.

Figure 161.

Moorish Ornament

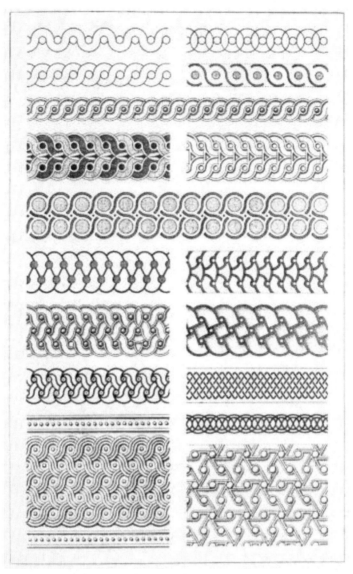

1 SIMPLE PLAIT, UNDULATED.
2 DOUBLE PLAIT.
3 SIMPLE PLAIT, INTERSECTED.
4 PLAIT, FROM A GREEK VASE.
5 REDOUBLED PLAIT, GREEK.
6 INFLECTED PLAIT, GREEK.
7 INFLECTED PLAIT, GREEK.
8 QUADRUPLED PLAITS, INTERLACED, SICILIAN.
9 SICILIAN.
10 TRIPLE PLAIT, GREEK.
11 TRIPLE PLAIT, GREEK.
12 DIVERSIFIED PLAIT, NEAPOLITAN.
13 GREEK.
14 GREEK.
15 ARABIAN.
16 PERSIAN (THREE PLAITS, INTERSECTED).
17 GREEK.

Figure 162.

Plate 65. Ornaments in Panels.

Plate 66. Ornaments over Arches at one of the Entrances.

Moorish Ornament

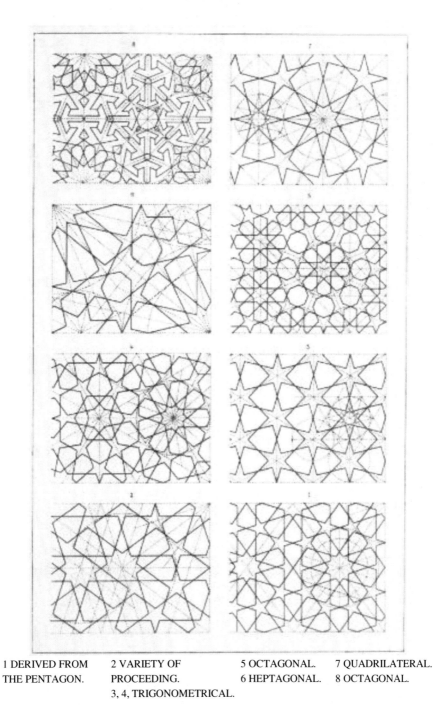

1 DERIVED FROM THE PENTAGON.
2 VARIETY OF PROCEEDING.
3, 4, TRIGONOMETRICAL.
5 OCTAGONAL.
6 HEPTAGONAL.
7 QUADRILATERAL.
8 OCTAGONAL.

Figure 163. Egypto-Arabian Knot, or Net-work.

1 SQUARES AND OCTAGONS.
2 DERIVED FROM SQUARES.
3 DERIVED FROM THE SQUARE: FROM THE CENTRE
A DODECAGON AND OTHER FIGURES ARE FORMED
BY SUB-DIVISION.
4 DERIVED FROM THE SQUARE: THE ANGLES BEING DIVIDED, THE RESULTING RAYS DETERMINE THE FIGURES BY INTERSECTION.
5 ANALOGOUS TO FIGURE 2.
6 TRIGONOMETRICAL.
7 HEXAGONAL.

Figure 164. Indo-Syro-Arabian Knot, or Net-work.

Moorish Ornament

Plate 67. Ornaments on the Walls.

Plate 68. Ornaments in Panels on the Walls.

212 *Albert F. Calvert*

1, 1', BRICK FACINGS FROM ROSETTA. 5 JAPANESE. 7 ARABIAN.
2, 3, 4, ARABIAN. 6 GRECO-ASSYRIAN. 8 CHINESE.

Figure 165.

Figure 166. 1 Arabian. 2 Ornamented Brick, Rosetta. 3, 4, 5, 6, Four Analogous Motifs, respectively Chinese, Arabian (Bis) and Greco-Assyrian. 7 Arabian. 8 Greco-Egyptian.

214 *Albert F. Calvert*

1 ARABIAN (DAMASCUS).
2 CEILING, LOUIS XIII.
3, 4, 5, ARABIAN (DAMASCUS)?
6 INDIAN.

Figure 167.

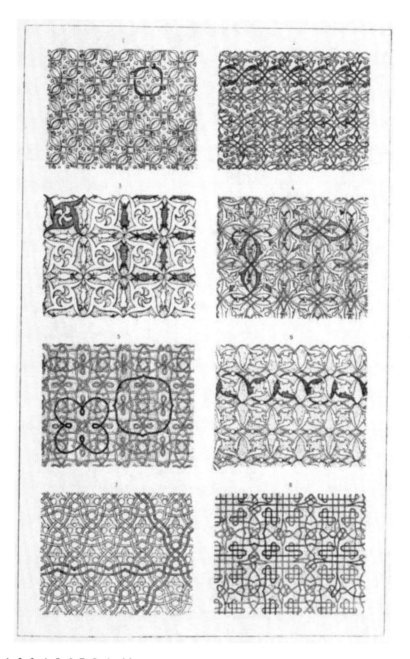

Figure 168. 1, 2, 3, 4, 5, 6, 7, 8, Arabian.

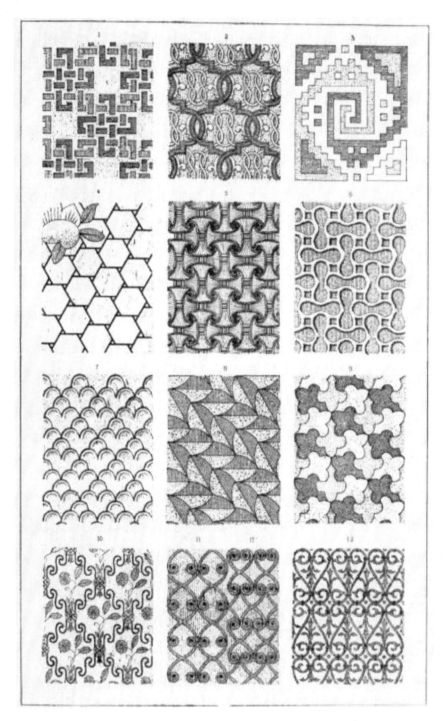

Figure 169. 1 Incrustation on Pottery, From Oiron. 2 Renaissance. 3 Mexican. 4 Chinese. 5 Egyptian. 6 Arabian. 7, 8, 9, Early Tiles, From Damascus, Rome, and Florence Respectively. 10 Italian. 11, 11', Egyptian. 12 Italian.

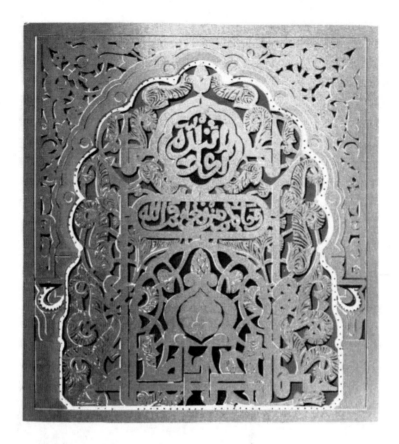

Plate 69. Small Panel in Jamb of a Window.

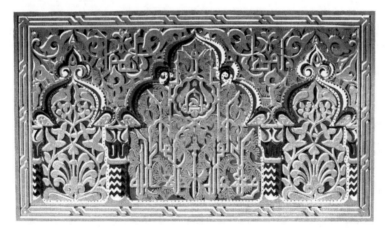

Plate 70. Small Panel in Jamb of a Window.

Figure 170. 1 Persian. 2 Arabian Ceiling, From Cairo. 3 Ceiling, Painted By Duban. 4 Byzantine. 5 Chinese. 6 Pompeian.

Moorish Ornament

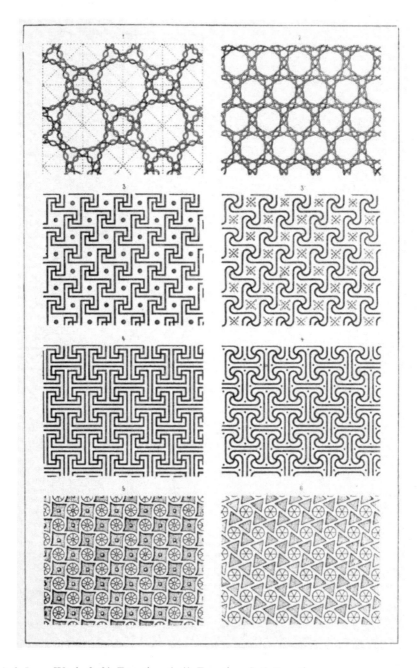

Figure 171. 1, 2, Lace-Work. 3, 3', Egyptian. 4, 4', Egyptian. 5, 6, Egyptian.

Figure 172. 1, 2, 3, Anglo-Saxon. 4 Egyptian. Strangely Analogous To Number 3. 5, 6, 7, Anglo-Saxon. 8 Egyptian.

Moorish Ornament

1 ARABIAN. 3 RENAISSANCE. 5 ARABIAN.
2 ITALIAN.   4 ARABIAN.   6 ARABIAN.

Figure 173.

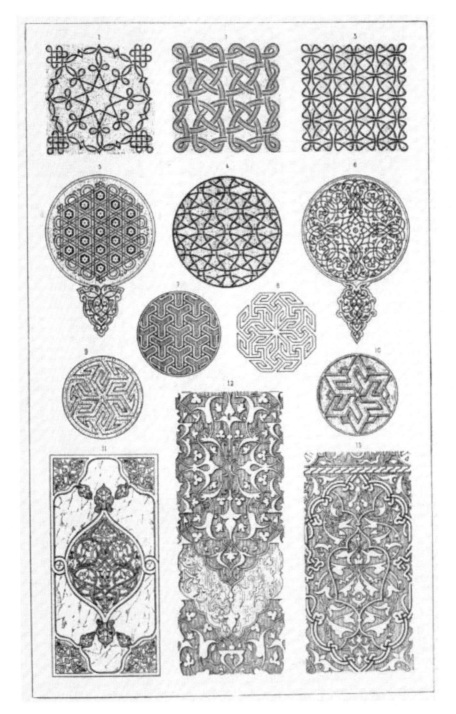

Figure 174. 1, 2, 3, From the Church Of St. Croix, Jerusalem. 4 Sicilian. 5, 6, 7, 8, Arabian. 9, 10, Chisellings on Stone, Jerusalem. 11 Marble Chasing, Jerusalem. 12, 13, Arabian Chasings, On Copper.

Figure 175. 1, 2, 3, "Palmettes" From the Prows of *Dahabiehs*. (Nile Boats). 4, 5, 6, 7, 8, Greek, From Examples at Athens.

Figure 176. 1-9. This Plate is Devoted to Curvilinear Figures, Chiefly from Athens. 7 is from a Mural Decoration at Pompeii.

Moorish Ornament

Plate 71. Panel in the Upper Chamber of the House of Sanchez.

226 Albert F. Calvert

DESCRIPTION OF THE PLATES

Hexagonal Family

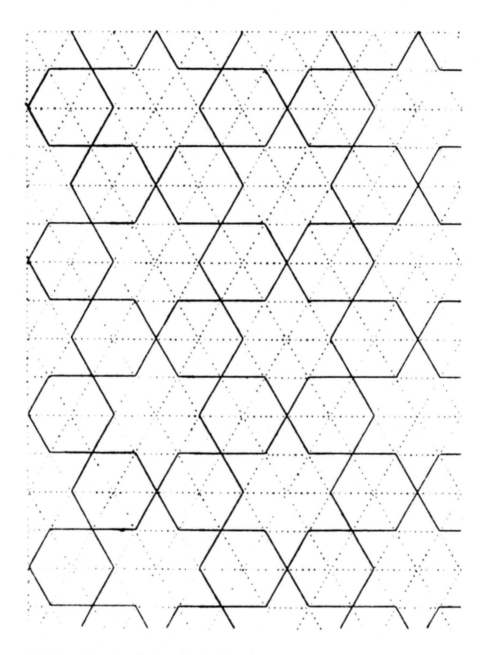

Figure 177. Plan, Triangular. To Describe the Hexagon.

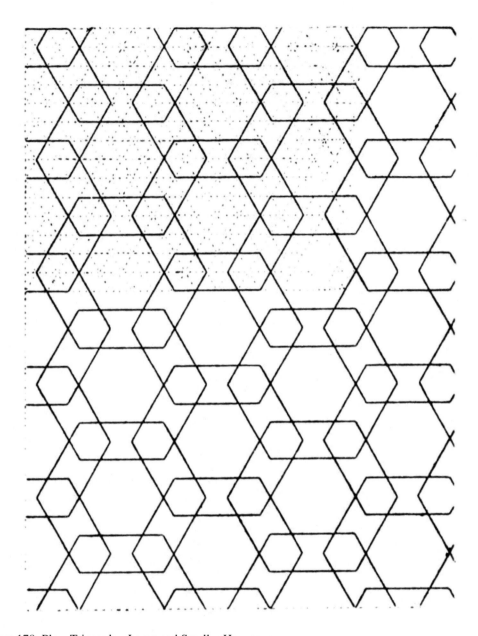

Figure 178. Plan, Triangular. Large and Smaller Hexagons.

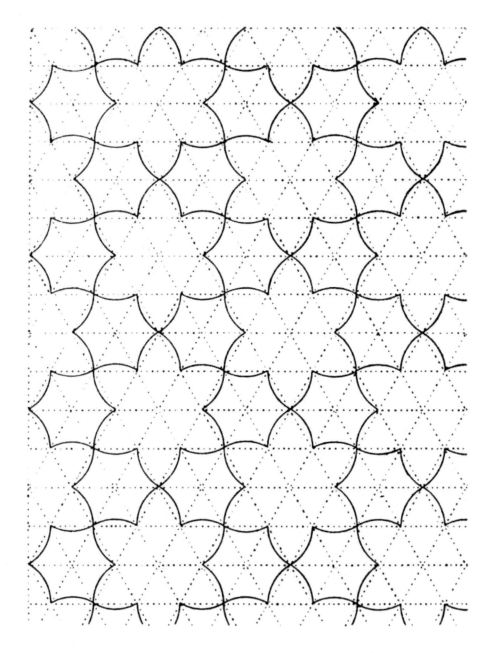

Figure 179. Plan, Triangular. Curvilineal Transformation of the Preceding Figure.

Figure 180. Triangles Curtailed; Or, Ternary Hexagons Intersected.

Plate 72. Spandril from Niche of Doorway at one of the Entrances.

Moorish Ornament

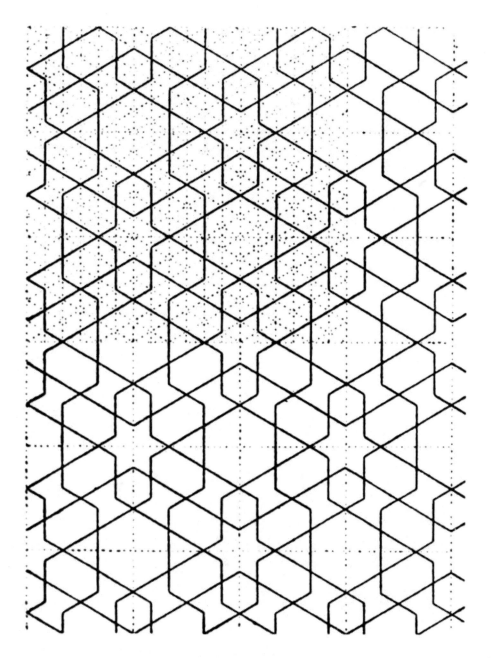

Figure 181. Intersections in Compartments. Five Figures—Large and Smaller Hexagon; Hexagon of Unequal Length; Dove-Tailed Hexagon; Hexagonal Star; Triangle.

Figure 182. Hexagons Intersected Circularly By the Six Points, the Apices United By a Triangle. Four Figures—Star, Pentagon, Triangle, Lozenge.

Figure 183. Hexagons, Intersected By the Apices. Three Figures—Star, Lozenge, Dodecagon.

Figure 184. Triangular Plan. From The Apices of the Triangles of Division Draw Hexagonal Stars. The Plan Is Intersected By Detached Hexagons Enclosing The Stars.

Moorish Ornament

Figure 185. Triangles Enclosed, and Leaving Hexagonal Stars, the Stars Being Joined By Zig-Zag Bands.

Figure 186. Hexagonal Star, of Which a Side from Each Apex is Extended in Revolving; Three Stars Thus Revolved are Joined by a Band.

Moorish Ornament

Figure 186. Bands Enveloping a Hexagon.

Figure 187. Rectangles Intersecting Regularly By Threes, and Interlaced By Their Smaller Sides, Their Extremities, Penetrating, Forming Three Pairs of Pentagons.

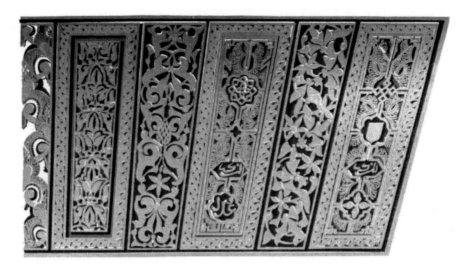

Plate 73. Lintel of a Doorway.

Plate 74. Capital of Columns.

Figure 188. From the Apices of Triangles of Division Describe Circumferences; Divide the Circumferences in Twelve Equal Parts, and Take the Diagonals of Five in Five Divisions; Thus Stars of Six Points are Obtained. These Stars Contain in the Enclosure a Hexagon of Ternary Symmetry, with Angles Alternately Right and Obtuse.

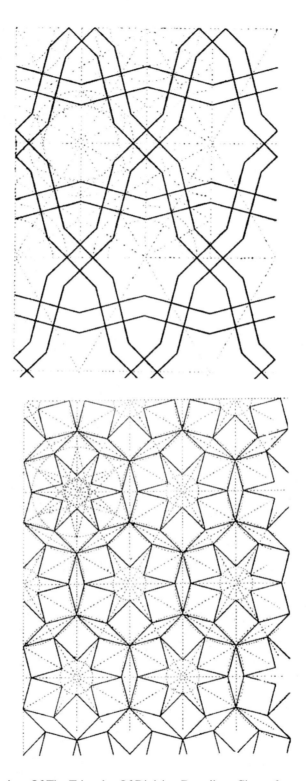

Figure 189. From the Apices Of The Triangles Of Division Describe a Circumference. With a Radius Equal To That of the Triangle. Inscribe a Dodecagon; Then Take the Diagonals of Three in Three Divisions from the Other Diagonals Which Form the Squares.

Figure 190. Figure Analogous To Figure 184. *q.v.*

Moorish Ornament

Figure 191. From the Apices of the Triangles of Division Describe Circumferences Having a Radius Equal to One-Third of a Side; Sub-Divide Them into Twelve Equal Parts, Then Take the Diagonals of Three in Three Divisions. The Radius of the Circumferences Would Be Smaller or Larger Than the One-Third of the Side; And Then, by Means of an Adjustment, the Squares Between the Apices Would Have a Side Equal to That of the Stars.

Figure 192. Dodecagons Intersected By Each Other, Which are Obtained by Sub-Division of the Angles of the Triangles into Four Equal Parts.

Moorish Ornament

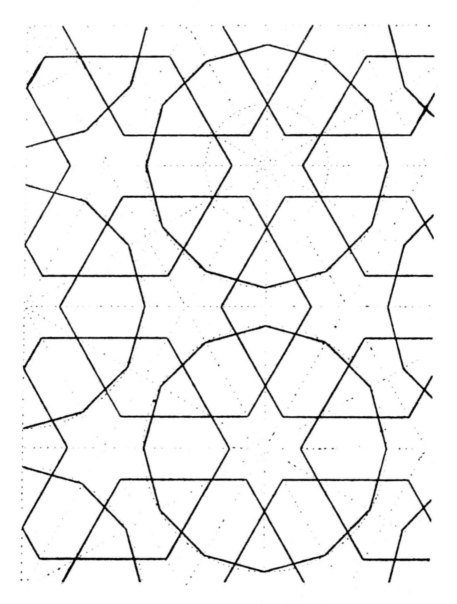

Figure 193. Dodecagons Containing Six-Pointed Stars Sub-Divided By Bands. The Radius of the Dodecagons is Equal to Half a Side of the Triangles of Division.

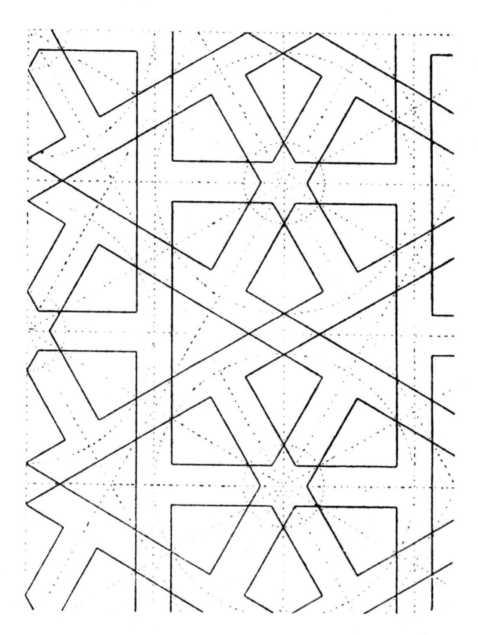

Figure 194. From the Apices of the Triangles Describe a Circumference, With Its Radius Equal to Half a Side of the Triangles. The Six-Pointed Stars and Bands Which are Derived From Them Could Be of Different Proportions.

Moorish Ornament

247

Figure 195. Distribution Proceeding From Hexagons and Triangles.

Figure 196. Six-Pointed Stars and Hexagons, From Which Proceed Band-Work and Lozenges.

Moorish Ornament

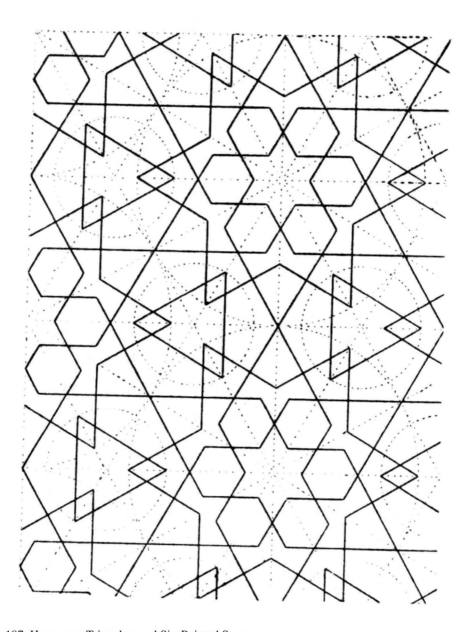

Figure 197. Hexagons, Triangles, and Six-Pointed Stars.

Figure 198. 24 Subject Similar to Figure 195.

Figure 199. Large Hexagons Crossed and Cut By Figures Quartered By Eight Sides; Horizontal and Vertical Bands Proceeding From Six-Pointed Stars.

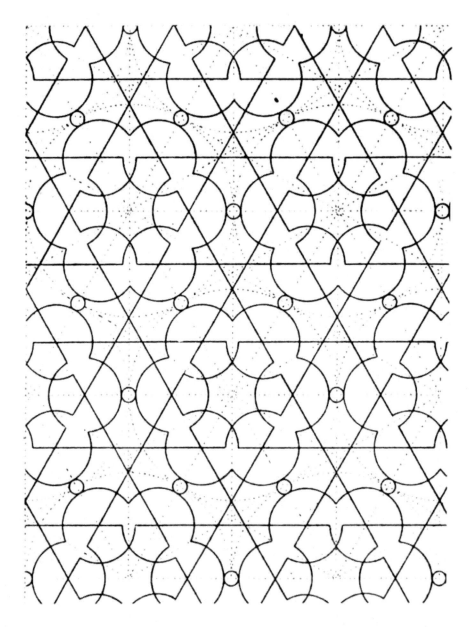

Figure 200. From the Apices of the Triangles of Division Describe the Circumferences, and Divide Them into Twelve Equal Parts. By the Points of the Star Thus Made, Describe Six Half-Circles, in Each Case Forming A Rosette. Small Intercalary Circles Unite the Rosettes.

Moorish Ornament 253

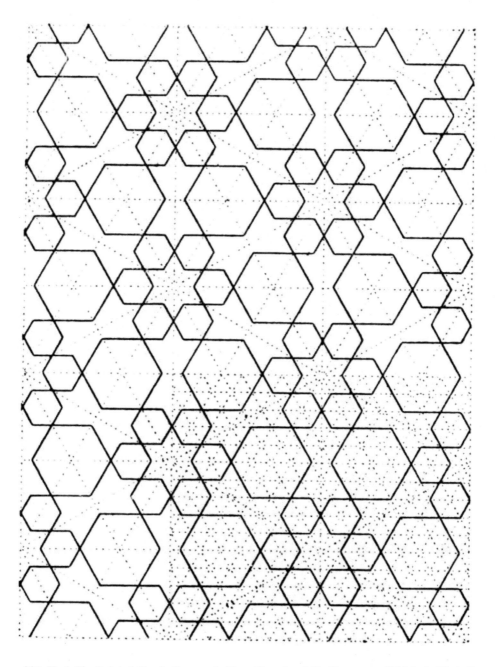

Figure 201. Each Six-Pointed Star is Surrounded by a Rosette of Six Hexagons, Which, in Their Turn, Distribute Their Lines to Form Larger Hexagons.

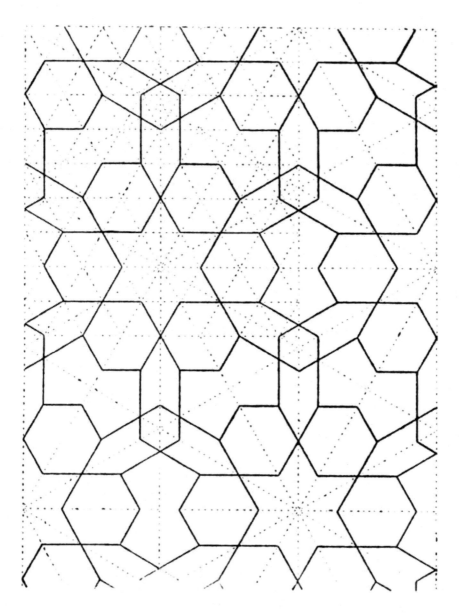

Figure 202. Each Six-Pointed Star is Surrounded by a Rosette of Six Hexagons, Which are Supplemented By Perpendicular Lines, Which, By Intersecting Octagons Themselves, are the Means of Completing Small Hexagons.

Moorish Ornament 255

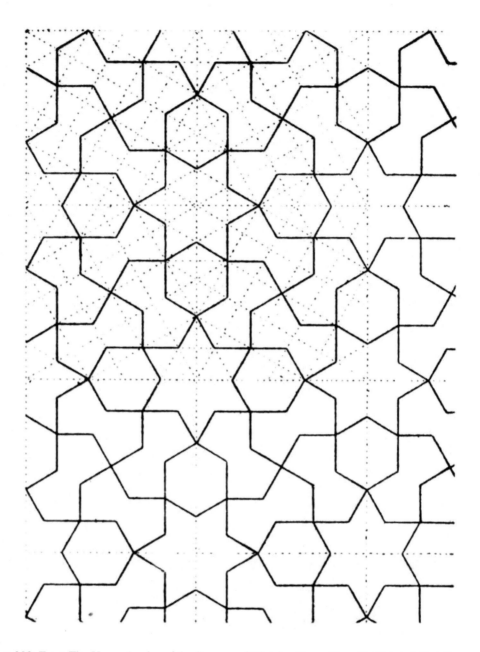

Figure 203. From The Upper Angles of the Squares of Division Trace Stars Six-Pointed, Rotating Alternately as Shown in Diagram. The Junction of the Lines of Division Determine the Points of the Figure.

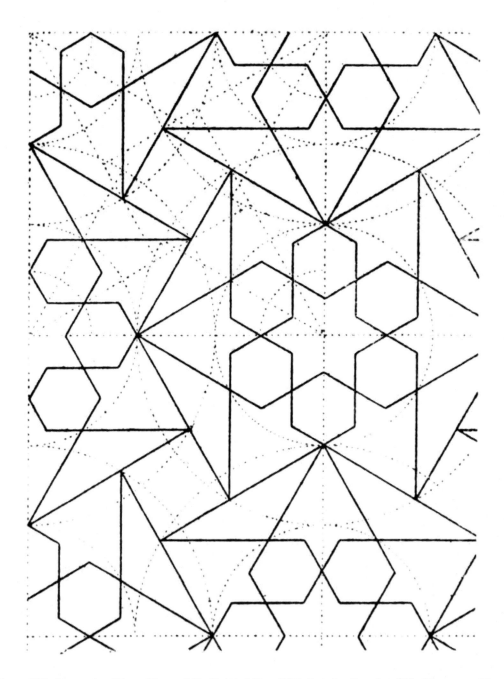

Figure 204. Alternating Dispositions of Six-Pointed Star, With Exterior Rosette of Six Hexagons. The Angles of the Square Being Divided into Three Equal Parts by a First and Second Radius, a Circumference is Made, Within Which Is Inscribed the Star of Six Points. The Rest Follows.

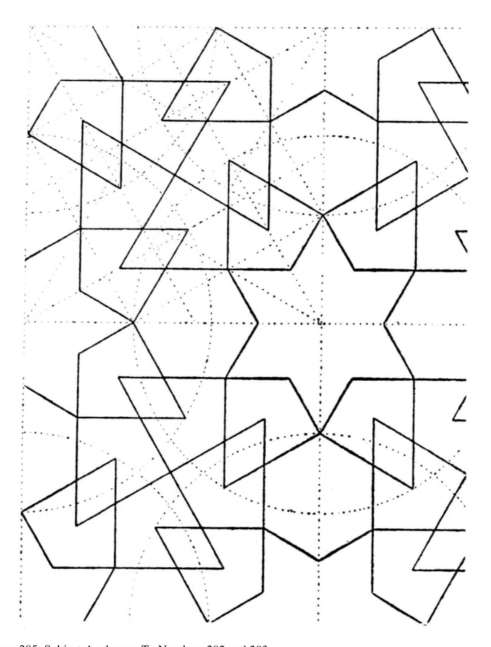

Figure 205. Subject Analogous To Numbers 202 and 203.

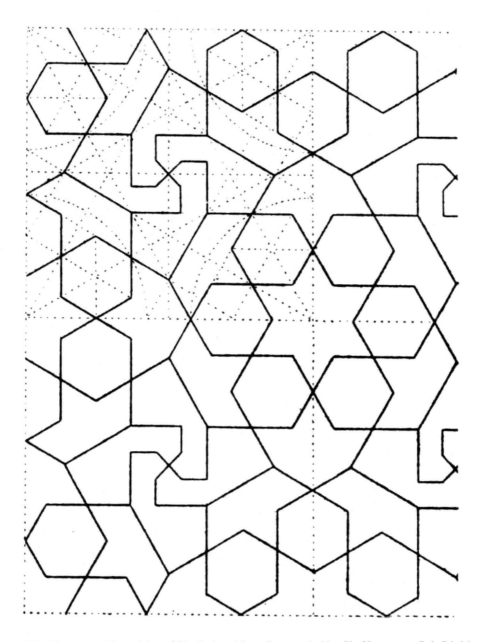

Figure 206. Alternating Disposition of Six-Pointed Star, Surrounded by Six Hexagons. Sub-Divide the Angles of the Square into Three Equal Parts. The Conjunction of the Radii With Them, and With the Medials of the Square, Make the Figure. In the Centre of the Square a Lineal Subject, Alternating.

Moorish Ornament 259

Plate 75. Capital of Columns.

Plate 76. Capital of Columns.

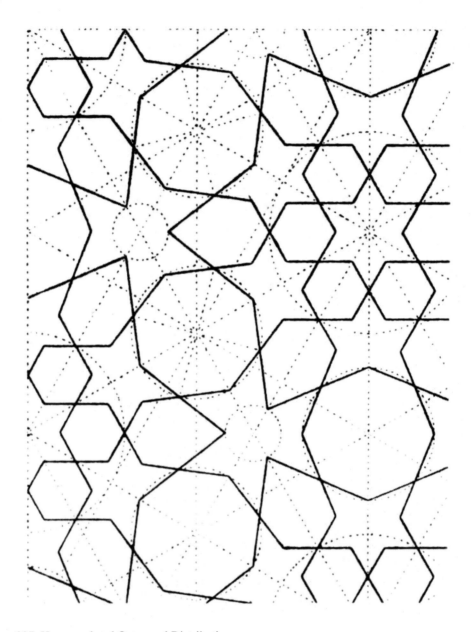

Figure 207. Hexagonal and Octagonal Distribution.

Figure 208. Hexagonal Distribution. Pentagonal Stars and Hexagons.

Figure 209. Hexagonal Star Inscribing a Second Six-Pointed Star. The Intersections Give Lozenges and Hexagons.

Moorish Ornament 263

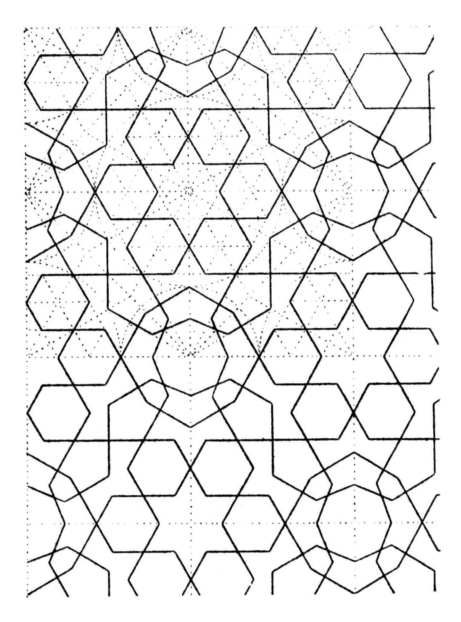

Figure 210. Square Plan. Divide Opposite Lines Into Three, and By the Centre of the Square Carry Two Cross Lines.

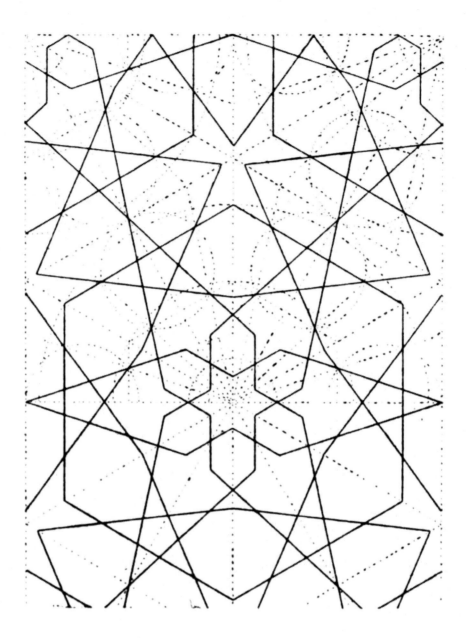

Figure 211. Triangular Plan. Hexagonal Star and Hexagonal Rosette Enclosed By Regular Hexagon.

Moorish Ornament 265

Figure 212. Hexagonal, Square, and Triangular Plan. Hexagonal Distribution. Dodecagon Star in Centres.

Figure 213. Triangular Plan. Hexagonal Disposition.

Figure 214. Triangular Plan. Hexagons and Triangles; Intersected Hexagons; Hexagonal Curvilinear Rosettes.

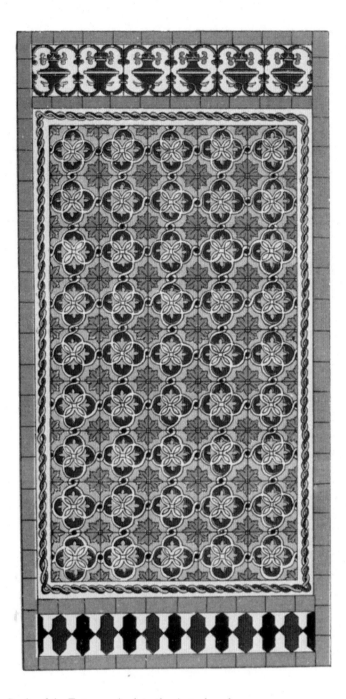

Plate 77. Seville. Socle of the Entrance Arch to the Antechapel.

Figure 215. Triangular Plan. Dodecagonal Stars; Hexagonal Stars Enclosed By Regular Hexagon.

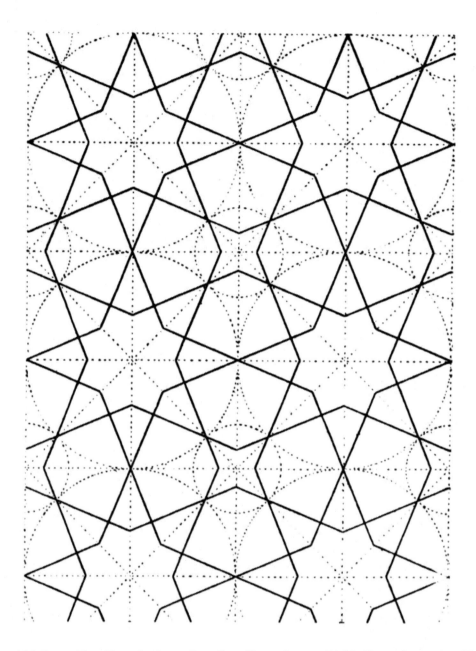

Figure 216. Square Plan. From the Centre Describe a Circumference; Divide Circumference into Eight Equal Parts, Starred Octagons are Thus Obtained, the Prolonged Sides of Which Determine Quadrilateral Stars.

Moorish Ornament

Figure 217. Curvilineal Transformation of Figure 216.

Figure 218. Octagonal Stars; Intersecting Lozenges, Squares, Trilaterals.

Figure 219. Divide the Square into Four Equal Parts. The Meeting of the First Line with the Median of the Square Gives the Radius of a Circumference. The Diagonal Lines Give an Octagonal Star.

Figure 220. Square Plan. From The Centre A Circumference, and By Diagonals a Starred Octagon.

Moorish Ornament 275

Figure 221. Curvilinear and Undulating Octagons and Pentagons.

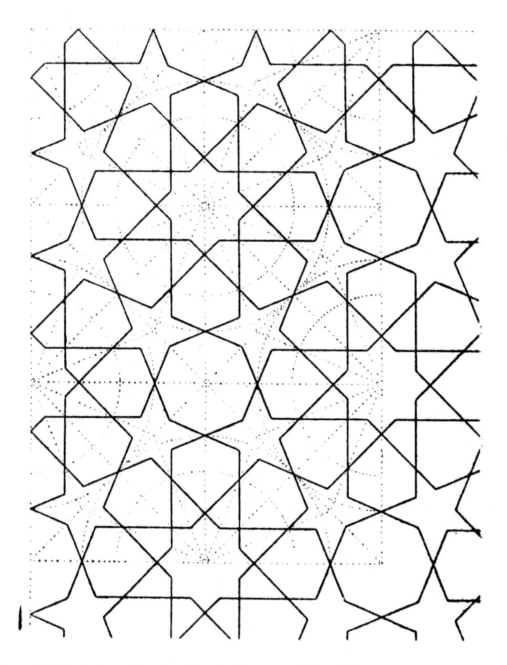

Figure 222. Distribution of Starred and Regular Octagons, with Starred Pentagons.

Moorish Ornament 277

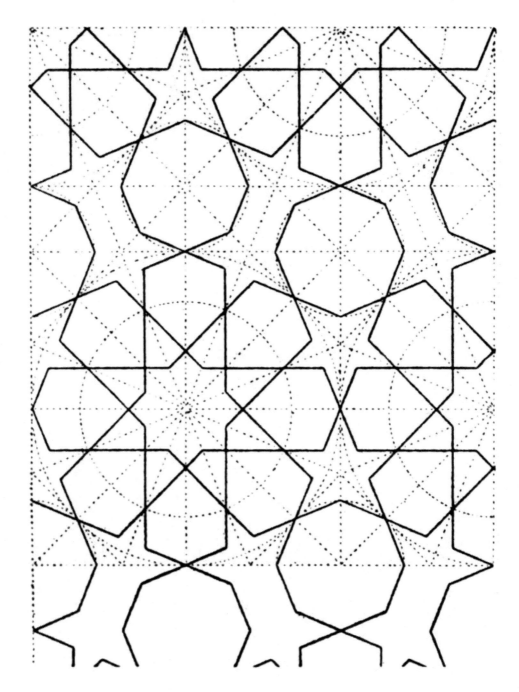

Figure 223. Octagonal Rosettes Following Isoceles Triangle with Pentagonal Stars and Regular Octagons Intercalary.

Figure 224. Describe Circumferences as Shown in Plan, in which are Carried Diagonals. From the Centre Inscribe a Square. The Intersections of the Lines of the Star Complete the Figure.

Figure 225. Describe Circumferences Equal and Tangent, and Divide into Sixteen Equal Parts. By the Angles of Division Describe a Pentagon Starred. By the Centre of the Square an Octagon Starred, from Which Emanates an Octagon Rosette. Hexagons Regular and Starred.

Figure 226. Divide Tangent Circumferences Into Sixteen Equal Parts. Similar Disposition to Figure Number 223, But With Different Treatment.

Moorish Ornament 281

Figure 227. Describe Circumferences as in Plan; Inscribe Therein by the Diagonals a Star, the Sides of Which, Prolonged and Intersected By the Octagonal Star, Determine the Rosettes.

Figure 228. Divide Circumferences as in Plan into Thirty-Two Equal Parts. From the Centre of the Square Inscribe a Star of Sixteen Points, the Prolongation of Its Lines Forming the Rosette of Sixteen.

Figure 229. Describe Circumferences as in Plan. From the Centre of the Plan By Radiating Lines Inscribe a Starred Octagon; the Prolongation and Meeting of Its Lines In Repetition Complete the Figure.

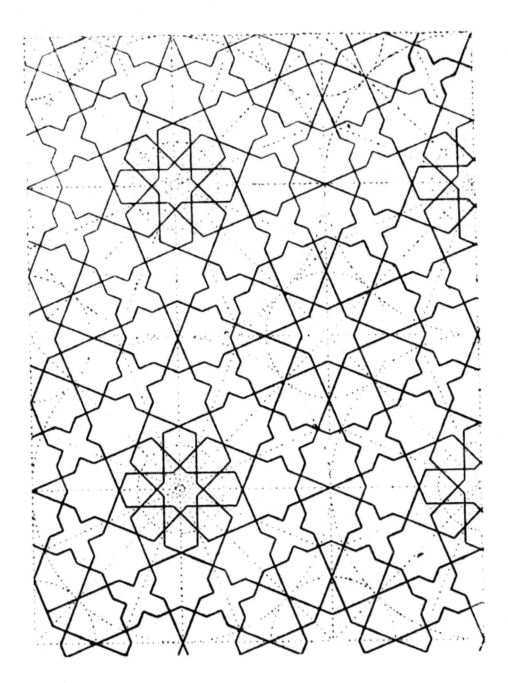

Figure 230. Describe Circumferences as in Plan. In The Centre of Four Equal Squares Trace an Octagonal Rosette, After Having Taken in the Large Rosette of Sixteen Points, Which Lends Its Lines to the Formation of Eight Surrounding Cruciform Figures.

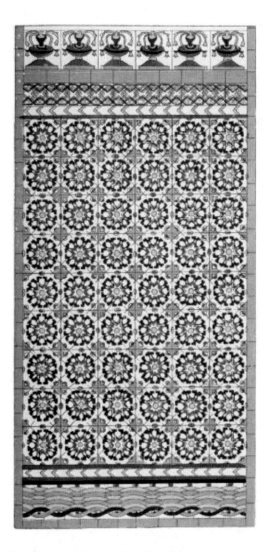

Figure 78. Seville. Socle of the Entrance Arch to the Chapel.

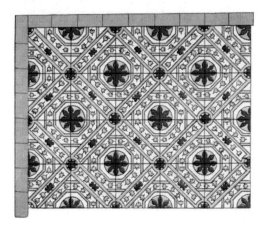

Plate 79. Seville. Detail of the Tiles of the Altar.

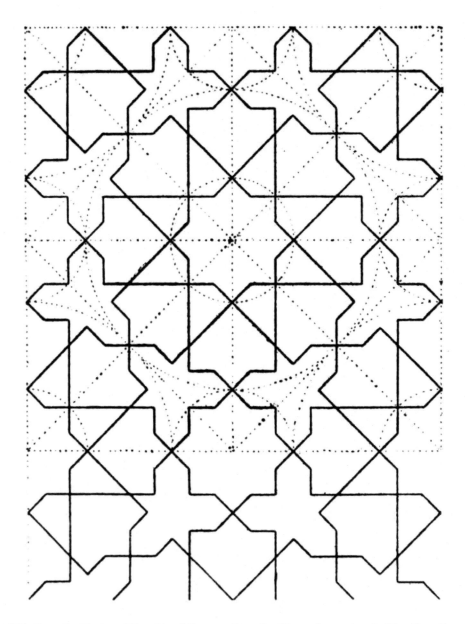

Figure 231. From the Centre of Four Equal Squares Describe Circumferences as in Plan. Inscribe Therein the Starred Octagon, the Prolonged Sides of Which Determine the Quadrilateral Rosette.

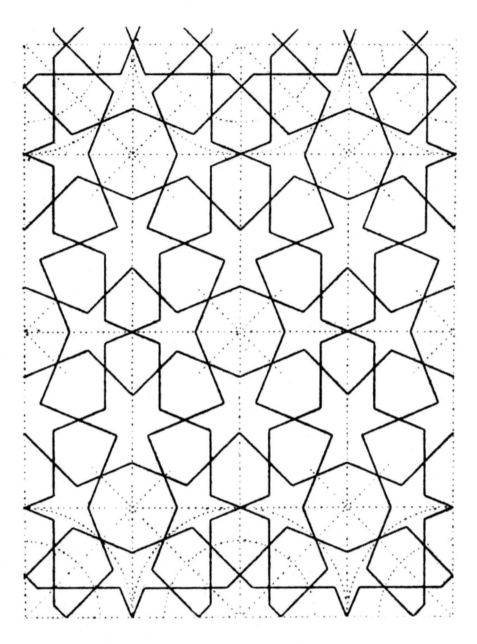

Figure 232. The Square of Distribution is a Rectangle Lengthened, From Which Octagons are Traced. Ternary Stars, yet with Six Points, And Paired Stars with Five Points Fill in the Rectangle.

Figure 233. Design of Four Figures. An Octagon, a Hexagon Paired, a Starred Pentagon, and a Starred Hexagon.

Moorish Ornament 289

Figure 234. Analogous to Number 232, with Closer Development.

Figure 235. A Starred Octagon, the Prolonged Lines of Which Form an Octagonal Rosette, Separated By a Regular Hexagon.

Figure 236. Divide Circumferences as in Plan into Sixteen Equal Parts. The Diagonals Will Give a Star of Sixteen Points, the Lines of Which, Extended, Form a Rosette of Sixteen Points Within a Square. The Angles of the Square Intersect Regular Hexagons.

Figure 237. Describe the Circumferences as in the Plan. Inscribe From a Centre a Starred Octagon Enclosed Within a Regular Octagon, A Starred Hexagon Within Alternate Hexagons, and a Cruciform Figure Within a Four-Pointed Star.

Figure 238. Describe Circumferences as in the Plan, and From a Centre Inscribe a Starred Octagon; From the Extended Lines Is Formed a Cruciform Figure. From Other Centres Inscribe Starred and Regular Hexagons.

Figure 239. Describe Circumferences as in the Plan. From a Centre Inscribe a Starred Octagon of Which the Sides are Prolonged. By These Prolongations, and By Octagonal Figures in Pairs, the Tracing is Complete.

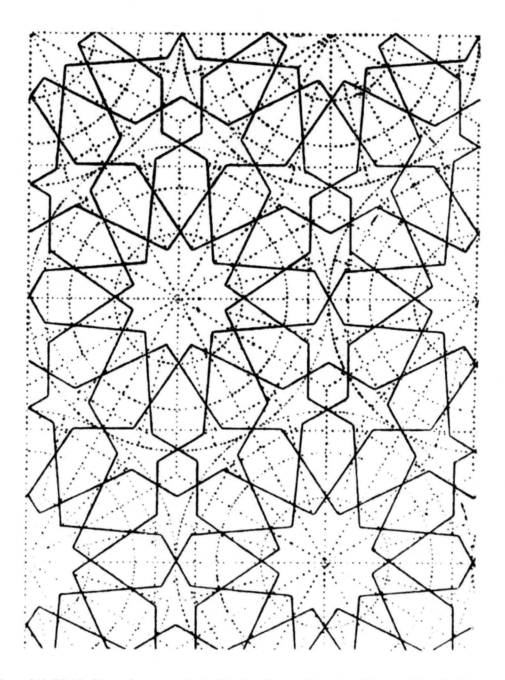

Figure 240. Divide Circumferences as in the Plan Into Twenty-Four Equal Parts, and Inscribe From a Centre a Starred Dodecagon, the Extended Lines of Which Determine the Intersecting Lines of the Rosette.

Figure 241. Describe Circumferences as in the Plan. From a Centre Inscribe a Starred Dodecagon Analogous to Number 240.

Figure 242. Triangular Plan. Describe Circumferences as in the Plan. From a Centre Inscribe a Starred Dodecagon, the Extended Lines of Which Form the Unequal Limbs of a Rosette, and a Cruciform Figure Within a Square.

Plate 80. Seville. Socle in the Interior of the Chapel.

Figure 243. Divide as in the Plan. Inscribe a Starred Dodecagon, the Sides of Which Prolonged Inscribe the Lines of the Rosette. Four Rosettes Penetrate Each Other, and Are Each Invaded by a Star Having Triangular Webs.

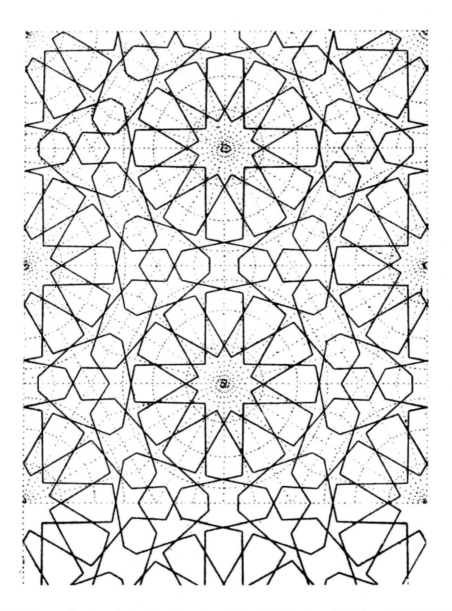

Figure 244. From a Centre as in the Plan Describe a Starred Dodecagon, the Sides of Which Prolonged Form the Lines of the Rosette. The Rosette, by Extending Lines, is Surrounded by Twelve Hexagons.

Moorish Ornament 301

Figure 245. Divide as in the Plan. Design Analogous To Number 244. By Extension of Lines of the Rosette Hexagons are Grouped.

Figure 246. Divide as in Plan. Design Analogous To Number 245.

Plate 81. Seville. Socle in the Interior of the Chapel.

Figure 247. Divide as in Plan. The Circumferences Divided into Twenty-Four Equal Parts Determine the Rosette, the Extended Lines of Which Describe the Starred Pentagon.

Moorish Ornament

Figure 248. Curvilinear Transformation of Number 247 by the Substitution of Arcs for Rectilineal Features.

Figure 249. Divide The Circumferences Into Twenty-Four Equal Parts. Inscribe The Starred Dodecagon, The Extended Lines Of Which Describe The Rosette.

Moorish Ornament 307

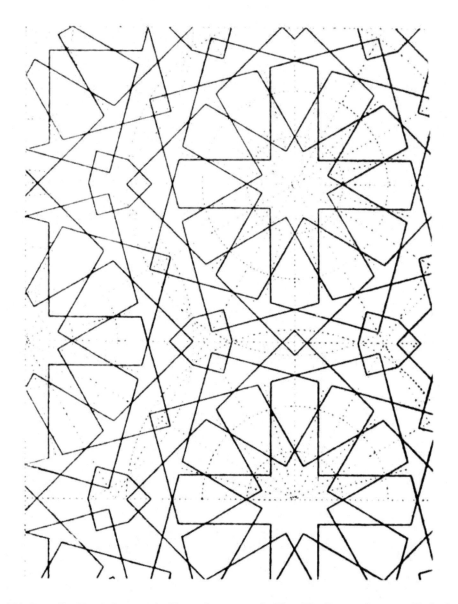

Figure 250. Describe Three Concentric Circumferences as in Plan. The Rosette Becomes Entire by Lines Extended from the Starred Dodecagon. Crossed Lines from the Rosette Determine the Square.

308 Albert F. Calvert

Figure 251. Transformation of Number 250. Rosette Identical. In the Centre of a Square Describe an Octagon, the Prolonged Sides of Which Invade the Square Which Figures Around the Rosette.

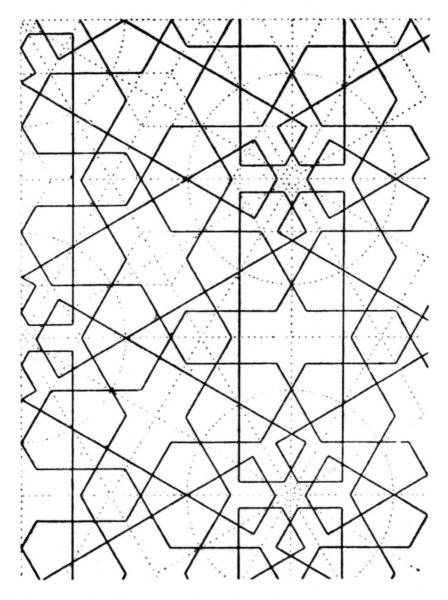

Figure 252. Divide as in Plan. From a Centre Trace a Starred Hexagon, the Extended Lines of Which Cut the Prolonged Lines of the Rosette.

Figure 253. Describe Circumferences as in Plan. From a Centre Trace a Starred Dodecagon. Thus are Determined Rosettes Placed End to End, Each in a Regular Hexagon.

Figure 254. Describe Circumferences as in Plan. The Rosette is Determined by the Starred Dodecagon. This Design is Most Diversified, and Capable of Exhaustive Forms of Ornament.

Figure 255. From a Centre Draw a Starred Dodecagon, Which Determines the Rosette, the Crossed Lines at the Points of the Rosette Determining the Many Regular Hexagons and *Tricèles*.

Moorish Ornament

Figure 256. Hexagonal Distribution. From a Centre Draw a Starred Dodecagon Determining the Rosette, the Alternately Crossed Lines of Which Form a *Tricèle*, within a Second Circumference, as in the Plan, Draw a Starred Hexagon, the Extended Lines Forming Six Regular Hexagons.

Figure 257. From a Centre a Starred Dodecagon. The Lines Extended Form an Outer Starred Dodecagon, and by Crossing Describes a Starred Hexagon and a Lozenge, within which is a Cruciform Figure.

Moorish Ornament 315

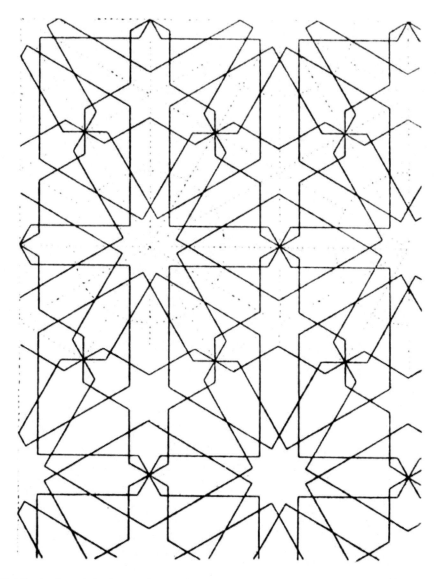

Figure 258. The Radius of the Circumference is Equal to a Third of the Height of the Triangle, and the Square Makes a Star of Four Points at Each Angle.

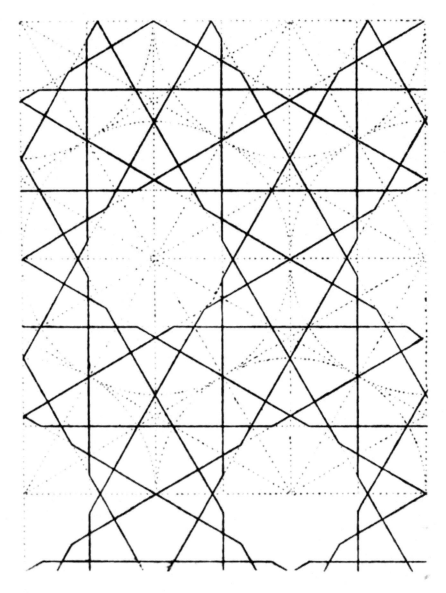

Figure 259. Draw Circumferences and Divide as in Plan. The Starred Dodecagon Determined by Intertwined Squares. The Lines of the Dodecagon, Extended at Intervals, Form a Star of Four Points.

Moorish Ornament

Figure 260. Describe Circumferences as in Plan. From a Centre an Inner and Outer Starred Dodecagon, The Lines of Which Extended Form a Starred and Regular Hexagon, Including a Starred Octagon Which Merges into a Cruciform Figure.

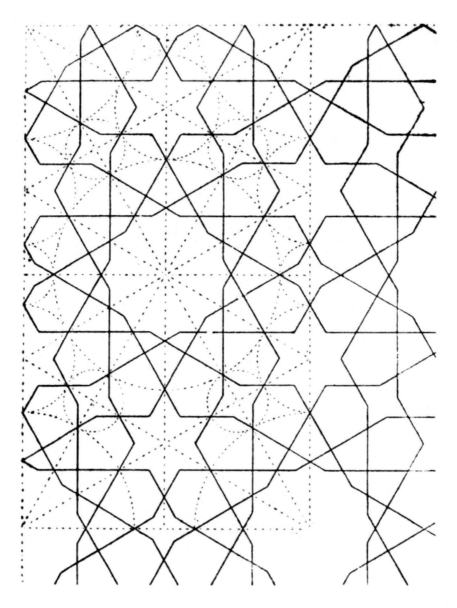

Figure 261. Trace The Net-Work of the Dodecagon, the Hexagon, and the Four-Pointed Stars. Follow Diagonals As In Plan.

Moorish Ornament

Figure 262. Draw Circumferences as in Plan. From a Centre an Inner and Outer Starred Dodecagon. Extended Lines of the Inner Dodecagon Form Six Squares Which Invade a Regular Dodecagon.

Plate 82. Mosaics from Various Halls.

Plate 83. Mosaics from Various Halls.

Moorish Ornament 321

Figure 263. Square Plan. An Inner and Outer Starred Dodecagon, and a Regular Dodecagon by Diagonals.

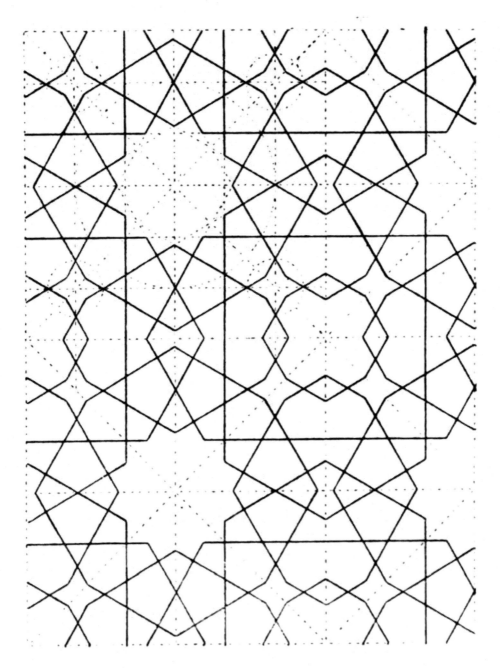

Figure 264. Square Plan. Describe Circumferences and Divide Them into Twenty-Four Equal Parts, and Draw the Diagonals of Eight in Eight Divisions. The Rest Follows.

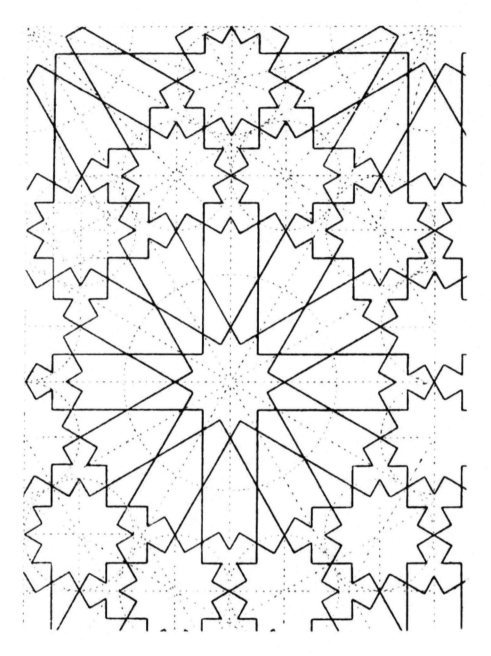

Figure 265. Net-Work of the Dodecagon and the Triangle Assembled. By Extended Lines of the Starred Dodecagon an Irregular Polygon, and a Rosette of Twelve Limbs are Formed.

Figure 266. Isoceles Plan. A Circumference is Drawn in a Square and Divided into Twenty-Four Equal Parts. A Circumference, Concentric to the First, Completes The Rosette by Means of Diagonals. The Small Hexagon and the Octagon are Traced.

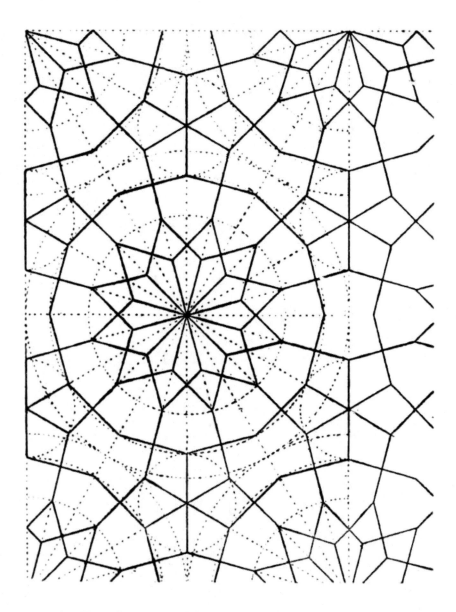

Figure 267. Describe Circumference and Divide into Twenty-Four Equal Parts. The Regular Dodecagon is Drawn. The Inner and Outer Starred Dodecagons are Described by Radiating Lines.

Figure 268. Net-Work of the Hexagon and the Triangle. The Rosette of Twelve Points Springing from a Starred Dodecagon is Enclosed by a Hexagon, Trellised, From Which The *Tricèles* Are Drawn.

Figure 269. Of Similar Intention to Number 268, But an Irregular Hexagon Receives Intercalary Lozenges.

Figure 270. Triangular Plan. Traced by Trellised Net-Work. The Hexagon Enveloped in Spirals.

Moorish Ornament

Figure 271. Triangular Plan. Hexagon Enveloped in Spirals. Analogous to Number 270.

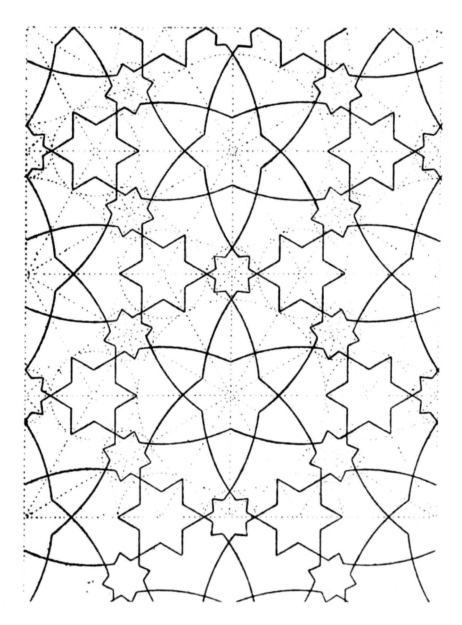

Figure 272. Net-Work of the Octagon, Hexagon, and Circle, Assembled. From the Starred Octagons a Curvilineal Rosette.

Moorish Ornament

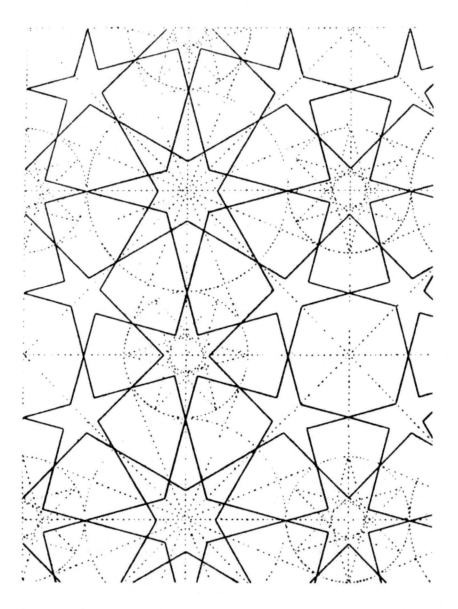

Figure 273. Square Plan. Stars and Rosettes. Describe Circumferences as Indicated. The Octagonal Stars Receive the Extended Lines of the Hexagonal and Pentagonal Stars. The Rest Follows.

Figure 274. Divide Circumferences as in the Plan. From the Centre of the Hexagonal Rosette Describe a Circumference Tangent to the First, and Divide into Twelve Parts. By the Aid of the Pentagon Comprised Complete the Rosette; Then, Depending on the Pentagon—Which, Though Irregular, Rules All—Trace the Pentagonal Figure Which Stands on the Points of the Rosettes.

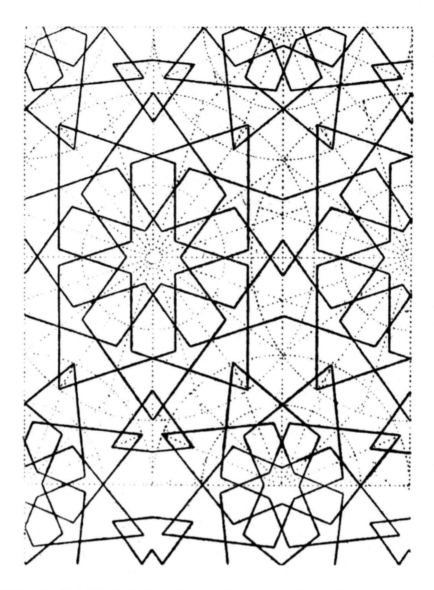

Figure 275. Isoceles Plan. Divide the Space Surrounding the Acute Apices of the Lozenge into Twenty Equal Parts, and of the Obtuse Apices into Sixteen. In the One Draw a Starred Decagonal, and in the Other a Starred Octagonal Rosette. The Adjustment of Two Types So Different is Not Considered Successful.

334   *Albert F. Calvert*

Figure 276. Diagram of the Dodecagon, Hexagon and Square. In the Centre of the Square a Regular Octagon, Which is Supreme. Then from the Starred Dodecagon Inscribe a Rosette of Twelve Points; Lastly, From the Starred Hexagon Inscribe a Rosette of Six Points.

Figure 277. Divide the Circumferences as in the Plan, the One Into Twenty-Four and the Other into Twelve Equal Parts. For the Rest, The Centres Being Indicated, It is Easy to Trace the Arcs, and So Complete the Figure.

Figure 278. The Lozenge and Trellised Rosette Emanating From Starred Hexagon, Alternating Row by Row with Dodecagonal Rosette Springing from Starred Dodecagon.

Moorish Ornament

Plate 84. Part of Ceiling of a Portico.

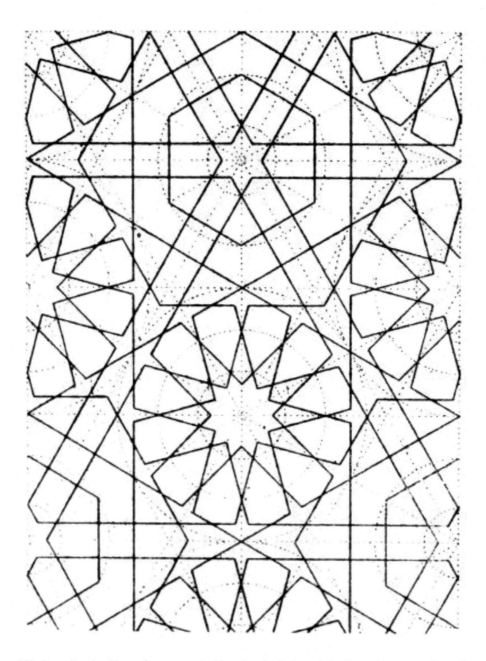

Figure 279. Describe the Circumferences as in Plan. By the Points of the Starred Hexagon Describe a Regular Hexagon. By Lines Extended from the Starred Hexagon the Twelve-Pointed Rosette is Formed, Constructing at the Same Time the Starred Dodecagon.

Moorish Ornament

Figure 280. Design Analogous To Number 279, But With Change of *Motif*.

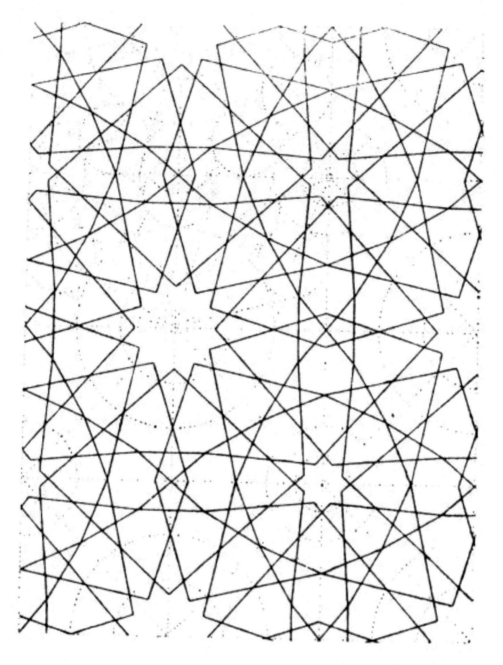

Figure 281. Square Plan. Divide as Indicated And Inscribe a Starred Dodecagon, the Extended Lines of Which Form an Outer Star Also of Twelve Points; The Starred Octagon is Constituted by Points Prolonged from the Dodecagon.

Moorish Ornament

Figure 282. Square Plan. Similar Ground-Work to That of Number 281. The Dodecagonal and Octagonal Rosettes are Described by Concentric Circumferences.

Figure 283. Square Plan. Similar Ground-Work to Numbers 281 and 282. The Treatment Considerably Changed.

Figure 284. Square Plan. Sub-Divide as Indicated. Inscribe the Pentagon, The Extended Lines of Which Establish the Octagonal Star and Rosette, as Well as the Dodecagonal Rosette and Star.

Figure 285. Square Plan. Divide as Indicated. The Flower-Work Which Accompanies the Irregular Octagon, Though Independent of Geometric Construction, Is Yet Within the Propulsion of the Lines.

Figure 286. Ground-Work Analogous to Number 284, But on a Triangular Plan. The Extended Lines of the Pentagon Govern the Enneagonal and Dodecagonal Star and Rosette.

Figure 287. Curvilinear Transformation of Number 286.

Moorish Ornament

Figure 289. Triangular Plan. Distribution of Enneagonal and Dodecagonal Stars and Rosettes. [The Dodecagon Only Partially Displayed.]

Figure 290. Triangular Plan. Similar Construction to Number 289. The Dodecagonal Star, Rosette, and Outer Star, Which are in the Diagram Number 289 Only Partially Seen, are Here Displayed.

Figure 291. Triangular Plan. From a Centre as in Plan Describe Circumferences, Which Rule the Dodecagonal Star, Rosette, and Outer Star. Many of the Figures are Drawn Independently, Though Governed By Divisions.

Figure 292. Divide as in Plan. Inscribe a Decagonal Rosette, From the Prolonged Lines of Which Proceed the Pentagonal Star, the Regular Octagon, and Other Figures.

Figure 293. Divide as in Plan. Two Different Rosettes, One of Twelve and the Other of Fifteen Points. [The Dodecagonal Rosette is, However, Only Partially Shown Here.]

Moorish Ornament 351

Figure 294. Describe Circumferences and Trace Rosette of Sixteen Points. The Lines Extended Will Complete the Figure.

Figure 295. Curvilinear Transformation of Number 294.

Moorish Ornament

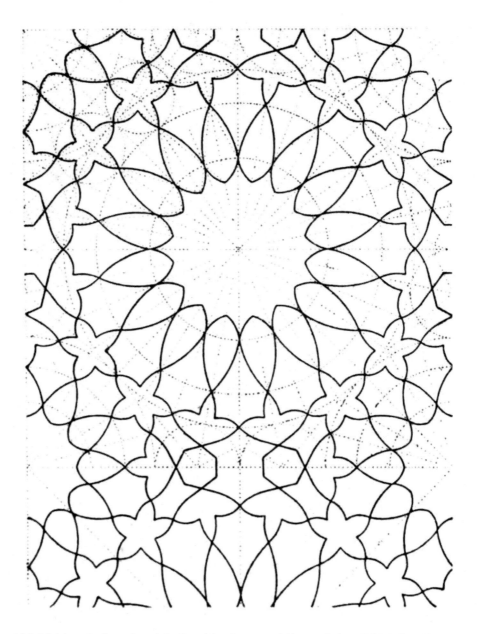

Figure 296. Divide as Indicated, and the Resulting Rosette of Sixteen Points, Which Would Naturally Be Rectilinear, May Be Easily Transformed To Curvilinear; While The Pentagonal Stars, Treated In Undulating Form, Become Flower-Work Or Foliage.

Figure 297. Same Ground-Work as Number 296. But Here the Rosette is Starred, End On End, About the Points.

Moorish Ornament   355

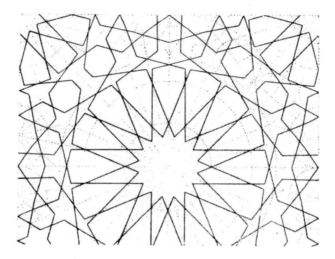

Figure 298. Sub-Divide as in Plan. The Circumference Governing the Heptagon is Divided into Equal Parts; By Prolonging the Sides of the Heptagon the Rosette of Sixteen Points is Inscribed.

Figure 299. Circumferences Tangent to Those of the Pentagon Inscribe the Rosette of Sixteen Points.

Figure 300. Transformation of the Rectilineal Rosette Number 299. The Figures in Other Respects Identical.

Figure 301. Divide As Indicated. The Extended Lines of the Hexagon Inscribe the Rosette of Eighteen Points and that of Nine Points. The Rest is but a Matter of Adjustment.

358   *Albert F. Calvert*

Figure 302. Design Analogous to Number 301. In This Arrangement, Two Sides of the Heptagon Prolonged Determine the Rosette of Eighteen and That of Twelve Points.

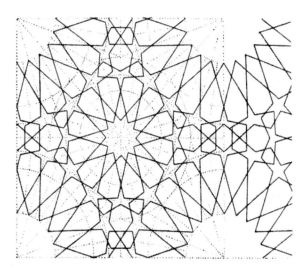

Figure 303. Square Plan. Divide as Indicated. Inscribe a Rosette of Twenty Points (The Half of Which Is Shown In the Diagram). In a Tangent Circumference Inscribe the Rosette of Twelve Points. The Rest Follows.

Figure 304. Distribution of the Dodecagon, Hexagon, and Square Assembled. By the Middle Points of The Sides of the Dodecagon Inscribe a Star and a Rosette of Twenty-Four Points. Within the Hexagon Inscribe Two Triangles from a Tangent Circumference. A Lozenge Is Inscribed Between Opposite Sides of the Square. Lastly, By Tricèles Révolvés, All the Prolonged Lines are Reconciled.

Figure 305. Distribution of the Dodecagon, Hexagon, and Square Assembled. In the Dodecagon Inscribe a Rosette of Twenty-Four Points; In the Hexagon a Rosette of Twelve Points; And, Lastly, In the Square a Rosette of Eight Points. A Little Pentagonal Star Reconciles the Prolonged Lines.

Moorish Ornament

Figure 306. Sub-Divide as in Plan. Dodecagon, Hexagon, and Square Assembled. In the Dodecagon a Rosette of Twelve Points. In the Tangent Circumference Six Hexagons. The Square Governs the Prolonged Lines.

362   *Albert F. Calvert*

Figure 307. The Rosettes are as in Number 306. The Smaller Hexagons Govern the Principal Figures.

Figure 308. Square Plan; Distribution Follows the Net-Work of the Octagon and Square. The Rosette Is Linked by the Smaller Octagons.

Figure 309. Analogous To Number 308.

Figure 310. Octagons and Squares Assembled. The Octagonal Rosette Governs.

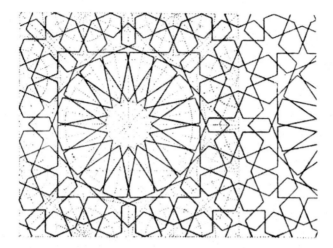

Figure 311. Sub-Divide as Indicated. Describe a Circle In Which Is Inscribed a Star With Sides Prolonged, Determining an Octagonal Rosette. By Concentric Circles, Somewhat Arbitrary, the Rosette of Sixteen Points is Determined.

Figure 312. Sub-Divide as in Plan. In a Circle is Inscribed an Octagonal Rosette, and Take a Tangent Circumference in Which to Inscribe the Rosette of Sixteen Points. The Rest Follows.

Figure 313. Distribution of the Octagon and Square. A Concentric Circle Contains Arcs Composing a Curvilinear Rosette, Within Which is a Rosette of Five Points. In the Centre of the Square Plan a Curvilinear Rosette Enclosing an Octagonal Rosette With Sides Prolonged, Bringing into Accord the Pentagonal Rosettes.

Figure 314. Sub-Divide The Main Circle into Thirty-Two Equal Parts, and Inscribe the Rosette of Sixteen Points. Other Circles are Inscribed, Each Containing a Perfect Octagon.

Figure 315. Net-Work of Octagon and Square. Inscribe a Rosette of Eight Points, and in a Circumference Tangent Inscribe a Rosette of Twenty-Four Points. The Rosettes are Brought into Accord by the Hexagons.

Figure 316. In a Circumference Indicated in the Square Plan Inscribe the Octagonal Rosette. Extended Sides Determine the Perfect Octagons.

Moorish Ornament 371

Figure 317. Square Plan. Octagonal and Square Distribution. Two Rosettes, One of Sixteen and One of Eight Points. The Diagonals from the Angles of the Pentagon Complete the Rosette of Sixteen Points, and the Extended Sides of the Pentagon Determine the Octagonal Rosette.

Figure 318. Square Plan. Net-Work of the Octagon and Square Assembled. Describe Circumferences as in the Plan. In Joining the Points of Division, There is on the One Part the Hexagon, And on the Other Part the Rosette of Sixteen Points. The *Tricèle Révolvé* Assists in Elucidating the Net-Work.

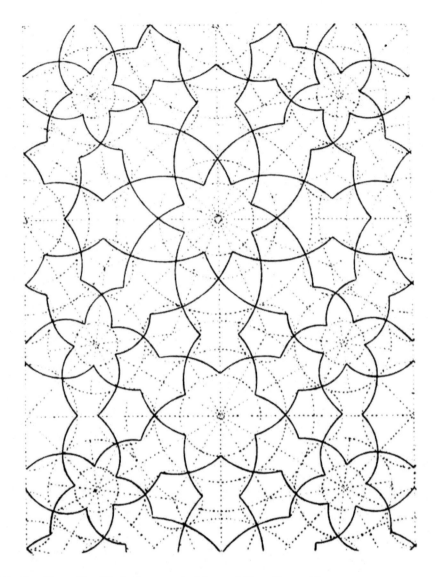

Figure 319. Curvilinear Net-Work Composed of Stars of Five, Six, and Eight Points. Describe the Circumferences as in the Plan. One Circle Describes the Star of Five Points; Another Circle Inscribes a Curvilinear Irregular Hexagon; Still Another Circle Inscribes a Star of Eight Points, and the Last Circle a Star of Six Points.

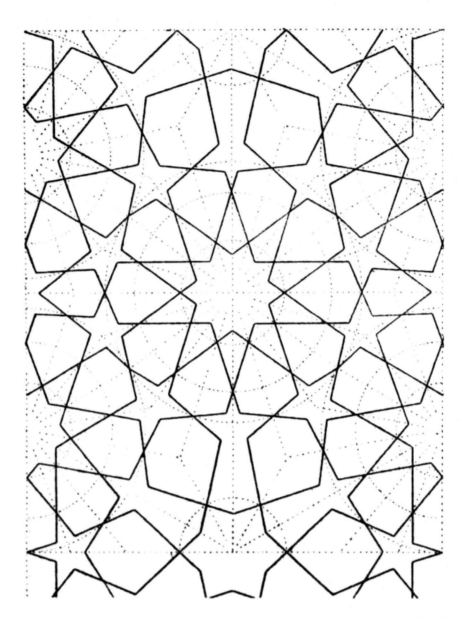

Figure 320. Sub-Divide as Indicated. The Prolonged Lines of the Pentagonal Star Determine the Decagonal Star and Rosette.

Moorish Ornament

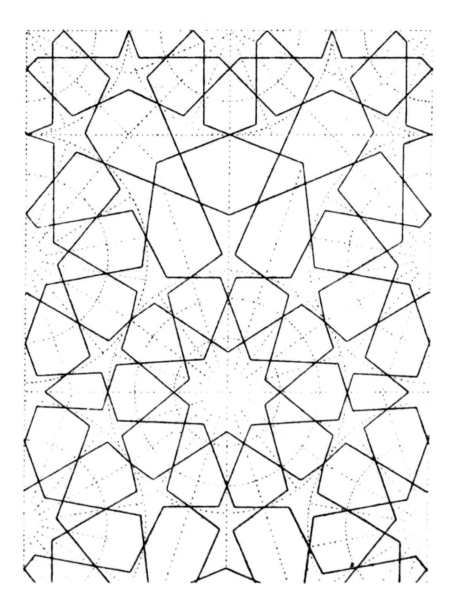

Figure 321. Divide as in the Plan. By Tangent Circumferences Inscribe the Rosettes. By Sides Extended the Rest Follows.

Figure 322. Octagonal, Decagonal, and Dodecagonal Stars and Rosettes. By Sides Prolonged the Rest Follows.

Moorish Ornament 377

Figure 323. Octagonal, Decagonal, and Dodecagonal Stars and Rosettes. By Extended Lines and the Adjustment of the Regular Octagons the Diagram is Completed.

Figure 324. In a Circumference as Indicated Inscribe a Star of Nine Points, and By Sides Prolonged a Rosette of Nine Points; In a Second a Star and Rosette of Twelve Points; and in a Third Circumference a Star and Rosette of Ten Points. The Rest Follows by Extension.

Moorish Ornament

Figure 325. The Central Circumference Divided Into Thirty-Two Equal Parts Produces a Star and Rosette of Sixteen Points. Divide Other Circumferences To Produce Stars and Rosettes of Twelve and Ten Points. The Rest Follows.

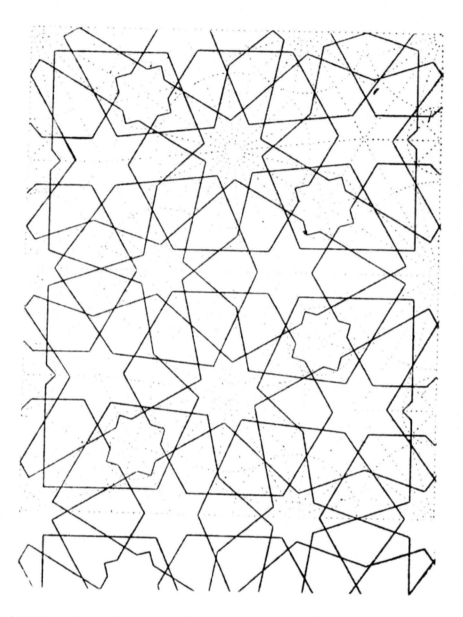

Figure 326. Circumferences Divided As Indicated. Inscribe Stars of Nine, Ten, and Twelve Points.

Figure 327. Net-Work Analogous To Number 325. The Lines of the Heptagon, Extended, Join the Lines of the Rosettes.

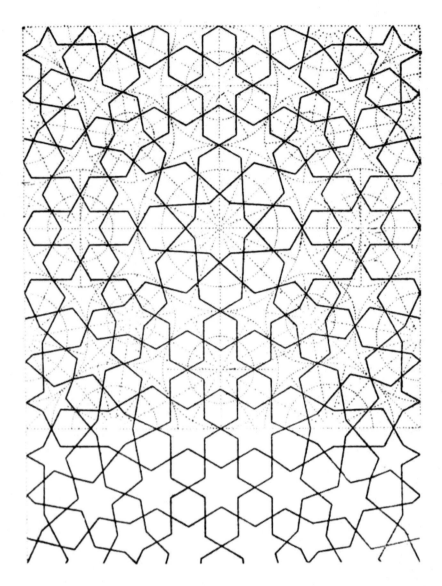

Figure 328. This Example Exhibits the Marvellous Ingenuity of the Arabian Designer in Composition, Rosettes of Five, Six, Seven, and Eight Points Being Adjusted. The Design Is Evidently the Production of an Art-Workman. If the Net-Work Is Not Actually Perfect, It Approaches Perfection So Nearly That It May Be Considered Exact.

Moorish Ornament 383

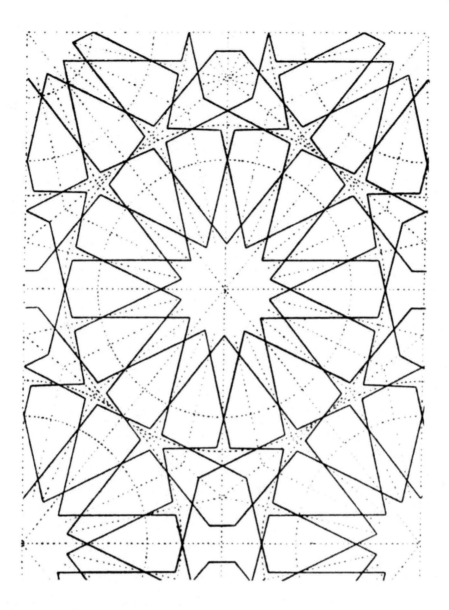

Figure 329. Isoceles or Lozenge Plan. The Rosette of Fourteen Points Result from the Extended Lines of the Heptagons.

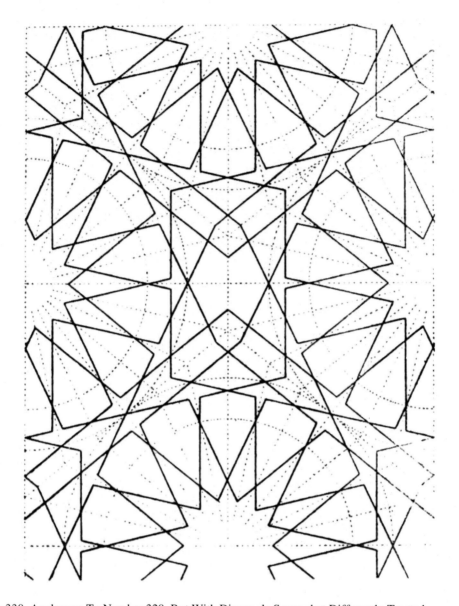

Figure 330. Analogous To Number 329, But With Diagonals Somewhat Differently Treated.

Figure 331. Rosette of Fourteen Points Governed By Heptagons.

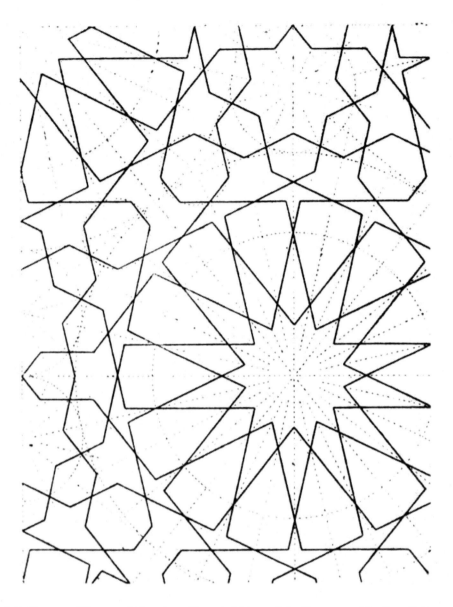

Figure 332. Rosette of Fourteen Points from Extended Lines of the Heptagons. The Rest Follows.

Figure 333. Pentagonal Adjustment. A Circumference Tangent to Those of the Pentagon Inscribes a Starred Rosette of Fourteen Points.

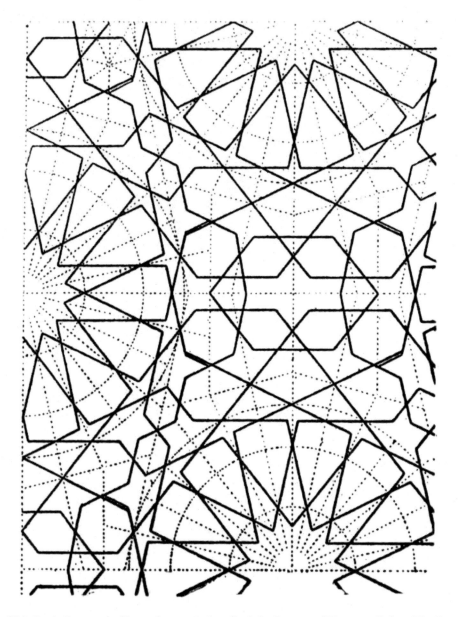

Figure 334. By A Concentric Circumference Is Inscribed the Rosette of Fourteen Points. The Pentagon Which Governs Has One Of Its Sides Extended To Greater Length Than The Six Others.

Figure 335. By The Aid of a Circumference, Indicated, Is Inscribed the Heptagonal Star From Which the Other Figures Proceed.

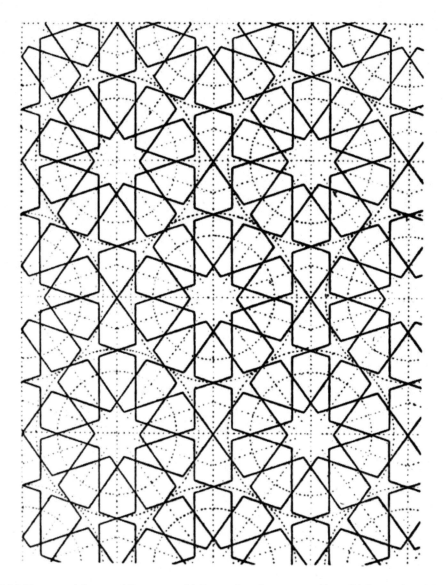

Figure 336. Decagonal Stars and Rosettes, with Intercalary Pentagons. Also with Intercalary Meshes, Which are Equal to Those of the Rosettes.

Figure 337. Analogous To Number 336.

Figure 338. Sub-Divide The Space Surrounding the Isoceles Triangle as Indicated. The Circumferences Being Described. The Diagonals Extended Complete the Figure.

Figure 339. Plan and Circumferences the Same as Number 338. The Aid of a Concentric Circumference Is Called In To Form the Rosette of Ten Points. The Rest Follows.

Figure 340. Describe Equal and Tangent Circumferences To Form a Star of Ten Points, and Take the Diagonals of Six in Six Divisions.

Figure 341. Describe Circumferences as Indicated, and Take the Diagonals of Six in Six Divisions. Draw a Horizontal Line at the Higher Line of the Little Pentagon, and Repeat the Construction Below the Line.

Figure 342. Divide Circumferences and Draw Parallel Lines as Indicated. Take the Diagonals of Six in Six Divisions, and the Rest Follows.

Figure 343. Describe Circumferences Equal and Tangent, and Take the Diagonals of Four in Four Divisions; Then in the Concentric Circumferences Take the Diagonals of Six in Six Divisions.

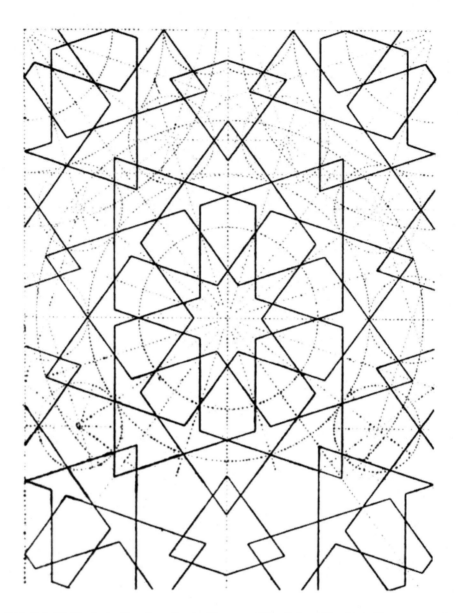

Figure 344. Sub-Divide As in Plan. Inscribe the Rosette of Ten Points; The Little Pentagons and Lozenges Follow, and the Rest Follows.

Moorish Ornament

Figure 345. Analogous To Number 344, But In Place of the Rosette Stars Are Formed.

Figure 346. Curvilinear Transformation of Numbers 344 and 345. The Points of Central Distribution are Marked by Minute Crosses.

Figure 347. Similar Ground Work to the Three Foregoing Diagrams. The Little Pentagons Govern the Design.

Figure 348. Describe the Circumferences as in Plan, and Inscribe the Decagonal Star. The Small Decagons in the Centre of the Triangles of the Plan, By Extended Lines, Form the Rosette.

Figure 349. Divide as in Plan. Upon the Lesser Side Trace an Isoceles Triangle. By the Apex of the Triangle Trace a Circumference, in Which Take the Diagonals if Three in Three Divisions.

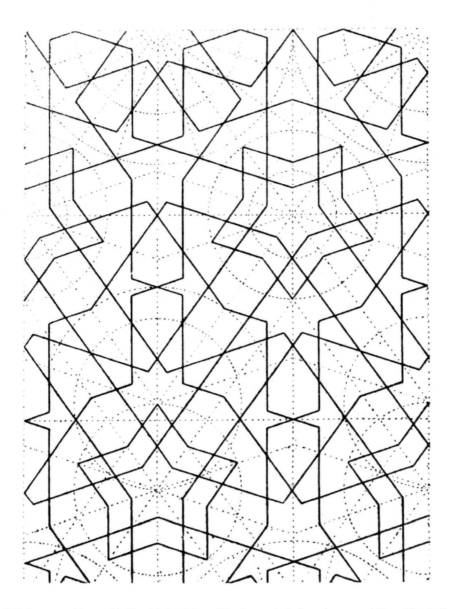

Figure 350. Lozenge Plan, with Combining Lines. The Lozenge is Imaginary, and Does Not Indicate the Radii in Extension One with the Other, But Only the Order of Sub-Division of the Pentagonal and Decagonal Rosettes.

Figure 351. Sub-Divide as in Plan the Space Surrounding a Point Into Twenty Equal Parts. At the Meeting of the Horizontal With the Vertical Line Draw a Concentric Circumference In Which Is Inscribed the Starred Decagonal Rosette. The Small Pentagon Is Dominant.

Figure 352. Same Ground-Work as Number 349, But With a Greater Interval between the Rosettes. One of the Rosettes, Instead of Being Rectilinear, Is Curvilinear.

Figure 353. Sub-Divide as Indicated. Describe Circumferences Equal and Tangent, and Take the Diagonals of Four In Four Divisions. Lastly, the Rosettes are Effected.

Figure 354. Draw Circumferences and Sub-Divide as In Plan. Take the Diagonals of Four in Four Divisions, Which, Prolonged, Complete the Design.

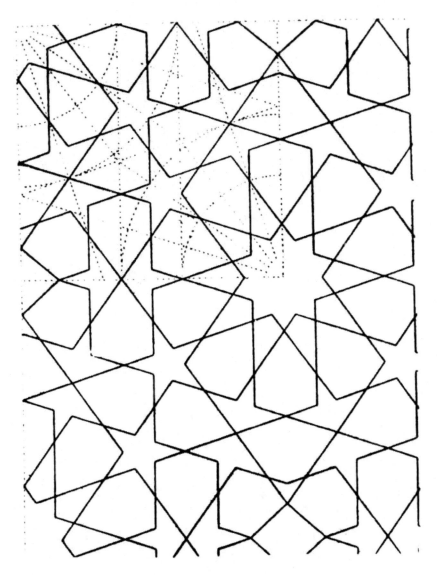

Figure 355. Describe Circumferences and Take a Perpendicular Line To the Border of the Radius; Take the Diagonals of Four In Four Divisions, Which Prolonged, Complete the Figure.

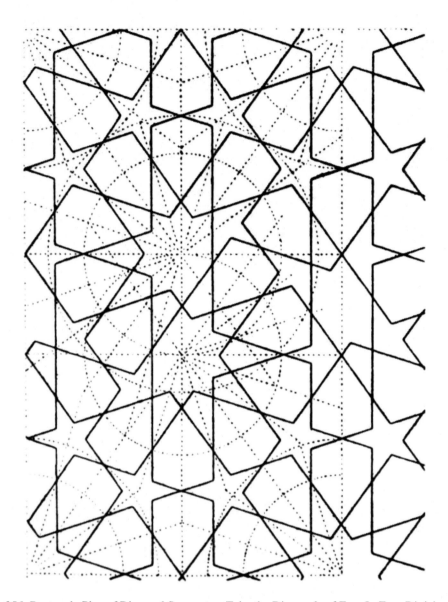

Figure 356. Rectangle Plan of Diagonal Symmetry. Take the Diagonals of Four In Four Divisions. Then By a Concentric Circumference. Set Out the Rosette. There Are, In Fact, Three Rosettes of Ten Points Equal and Tangent.

Figure 357. Lozenge Plan, With Combining Lines a Concentric Circumference Describes a Star the Rosette Is Then Drawn. Then Gradually, By the Aid of the Pentagonal Adjustment, The Net-Work Is Described.

Figure 358. Lozenge Plan, Where the Great Axis Is Three Times That of the Lesser Axis. Sub-Divide As In Plan. Trace Circumferences Equal and Tangent, In Which Are Inscribed Regular Pentagons. The Rest is Easily Followed. The Net-Work is Composed of Five Series of Lines.

INDEX

A

Africa, xxiv, xxvii, 7, 17, 20, 91, 99, 101, 146

Alcazar, vii, viii, 7, 67, 94, 95, 96, 97, 98, 100, 102, 103, 105, 106, 107, 108, 109, 111, 112, 113, 114, 115, 116, 118, 119, 121, 122, 123, 124, 126, 127, 128, 129, 131, 132, 134, 135, 136, 137, 140, 141, 143, 144, 146, 147

Alcazar at Seville, vii, 67

Alhambra, vii, viii, xxviii, 67, 71, 104, 105, 109, 112, 113, 118, 135, 155, 189

ambassadors, xxiii, 86, 87

ancestors, xxiii, 70, 104

Andalusia, vii, xi, xii, xiv, xv, xx, xxiii, xxv, xxvii, 6, 35, 82, 91, 96, 97, 99, 130, 143, 145, 147, 171

Arabian art, ix, 188, 189, 190

Arabian tower, viii

architect, 7, 21, 41, 67, 138, 152

architecture, 42, 58, 64, 67, 80, 83, 101, 105, 106, 109, 111, 118, 120, 125, 129, 130, 154, 155, 156, 161, 174, 182, 183, 184, 189, 190

Asia, 7, 18, 110

assassination, xxiii, xxiv, 93, 163

Athens, viii, 223, 224

atmosphere, 161, 166

Austria, viii, 111, 121

B

Baghdad, viii, xxi, 1, 97, 144

banks, xii, 1, 3, 18, 82, 97, 164

baths, 82, 92, 96, 103, 125, 126, 130, 133, 144

benefits, 76, 93, 137, 138

birds, 2, 3, 86, 104, 120, 180

blood, xv, xxiv, 5, 6, 35, 70, 76, 89, 162, 163, 174, 182, 184

C

Cairo, 118, 144, 218

Carthage, viii, xi, 83, 163

charm, xxiii, 2, 105, 173, 185

children, 56, 72, 78, 104

Christianity, viii, xi, xxi, 75, 165, 167

Christians, viii, xiii, xv, xxi, xxii, xxiii, xxiv, xxvii, 5, 6, 7, 9, 40, 57, 64, 76, 93, 100, 121, 139, 174, 175, 176, 182, 184, 187

cities, viii, xxi, xxv, 1, 5, 91, 96, 143, 144, 156, 187

citizens, 174, 175

communication, 25, 63, 143

composition, 114, 121, 189, 193

construction, 21, 36, 45, 67, 101, 104, 119, 131, 132, 138, 139, 153, 154, 155, 189, 198

Cordova, v, vii, viii, ix, xiv, xv, xvi, xvii, xviii, xix, xx, xxi, xxii, xxiii, xxv, xxvi, xxvii, xxviii, 1, 2, 3, 4, 5, 6, 7, 8, 9, 10, 11, 12, 13, 14, 15, 17, 18, 19, 20, 21, 22, 23, 24, 25, 26, 27, 28, 29, 30, 31, 32, 33, 34, 35, 36, 37, 38, 39, 40, 41, 42, 43, 44, 45, 46, 48, 49, 50, 51, 52, 53, 54, 55, 56, 57, 58, 59, 60, 61, 62, 63, 64, 65, 66, 67, 68, 69, 71, 72, 73, 74, 75, 77, 78, 79, 80, 81, 82, 83, 84, 85, 87, 88, 89, 91, 96, 97, 98, 99, 101, 103, 106, 117, 125, 139, 152, 164, 171, 172, 175, 176, 183, 187

corruption, 101

covering, 7, 8, 34

Cristo de la Luz of Toledo, vii

414 *Index*

crowns, 169
culture, xxi, 114, 166, 171, 177, 188

D

Damascus, viii, xiv, xv, xx, 1, 28, 80, 81, 82, 93, 95,
169, 171, 216
danger, xxiv, xxvii, 6, 99, 123
decoration, ix, 17, 21, 38, 42, 51, 62, 103, 105, 106,
110, 112, 115, 121, 156, 185, 188, 189, 190, 193,
195
degenerate, xi, xxiv, 28, 119
destruction, xxi, 1, 5, 7, 64, 93
distribution, 50, 51, 69
doctors, 3, 82, 88
drawing, 6, 139

E

education, 6, 166, 187
Egypt, 111, 115, 179
enamel, 28
enemies, xii, xxi, 78, 99, 177
England, 122
enlargement, 42
Europe, vii, viii, xi, xiv, xxi, xxvii, 1, 82, 88, 187
European civilisation, viii
execution, xxii, 151, 176, 177, 188

F

faith, viii, xii, xxi, xxiii, 6, 64, 70, 79, 128, 156, 161,
175, 184, 188
families, xxi, 93, 139
famine, xxii, 175, 176
fanaticism, xxii, 167
fear, xxiv, 6, 29, 43, 99, 167
Ferdinand III, vii
fertility, 144, 145
fine arts, 196
flame, 76, 175
flowers, 3, 8, 82, 174
foundations, 7, 21, 29, 40, 45, 106, 153, 158
framing, 69, 110
France, 178, 181
freedom, viii, xv, xxii
freezing, 125
friendship, 170

fruits, 5, 81, 82

G

geometry, 189, 191, 198
Giralda, viii, 103, 109, 128, 148, 149, 152, 153, 154,
155, 156, 157, 161
God, xi, xv, xx, xxiii, 6, 20, 28, 34, 54, 56, 64, 76,
78, 79, 82, 86, 95, 136, 137, 138, 152, 162, 163,
184, 204
Goths, viii, xi, xv, 1, 163, 165, 166, 167, 170, 184
governor, 93, 151, 170, 172, 173, 174
Granada, vii, viii, xxv, xxviii, 1, 67, 71, 81, 97, 101,
103, 105, 109, 113, 120, 121, 122, 125, 135, 137,
138, 139, 140, 149, 154, 156, 187, 204
Greece, 188

H

happiness, 23, 125, 136, 138
harmony, 2, 105, 188, 189
height, 7, 41, 46, 61, 110, 120, 158, 161
historical data, viii
history, xi, xxiii, xxvii, xxviii, 88, 91, 93, 101, 130,
147, 163, 165, 169, 170, 172, 174, 179
Holy Inquisition, viii
hospitality, 173, 176
host, xiii, xxvii, 122, 145, 167
hostility, 1
House, 20, 118, 121, 151, 152, 154, 155, 157, 158,
162, 193, 225
human, 92, 170, 175, 189
human nature, 175

I

imagination, 72, 73, 75, 86, 88, 104, 125, 143, 163,
191
imitation, 115, 117, 130, 161, 162
independence, xiv, xxii, xxv, 98, 172, 174, 176, 180
intelligence, 82, 135
iron, xi, xii, 2, 83, 141, 143, 157, 161
Islam, 3, 7, 9, 75, 76, 139, 161, 175
Islamism, 135, 137, 189

J

Janus, viii
Jews, xv, 56, 58, 165, 174, 175, 182

K

Kaaba of Mecca, viii

L

La Tierra de Maria Santisima, viii
laws, xi, xv, 147, 189, 191
learning, viii, 82, 88, 99
legend, xii, 116, 138, 182
leisure, xiv, 5, 147
lifetime, xxii, 160
light, viii, xiii, xxi, 2, 4, 8, 12, 18, 27, 28, 58, 60, 67,
    72, 101, 120, 132, 138, 148, 150, 151, 162, 187
love, xii, xxiii, 17, 20, 72, 81, 101, 191

M

Malaga, viii, xiv
mantle, 161, 174
marriage, 130, 150
masterpieces, 161, 169, 185
matter, iv, 6, 67, 175
memory, 5, 83, 128, 156, 167
metals, 34
Middle Ages, ix, 41
military, xxii, xxiii, 2, 5, 99, 180
Moor, vii, viii, xi, 96, 104
Moorish Art, vii
Moorish citadel, viii
Moorish fountains, viii
Moorish masonry, viii
Moorish monument, viii, xxviii, 105, 156, 193
Moorish wizardry, vii
Morisco decoration, ix
Morocco, xxvii, 110
mosaic, 24, 27, 28, 34, 47, 125, 127, 193
Moslem, vii, viii, xii, xiv, xxi, xxvii, 1, 82, 95, 139,
    158, 170, 172, 174, 175, 176, 187
mosque, vii, viii, xvi, xviii, xix, xx, xxiv, xxvi, xxvii,
    5, 7, 8, 9, 10, 11, 18, 19, 20, 21, 22, 23, 24, 25,
    26, 27, 28, 29, 30, 31, 32, 34, 35, 36, 37, 38, 39,
    40, 42, 43, 44, 45, 46, 49, 50, 51, 52, 54, 55, 56,
    58, 59, 60, 64, 66, 67, 68, 69, 70, 71, 72, 73,74,
    75, 78, 80, 81, 82, 83, 84, 89, 93, 96, 101, 103,
    106, 125, 139, 147, 152, 153, 157, 182, 183, 203,
    204
Mosque at Cordova, vii
moulding, 34, 101, 116
murder, xv, xxi, 93
music, xxi, 2, 52, 99
musicians, 99, 104
mythology, xi, 91

N

nationality, 152
nobility, xii, 44, 97, 163, 167
North Africa, xi, xv, xx

P

painters, 105, 151, 161
peace, xi, xv, xxiii, xxv, 5, 8, 28, 80, 136, 139, 150,
    184
Pentagon, 232, 279, 288, 304, 332, 343, 345, 355,
    371, 387, 388, 395, 405
personality, vii, xxiv, 125, 167, 174
pleasure, xxi, 2, 29, 72, 144, 174, 179
poetry, xxi, 18, 82, 88, 99, 147, 187
population, xv, 3, 144, 145
portraits, 112, 120, 121, 130
prayer, 18, 38, 54, 56, 93, 95, 103
principles, xiv, 101, 109, 172, 177, 188, 189
project, xx, 5, 67, 175
propagation, 8
proposition, 177
prosperity, xi, xv, xxiii, xxv, 23, 101, 137, 139, 174,
    181
protection, 50, 138, 176

R

race, xv, 101, 138, 167, 174
reading, 76, 123
reception, 122, 162
recommendations, iv
reconstruction, 110
Red Palace of Granada, vii, xxviii
relief, 22, 47, 67, 69, 114, 127, 130, 180, 188

416   *Index*

religion, xv, xxii, xxiii, 6, 8, 20, 47, 72, 95, 104, 138, 161, 165, 189, 191
religious beliefs, 166
religious observances, 175
renaissance, 101, 184
reproduction, 104, 105, 183
requirements, 104, 113
resources, 9, 18, 189
restoration, 133, 153
Roman, viii, xi, xv, 1, 8, 91, 101, 110, 119, 120, 153, 158, 162, 163, 178, 182, 184, 187, 189, 190
Rome, viii, xi, 83, 153, 160, 163, 170, 216

S

school, 6, 9, 52, 67, 105, 121, 129, 187, 188, 190
science, xv, xxiii, 1, 82, 99
sculptors, 161
security, xi, xiv, 25, 139, 175
Seville, v, vii, viii, xiv, xx, xxii, xxv, xxviii, 1, 91, 93, 94, 95, 96, 97, 98, 99, 100, 101, 102, 103, 105, 106, 107, 108, 109, 111, 112, 113, 114, 115, 116, 117, 118, 119, 121, 122, 123, 124, 126, 127, 128, 129, 130, 131, 132, 134, 135, 136, 137, 138, 139, 140, 141, 142, 143, 144, 145, 146, 147, 148, 149, 151, 152, 154, 155, 156, 157, 158, 160, 161, 162, 164, 171, 188, 268, 285, 298, 303
silk, 35, 87, 88, 99
silver, 20, 22, 28, 34, 36, 53, 56, 161, 162, 169, 170
smoothness, 86, 92
sovereignty, xi, xxiii, 96, 145
Spain, vii, viii, xi, xii, xiii, xiv, xv, xx, xxi, xxii, xxiv, xxv, xxvii, xxviii, 1, 5, 17, 41, 52, 75, 81, 83, 89, 93, 96, 98, 103, 104, 109, 112, 117, 120, 132, 139, 153, 156, 161, 165, 167, 169, 172, 179, 181, 182, 184, 187, 193
Spanish-Morisco art, viii
speech, 88, 170, 174
stars, 114, 120, 130, 144
stretching, 44, 114, 141, 145
strictures, 104
structure, 17, 86, 103, 112, 152, 154, 176, 181, 184, 185, 188

style, xii, xxi, 56, 62, 67, 70, 101, 106, 109, 110, 112, 113, 114, 115, 116, 118, 119, 120, 121, 123, 125, 128, 129, 130, 132, 133, 154, 161, 162, 184, 188, 190
symmetry, 40, 86, 188
sympathy, 175
Syria, 8, 20, 115

T

temperament, 147
theatre, 123, 125
thoughts, 80, 156
Toledo, v, vii, viii, xii, xiv, xv, xxi, xxii, xxviii, 1, 5, 56, 97, 120, 130, 138, 163, 164, 165, 166, 167, 168, 169, 170, 171, 172, 173, 174, 175, 176, 177, 178, 179, 180, 182, 184
traditions, 64, 67
training, xxiii, 174

U

uniform, 45, 120, 161

V

Vatican, 170
Visigoth, viii, 167, 178
vocabulary, vii

W

war, xiii, xiv, xxiv, 9, 76, 78, 145, 161, 176
water, ix, 21, 39, 80, 81, 86, 127, 143, 169, 178, 179
wealth, ix, xv, xxv
weapons, 169
windows, 2, 7, 22, 47, 58, 63, 67, 72, 110, 114, 116, 119, 120, 121, 127, 133, 136, 154, 162, 178, 202
wood, 7, 34, 51, 67, 125, 138, 143, 181, 190
workers, 88

Related Nova Publications

The Chief Periods of European History

Author: Edward A. Freeman

Series: Political Science and History

Book Description: The Chief Periods of European History is about the birth of modern Europe, tracing the history from the end of the Middle Ages and the Renaissance into the modern era. The book contains six lectures read in the University of Oxford in Trinity Term, 1885. It also contains the essay "Greek Cities under Roman Rule," as an appendix.

Softcover ISBN: 978-1-53615-723-9
Retail Price: $95

Nationalism, National Identity and Movements

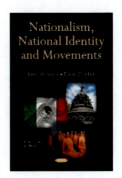

Editors: Joel Jensen and Dale Carter

Series: Political Science and History

Book Description: *Nationalism, National Identity and Movements* begins by presenting an examination of how forced migratory movements, although seeming to question traditional national principles of the sovereign state as well as undermining or even eroding nationalist value systems, ended up strengthening the power of the nation-states during the period after the Second World War.

Softcover ISBN: 978-1-53614-117-7
Retail Price: $95

To see a complete list of Nova publications, please visit our website at www.novapublishers.com

Related Nova Publications

The Russian Turmoil: Memoirs: Military, Social, and Political

Author: Anton Denikin

Series: Political Science and History

Book Description: Anton Denikin was an officer in the Russian army stationed in the Western Front during the Revolution. This memoir deals chiefly with the disintegration of the Russian army and its participation in the progress of the Revolution.

Hardcover ISBN: 978-1-53615-727-7
Retail Price: $230

Vagabonding Through Changing Germany

Author: Harry A. Franck

Series: Political Science and History

Book Description: Vagabonding Through Changing Germany is an account of the author's travels in Germany in 1919, a few months after World War I. The author highlights the economic hardships and growing anti-Semitism of the that time.

Hardcover ISBN: 978-1-53614-920-3
Retail Price: $230

To see a complete list of Nova publications, please visit our website at www.novapublishers.com